The Business of
Economics

The Business of
Economics

JOHN KAY

OXFORD UNIVERSITY PRESS
1996

Oxford University Press, Walton Street, Oxford OX2 6DP
Oxford New York
Athens Auckland Bangkok Bogata Bombay
Buenos Aires Calcutta Cape Town Dar es Salaam
Delhi Florence Hong Kong Istanbul Karachi
Kuala Lumpur Madras Madrid Melbourne
Mexico City Nairobi Paris Singapore
Taipei Tokyo Toronto
and associated companies in
Berlin Ibadan

Oxford is a trade mark of Oxford University Press

Published in the United States
by Oxford University Press Inc., New York

British Library Cataloguing in Publication Data
Kay, J. A. (John Anderson)
The business of economics / J.A. Kay.
Includes bibliographical references and index.
1. Economics. 2. Business. I. Title.
HB171.K37 1996   330—dc20 96–31302
ISBN 0–19–829222–8

Library of Congress Cataloging in Publication Data
Data available
ISBN 0–19–829222–8

1 3 5 7 9 10 8 6 4 2

Typeset by Hope Services (Abingdon) Ltd.
Printed in Great Britain
on acid-free paper by
Biddles Ltd., Guildford & King's Lynn

PREFACE

THIS book is a collection of essays, articles and lectures on the application of economics to business issues. In an endeavour to make the whole more than the sum of the parts, I have organised it around four themes.

The first section is concerned with the uses of economics. Most business people think economics is about forecasting inflation, growth, and interest rates. These are not the subjects of this present volume. The only references to these activities are in chapter 2, where I examine the track record of macro-economic forecasters I show not just that the record is abysmal, which most people already suspected, but that—in contrast to the prevailing view that economists always disagree—all the forecasts available at any time are much the same. It is just the economy that is different. This book stresses the priority of microeconomics—the study of markets, industries and firms—over macroeconomics—the analysis of monetary and fiscal policies.

Like most students, I was attracted to economics by the prospect of learning how to conquer inflation and unemployment. But I discovered that microeconomics was not only more interesting: it also offered more answers, even to these macroeconomic problems.

Most people—including many economists—still think that macro relates to the big issues, micro to the small. The essay in Chapter 4, which suggests that the Chancellor's so-called Wise Men would do better to consider the level of taxi fares than the level of taxes, was written to tease. But it was also written to make a serious point.

Take the greatest of all economic experiments—the fifty-year division of Germany into two economic zones. There are not many people who believe that the main reason why income levels in the West ended at levels more than twice as high as those in the East was the Bundesbank's exemplary management of West Germany's interest and exchange rate policy. What really mattered was the different ways in which the two zones organized their industries and their markets. Or we might ask why have the tiger economies of east Asia shown such rapid growth while most of Africa has experienced economic decline? Here too, the key issues are not to do with the growth of the money supply, but with the behaviour of firms and the functioning of markets.

Even in the UK, the most important macroeconomic developments of the last decade—the rise in manufacturing productivity, the widening of income differentials, the rise in long-term unemployment, the boom and bust of the late 1980s and early 1990s—are all best understood by observing what has been happening in firms and how industries have responded to competition. And while macroeconomic commentators have persistently overestimated the inflation rate over the last five years, an appreciation of the changes that have occurred in individual markets explains why today's pricing behaviour is very different from that which underpins econometric relationships based on data from earlier decades.

The second section examines the application of economics to the central strategic issues facing firms—their choice of activities and markets. It provides an exposition of the resource-based theory of strategy, which examines the dynamics of the successes and failures of firms by reference to their distinctive capabilities—the factors, often implicit and tangible, which differentiate them from competitors in the same markets and which cannot be reproduced by these competitors even after the advantages which they offer are recognized. This approach emphasizes that the purpose of business is to create what economists call 'rents' and what I prefer to describe as 'added value'. This links the resource-based theory of strategy to the financial reporting of the corporation.

The third part of the book develops some broader themes which are suggested by the resource-based view of strategy. That theory leads to an emphasis on the importance of corporate personality, the routines and cultures, relationships and reputations, which are not simply associated with successful companies but which are the essence of what makes them successful. But if these are what a corporation consists of, how can we talk about the ownership of a corporation? It is simply not possible to talk about the ownership of routines and relationships, at least in any ordinary sense of the word 'own'.

This perception, which implies that large companies are fundamentally social institutions, not creations of private contract or vehicles of the capital market, has wide-ranging implications for the way corporations are governed and for the politics we adopt towards them. Stakeholding became a term of political debate when Tony Blair put it forward as a central component of New Labour thinking. Section three illustrates how the theory of stakeholding has evolved and the last chapter in this section explores some consequences of this philosophy for economic and social relationships, not just those of the corporate sector.

Section four is a collection of mostly shorter essays. It is designed to illustrate how business economics can be used to analyze a range of individual commercial issues, such as pricing, positioning, and the evolution of industry structure.

The origins of this book go back ten years, when I decided to take on the challenge of demonstrating that economics was capable of illuminating business issues. That decision led me to accept a professorship and the opportunity to run a research group at the London Business School. With a colleague, Nick Morris, I established a commercial company, London Economics, to sell economics to business. And I agreed to contribute a regular column to the *Daily Telegraph*.

I embarked on each of these ventures with some trepidation. I was uncertain about the nature of the academic environment of a business school: I did not know whether business would pay for economics: I was not sure whether I could retain the freshness and vitality, or meet the deadlines, which journalism requires.

For me, this volume is a celebration of at least partial success in each of these. My research led to the publication *Foundations of Corporate Success* in the UK in 1993, followed by *Why Firms Succeed* in the United States. London Economics now employs seventy people in the UK and has offices around the world. I have continued to write a fortnightly newspaper column, which appeared in the *Daily Telegraph* for several years and more recently in the *Financial Times*. The material here is based on analysis derived from the academic environment of the London Business School and experience gained from working with clients at London Economics, and it includes around twenty articles on business themes which appeared first in the *Daily Telegraph* or *Financial Times*.

The different approaches of the pieces published here reflect their different origins—as newspaper columns, as essays, as lectures, and as articles in more scholarly journals (although I have not included any aimed solely at an academic audience). I have edited to remove duplication of content or to shorten, but not otherwise: where this editing is substantial, I note the fact. I hope that some readers will find, as I do, the mix of the more accessible and the more technical stimulating.

I am grateful to David Musson, whose idea this volume was: to Barbara Lee, Helen Pryke and Mary Barton, who helped to put it together: and to Nick Morris, now a colleague for nearly twenty years, without whom none of this would have happened.

CONTENTS

LIST OF FIGURES

LIST OF TABLES

I

ECONOMICS IN BUSINESS

The five chapters in this section are all concerned with how economics is, and should be, used in business. The recurrent theme is that the value of economics lies in conveying an understanding of how markets and industries work, not in foreseeing the future. I give some examples of what economics can and cannot do. Chapter 5 attempts to rebut the claim that the scientific study of business behaviour is simply impossible.

1

Economics and Business

Chapter 1 was written for the centenary issue of the Economic Journal. *Its purpose was to explain why economics had so little impact on business, and what should be done about it.*

The article is the only one in this book which was addressed exclusively to professional economists, and its style to some extent reflects that. But I have nevertheless chosen to place it first because its arguments are central to everything that follows. Economics is not about forecasting, and economists should not be judged by the accuracy of their forecasts. The economics which is principally relevant to business is the economics which deals with firms and with markets, not the economics which tries to tell politicians whether interest rates go up or down. Most people in business have little knowledge that the former economics even exists. This chapter outlines its scope.[1]

If you ask most business executives what they think economics is about, their answer will be economic forecasting. They do not think very much of economic forecasting—although they go on thinking they need it—and so they do not think very much of economists. Every day they are concerned to analyse their costs—which is done by their accountants. They determine their prices—this is the responsibility of their marketing department. They need to interpret the business environment they face—the task of their corporate planners and strategic advisers. The economic input into any of these functions is minimal.

Yet costs, prices, industries, and markets are the very lifeblood of microeconomics, just as inflation, output, and growth are the lifeblood of macroeconomics. Economics dominates public policy and every country's chief executive regards his (or her) macroeconomic adviser as a vital aide. But economics has almost no influence on business policy, and in only a small

---

[1] 'Economics and Business', *Economic Journal*, 101/404 (Jan. 1991), edited.

minority of companies does the chief executive have an economic adviser at all. The evolution of microeconomics over the past century provides a partial answer. The year 1990 is not only the centenary of the *Economic Journal*; it is also the centenary of the first edition of Alfred Marshall's *Principles of Economics*. It was Marshall who set the agenda for much of the economics that was to occupy the *Journal* for the subsequent 100 years. Marshall's analysis, and his understanding of the commerce of his day, was sophisticated and wide-ranging. Indeed Marshall probably knew more about the day-to-day functioning of business than any leading economist this century. Yet his approach barely scratched the surface of the firm. Marshall's key tool of analysis is 'the representative firm'. His famous metaphor of the trees in the forest is designed precisely to play down the role of individual agents and the importance of their distinctive characteristics. It is no accident that his second landmark work is entitled *The Economics of Industry*, not the economics of the firm. The imperfect competition revolution of Chamberlin and Joan Robinson changed this direction little. In the models they develop, firms do differ from each other, but the ways in which they do so are essentially trivial.

The structure-conduct-performance paradigm

Since the Second World War, the dominant tradition in industrial organization has been based on the strongly empirical structure–conduct–performance paradigm. The focus of this work is clearly set out by Bain (1959: pp. vii–viii):

I am concerned with the environmental setting within which enterprises operate and in how they behave in these settings as producers, sellers and buyers. By contrast, I do not take an internal approach, more appropriate to the field of management science, such as could inquire how enterprises do and should behave in ordering their internal operations and would attempt to instruct them accordingly . . . my primary unit for analysis is the industry or competing groups of firms, rather than the individual firm or the economy wide aggregate of enterprises.

Fig. 1.1, drawn from Scherer's (1970) definitive survey of that tradition, illustrates its essential features. All of the factors in it are external to the firm; nothing explains why one firm in an industry differs from another. True, Scherer's work is also a rich encyclopedia of information about American business, but it is precisely that which distinguishes it so clearly from other contributions in its genre. His unit of analysis is emphatically the industry, not the firm. For industrial economists in this tradition (and, indeed, for those of the Chicago school which represented its principal alternative) the policy issues of interest were those of public policy, not business policy.

This inability, or unwillingness, to probe within the boundaries of the firm itself has serious weaknesses even in its own terms. If opportunities are equally available to all they are available to no one in particular. This problem, most clearly articulated by Richardson (1960), lies a little beneath the

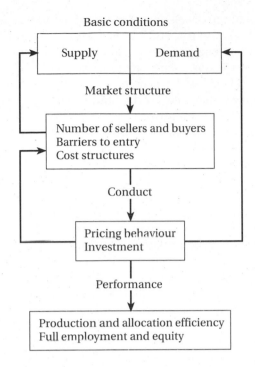

Fig. 1.1. A Model of Industrial Organization Analysis
Source: simplified from Scherer (1980: fig. 1.1).

surface. But the failure to resolve it creates a theory of industrial organization of limited value to practical businessmen. Reviewing the state of oligopoly theory in 1975 Joskow comments that 'the ultimate test of the utility to the various models is whether they prove useful to people involved in analysing problems involving actual markets or groups of markets. I suggest that not only aren't they particularly useful but also that they aren't really used.'

The development of business strategy

The vacuum that this leaves has been filled. Igor Ansoff is generally credited with founding the subject of corporate strategy. Although such a development is clearly foreshadowed by Chandler's contributions to business history, Ansoff (1965: 16) is explicit that his work is motivated by the deficiencies of contemporary microeconomics:

Study of the firm has been the long time concern of the economics profession. Unfortunately for our present purpose, the so-called *microeconomic* theory of the firm which occupies much of the economists' thought and attention, sheds relatively little light on decision-making processes in a real world firm.

It cannot be said that the development of a distinct discipline of strategy has enjoyed such success. The tools of the strategist—the experience curve and the portfolio matrix—are jejune at best, and much of what passes for strategy is platitude or pious exhortation. The most substantial body of empirical research to be found under the heading of strategy is based on the PIMS database (Buzzell and Gale 1987) and would fit comfortably into the structure–conduct–performance tradition.

The most widely read and influential management book of the 1980s is probably *In Search of Excellence*, a journalistic account of the characteristics of leading American corporations (Peters and Waterman 1982). The two most important contributors to the development of strategic thinking in the last decade are probably Porter and Moss Kanter, whose work has recognizable antecedents in economics and organizational sociology respectively. Strategy has even developed its own counter-culture, based largely around the engagingly eccentric Henry Mintzberg, who denies the possibility, or at least the relevance, of a rational strategy.

Michael Porter stands out from this field in having taken economics to business leaders and in having based strategy firmly in economics. Yet the economics he uses is economics with which Bain and Mason would have been comfortable and familiar. Porter's 'five forces'—suppliers, substitution, entry, customers, rivalry—have an obvious affinity with Scherer's S–C–P presentation in Fig. 1.1. And this should come as no surprise, since what Porter has done is to cross the Charles River, metaphorically and literally, and bring together the traditions of Harvard economics with those of its Business School. It is notable, but consequential, that the approach is decidedly less successful when applied to the firm (in *Competitive Advantage* (1985)) than when applied to the industry (in *Competitive Strategy* (1980)).

The absence of a well-ordered body of knowledge is most clearly reflected in the way in which the subject is taught. This is based largely on the case method—a kind of classroom learning by doing. No one teaches physics by cases and, interestingly, the technique is not much used in law either. But if economics might lay claim to providing that well-ordered body of knowledge which strategy lacks, it is not a claim that has been widely recognized. While business education as a whole has been expanding, the role of formal economics within it has generally been contracting.

The new industrial economics

But while all this has been going on, and following directly on the pessimistic comments of Joskow cited above, the subject of industrial economics itself has undergone massive changes. Those that are relevant to the themes of this article fall into two broad areas. Each reflects the resurgence of formal methods in industrial economics: in reaction to, or perhaps in development of, the strongly empirical traditions of the structure–conduct–performance paradigm.

One of these areas is the development of models rooted in game theory. An economist who knew nothing of business strategy might well suppose that it would be centred around the theory of games. He or she would be quite mistaken. A recent volume (Oster 1990) is the only major textbook on strategy I know even to mention the subject and even that apologizes for its novel content by beginning with the slightly shamefaced confession that 'this is a book about competitive strategy by an economist'. Now it is perhaps true that game theory has never quite lived up to the potential which its initial development appeared to offer. One recent text on the subject (Rasmussen 1989) describes it as the Argentina of economics, in terms of the gap between potential and achievement. If game theory seemed to offer the key to analysing oligopolistic interactions, the lock proved obdurately hard to turn. But from the mid-1970s it did begin to move, and modern textbooks in industrial organizations such as Tirole (1988) are very largely based on game theory, at least in the broad sense.

The second important area of change is in that group of issues concerned with asymmetry of information, with principals and agents, and with the nature of contracts and ownership. This area of study is currently developing in many different directions, and at present enjoys little coherence taken as a whole. This hardly matters. It is evidently a fertile area of study and has attracted many of the most fertile minds in the profession. It holds out the prospect of a theory of the internal organization of firms, and of the relationships between firms, which is both more comprehensive and more powerful than anything that has existed until now.

The future of economics in business

The firm is a collection of contracts. Its internal organization is a set of arrangement between principals and agents. Its relationships with its competitors are non-cooperative games and those with its suppliers and customers are co-operative games. All these are subjects which have been at the centre of research in economic theory in the past fifteen years. The key issue for the development of microeconomics in the next century is whether they can be expressed and developed in ways which gives them relevance to business policy. This requires change in the attitudes of both business executives and economists.

It is, of course, easier to say what business executives must do. Distinguish insight from cliché. Discover that learning comes not from hearing the felicitous reiteration of what one has oneself just said—the mainstay of most consultancy and business seminars—but from experiencing challenges to one's preconceptions. Most of this will happen as the educational level of management rises.

Microeconomics has potentially the same role to play in relation to management issues that macroeconomics currently has for political issues.

Because of the ways in which the subject has evolved over the past 100 years, it has conspicuously failed to play that role. Today business executives' expectations of what economics can offer are not related to microeconomics at all—they look to economists mainly for their forecasts (and are inclined to look at them less).

Yet the present state of knowledge in microeconomic theory is one which makes the time particularly apposite to assert that economics has a much wider range of practical uses. Economics is the natural integrative discipline for much of management science. But its past relative neglect of the firm as the unit of organization has severely limited the role which it has to play. That is now changing, and that can mean that economics in the next hundred years will have a quite different, and much wider, range of policy applications than those it has exercised in the century that has passed.

The two key groups of question of interest to business executives—the internal organization of the firm and the relationship between its suppliers and customers, and the nature of strategic interactions between small groups of firms—are clearly on the agenda of modern economics in a manner which has not been true for most of the last century. First-year students are still puzzled when they are faced with models of atomistic perfect competition and wonder which real world industries this actually describes. It is a safe bet that they will not be presented with the same material in the next century.

2

···

The Failures of Forecasting

This essay, which appeared in the Financial Times, *attracted more letters in response than any piece in that paper for many months.[1] Two were published: one asserted that his unpublished forecasts were far more accurate than those which appeared in print (but did not disclose what they had been), the other that economists did not really forecast at all. Neither did much to restore the reputation of economists.*

A better reply came from Wynne Godley, who retired soon after from his position as one of the Chancellor's 'Wise Men'. Godley noted that the article ignored the conditionality which is attached to many forecasts, including his own: the forecasters state that their estimates are contingent on other factors, in particular on assumptions about government policy. Godley has a point in relation to his own forecasts, whose purpose is to influence that policy. But the vast majority of business and city forecasters are in business to tell their clients what is going to happen: and even if conditions are attached (they rarely are) such conditions are generally ignored by those who use their forecasts. For them there is no defence.

It is a conventional joke that economic forecasters always disagree, and that there are as many different opinions about the future of the economy as there are economists. The truth is quite the opposite. Economic forecasters do not speak with discordant voices; they all say more or less the same thing at the same time. And what it is that they say is almost always wrong. The differences between forecasts are trivial relative to the differences between all forecasts and what actually happens.

My assessment of the performance of forecasts is based on an analysis by London Economics of the performance of all major forecasting groups since 1987. The forecasts used are the latest made, so that for 1990 I have selected the last forecast made by each group in 1989. Take their forecasts of growth in the economy in 1994, for example. We now know that it was around 4 per cent. The best estimates were made by Patrick Minford of Liverpool

---

[1] *Financial Times* (29 Sept. 1995).

University, and a commercial firm, Business Strategies Limited. Both predicted that the economy would grow by 3.3 per cent. But these were not just the best forecasts. They were also the highest. Of the thirty-four forecasts I have obtained, every one was substantially below the outcome. In fact, almost all were between 2 per cent and 3 per cent.

Perhaps 1994 was a bad year for forecasters, if not for the economy. It was not an untypical year, however. The same thing happened in 1993. Growth then was 2 per cent. One forecasting group—the National Institute for Economic and Social Research—was spot on. Every other forecaster—every single one—was below the outcome.

Perhaps forecasters are by nature pessimistic. But they were not in 1992. Growth was actually negative that year. That outcome was worse than anyone had predicted. And the same was true in 1991. In not one of these four years did the outcome lie within the range of *all* the forecasts made (Table 2.1).

It was dissatisfaction with the outcome of forecasts, and particularly his own, that led the Chancellor to establish his panel of independent economic forecasters—the so-called Wise Men. He need not have bothered. In both the last two years, the average forecast from the Wise Men has been exactly equal to the Treasury's own forecast, and exactly equal to the average of all forecasters (Table 2.2). The degree of agreement among the forecasts is astounding. It is just the economy that is different.

Perhaps the forecasters do better with other economic variables. Table 2.3 shows how they did on the retail prices index. In 1993 and 1994, virtually everyone overestimated inflation. In 1991, virtually everyone underestimated it. Only in 1992—oddly enough, the most dramatic year of the four, the one in which Britain was forced out of the ERM—were the forecasts close to outcome. Even a stopped clock is right sometimes.

Nor have the last four years been worse than usual for the forecasting profession. They did no better in the 1980s (Table 2.4). And although 1995 is only two-thirds over, it already looks likely that the consensus will be too high on both inflation and growth.

There is a consensus forecast, to such a degree that it is barely worth distinguishing between one forecast and another. Yet the consensus forecast failed to predict any of the most important developments in the economy over the past seven years—the strength and resilience of the 1980s consumer spending boom, the depth and persistence of the 1990s recession, or the dramatic and continuing decline in inflation since 1991.

Now there are several reasons for this clustering around a consensus. While some forecasts—such as those of the Treasury, the National Institute, and the London Business School—are based on elaborate econometric models of the economy, many City and business forecasts are based only on an assessment of the opinions and forecasts of others. So it is not surprising that they are not far apart. And it is always safer to be wrong in a crowd. It is striking that the commercial and City forecasters, whose jobs may be on the line, rarely stray far from the consensus, while the outliers are more often academics. Patrick

Table 2.1. Growth forecasts, 1991–1994

	1991	1992	1993	1994
Average forecast (%)	0.8	1.9	1.0	2.6
Outcome (%)	−2.5	−0.6	2.0	3.9
Number of forecasts				
Too high	29	30	0	0
Too low	0	0	29	34

Table 2.2. Growth forecasts, 1993–1994 (%)

	1993	1994
Treasury	1.0	2.7
Average of Wise Men	1.0	2.7
Average of all forecasts	1.0	2.6
Outcome	2.0	3.9

Table 2.3. Inflation forecasts, 1991–1994

	1991	1992	1993	1994
Average forecast (%)	5.2	4.0	3.3	3.7
Outcome (%)	5.9	3.7	1.6	2.7
Number of forecasts				
Too high	3	15	26	29
Too low	20	8	0	1

Table 2.4. Growth forecasts, 1987–1990

	1987	1988	1989	1990
Average forecast (%)	2.8	2.5	2.5	1.7
Outcome (%)	4.5	4.2	2.1	1.0
Number of forecasts				
Too high	0	0	15	18
Too low	17	19	3	3

Minford and Wynne Godley are no more often right than other people, but they are more likely to be different from other people—so Minford's growth forecast won the golden guru award in 1990 and 1994, but the wooden spoon in 1992.

Even in retrospect, it is important to maintain the consensus. It is an article of faith among banks, for example, that the depth of the recent recession and the magnitude of the property market collapse could not have been predicted, since if it could have been predicted those responsible for the lending excesses of the 1980s would be guilty of gross negligence rather than helpless victims of events. Tim Congdon, whose maverick predictions anticipated the events of the last boom and recession better than anyone, parted company with Shearson Lehman just as events began to prove him right. In large organizations, it is often more important to be wrong for the right reasons than to be correct, and nowhere is this more true than in the Treasury and Bank of England.

But another reason for the near identity of all the major forecasts can be found by looking more carefully at the tables. If you want to add to the forecasts by predicting what the consensus forecast will be, it is not very difficult. The consensus forecast can be derived by taking the average of the present and the past. Today, inflation and interest rates are at historically low levels, and so the consensus is that they will rise. Growth is pretty much in line with its historic average, and that is why most forecasters think that it will stay there. Many so-called forecasters derive their predictions in this way, and if they use the same principle and the same method it is no surprise that they come up with the same answer. What is less obvious is that the Treasury model, and other systems like it, have the same property. In the absence of external shocks, or after them, they revert quickly to the long-run trend.

Now if you know very little about what you are forecasting—and when we make macroeconomic predictions we do know very little about what we are forecasting—then there are worse rules of thumb than expecting that the future will be like the past, although it is difficult to see why anyone should command the deference accorded to the Chancellor's Wise Men or the salaries paid to City economists for enunciating this principle. Yet the fundamental weakness of the approach is that it is intrinsically incapable of identifying structural changes in the economy. Changes in asset prices played a role in the boom of the 1980s and recession of the 1990s which had not been seen in previous economic cycles. It was that phenomenon which the consensus forecast almost entirely missed. And the most important current economic policy issue is whether a combination of changes in expectations and microeconomic deregulation has finally brought to an end the fifty-year age of inflation. I do not know the answer to that question. But I do know that the consensus forecast, which predicts that inflation will rise because in the past it always has, sheds absolutely no light on the matter.

The next chapter explains why reliable macroeconomic forecasts for more than a short period ahead are, in principle, impossible. Despite that, they will continue to be made, just as astrologers and quack doctors stay in business. The hope that what they say might be true overrides innate scepticism, and despite the low opinion which both politicians and business people profess for economic forecasts, they continue to listen to them with extraordinary credulousness. Yet once we realize the limitations of our knowledge, there is much that can more sensibly be said. The fall in inflation, and the revival of manufacturing—two current structural changes—both have wide-ranging effects on business and finance, and economic analysis can illuminate what they are. But when someone tells you what inflation will be in the third quarter of 1996, or predicts the growth of manufacturing output in 1997, do not listen. He does not know.

3

Economic Models

No well respected professional economist would be without models: but few
people who are not economists understand what an economic model is.
This chapter is designed to explain the answer. The first part, edited from
Daily Telegraph *and* Financial Times *articles, describes the uses and*
limitations of macroeconomic models. The second part of the chapter,
which is an extract from the essay in Chapter 1, explains more fully the uses
of economic models in business.

WHAT IS A MACROECONOMIC MODEL?

Macroeconomic models are in the news again.[1] The Treasury is talking
of privatizing its macroeconomic model. The Chancellor's Wise Men
(strictly his panel of Independent Forecasters) are already, if predictably,
quarrelling among themselves over whose model is best. What is a macroeconomic model?

The very word 'model' which creates great confusion. When we think of a
model, we tend to think of the kinds of models you buy in toy shops. A model
of a B52 bomber looks like a scaled-down version of a B52 bomber, and the
more it looks like a B52 bomber the better model it is.

Economic models are not like that at all. The Treasury model is not one in
which you and me, and ICI and Glaxo, all make our miniaturized decisions
like miniaturized men in a model village. In fact, the Treasury model does not
acknowledge that ICI or Glaxo exist, far less find a role for you and me. You
could conceivably build a macroeconomic model which did incorporate individual decisions and some attempts have been to develop ideas in this direction, but it is still miles away from what people actually do.

The confusion over the meaning of the word model is responsible for misunderstanding of what it is that a macroeconomic model can do. Many

---

[1] *Daily Telegraph* (26 Apr. 1993), edited, and *Financial Times* (29 Sept. 1995).

people (including some of the modellers themselves) think that as we build bigger and more elaborate models we will arrive at more and more realistic descriptions of the world, and that forecasts and predictions derived from them will become more and more accurate. That probably would be true if you were building a model of a B52 bomber, but it is not true of a macroeconomic model at all. Since it is not an attempt to replicate the economy, but rather a way of organizing thoughts about the economy, the quality of the answers that emerge from it depends on the quality of that basic thinking, not on the elaboration of the model.

I met my first macroeconomic model twenty years ago. The lecturer was writing on the blackboard, talking rapidly with his back to the audience (this was before the days of performance appraisal for university staff). What he wrote was:

$$Y = C + I$$

followed by:

$$C = a + bY$$

Anyone who can pass Mr Patten's tests, either in mathematics or in economics, will recognize the denouement:

$$Y = \frac{a + I}{I - b}$$

The first line says that there are two components to national income—consumption and investment. The second says that consumption itself depends on the level of national income. And the third deduces from these that national income will be determined by the level of investment. Not only will national income be determined by the level of investment, but it will be extremely sensitive to that level. This is the basic Keynesian macroeconomic model, to which every beginning student of economics is (even now) still introduced.

Is it really possible to say something significant about a national economy, made up of over fifty million people, with hundreds of thousands of firms beset by recession, and a troubled international economy, with a model as simple as that? Not only is the algebra about as trivial as it is possible to imagine, but the model says nothing about trade or about government, it assumes that there are no constraints on resources, it does not allow any role for money and inflation.

Despite his unprepossessing style, the lecturer convinced me that the answer to that was yes, and I still believe not only that models of that kind can give insight into the economy but that this particular model does. We do not consider it impossible that someone might, in two or three sentences, say something incisive about the economy, or the natural or physical world.

Since mathematics is only another language there is absolutely no reason why the same person should not say something incisive about the economy, or the natural or physical world, in two or three lines of algebra. (Although we should not fall into the trap, which does beset many economists, of thinking that a statement which would be banal if it was expressed in words becomes profound when it is translated into mathematics.) Mathematics for economists, as it is for scientists, is simply another language—a way of expressing things which would become impossibly cumbersome to describe if ordinary verbal communication were used instead.

A macroeconomic model of the economy is a consistent system of relationships, based on past data, which describes the interactions between the main economic variables. For example, investment expenditures by business might depend on the rate of growth of demand for output, the level of interest rates, and the cash flow of firms; wages might be affected by unemployment and by inflation expectations, which might in turn be determined by past inflation. Each of these elements of the model is validated by examining how well it would have predicted the variable concerned—investment or wages—in previous years.

The Treasury model consists of a long list of mathematical equations which are expanded versions of that $Y = C + I$ relationship. In fact, the Treasury model, and most macroeconomic models, still follow the basic structure that my lecturer expounded quite closely.

Structural changes in the economy can raise major problems for this approach. For example, there has been a strong relationship over twenty years between house prices and average incomes. When the affordability ratio has been attractive, house prices have gone up; when the ratio of prices to incomes is too high, they rise less quickly. But this relationship was observed in a period when house prices always went up, so that what you would pay for a house was often limited only by what you could borrow.

So will this historic relationship persist in an era of lower inflation? No one really knows. Ideally, one could construct a mega-model which delved deeper into underlying behaviour and would describe both inflationary and non-inflationary periods. But most models are very far from achieving this degree of sophistication. Until then, however, all macroeconomic models will be biased towards expecting the future to be like the past and will often fail to identify the most important changes in economic behaviour.

So in the 1980s, forecasters like Tim Congdon, who emphasized the role of asset prices in the economy, did better than others who did not, including the Treasury. That is not because his model was better in the technical sense that it had more and better-determined econometric equations—it did not—but because the basic insight into how the economy worked was, at least at that time, a better one. That insight, and that forecaster, might, or might not, be right next time.

Chaos theory is currently one of the most fashionable branches of mathematics—to be found in Stephen Spielberg's *Jurassic Park* and Tom Stoppard's *Arcadia* as well as in more prosaic textbooks. One of its key insights is that in non-linear systems, which have curves or discontinuities—which certainly include economies and businesses—small differences in initial conditions may lead to large differences in final outcomes.

Consider the effect of dropping a marble into the system shown in Fig 3.1. Whether it ends up at A, B, or C is a matter of chance—strictly, it depends on the angle and speed at which you drop the marble. These small differences determine whether what happens is A, B, or C. There is no way of predicting where it will end up, but if you are forced to make a prediction, you should guess C, because it will end up there twice as often as at A or B. This is the phenomenon of the consensus forecast.

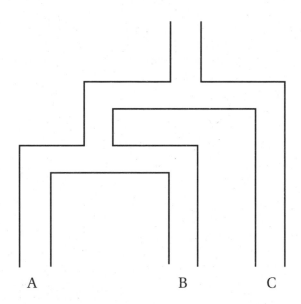

Fig. 3.1. An Unpredictable System

You can, of course, hire someone who guessed right last time—usually someone who guessed C. You can hire a panel of wise men to pronounce on why they were right or wrong, last time. Or you can recognize that the marble will end up one-quarter of the time at A, one quarter at B, and the rest of the time at C, and that no one can tell you what will be the outcome this time around. Then prepare a strategy which copes with these different outcomes and which reflects the probabilities they will occur. That is what I recommend—both to business people and to chancellors of the Exchequer.

Britain's exit from the ERM in September 1992 raises similar issues. That

Britain might be forced out at some time was quite likely. The exact timing of the débâcle was the product of chance events—a run on the lire, statements from the Bundesbank, uncertainty about the outcome of the French referendum. Even in summer 1992, no one could have predicted with any confidence that nemesis would come in the autumn, rather than in November or the following spring. In turn, no one could have predicted the course of interest rates, growth, or inflation in 1993. In practice, most forecasters simply assume such discontinuities as ERM exits will not occur—which is, in part, why they are so often the same and so often wrong.

In the end, no economic model tells you anything you have not already told it, although since the implications of what you have told it may be quite complex, a computer may be a useful way both of working out these implications and ensuring that what you have told it amounts to an internally consistent story.

Economic models are genuinely useful tools, but only for people who realize the limitations of what they can do. Most people are absurdly optimistic about what economic models might do and absurdly critical when they fail to do it; I could blame them more if so many economists did not encourage their optimism.

THE USES OF MODELS

If strategy has boomed in the last two decades, so has the activity of modelling.[2] All sophisticated firms now have sophisticated models of their operations. Most of these models are of a very different kind from the models typically built by economists. They are deterministic, they are numerical, they are complex, and they are used for computer simulation of future scenarios.

In the early 1970s, this activity was the province of specialists, because the computing power required was so substantial that only skills in new types of program languages made the development of such models feasible. But computing power is no longer a problem, and the development of spreadsheets means that anyone can become a modeller.

This activity has developed to meet a perceived need for forecasts. And forecasts are what the models provide. Output in 1995, costs in 1997, profits in 1999, all come in pages of computer printout at the touch of a button. It is as easy to see why, in a turbulent world, everyone would like the aid of a crystal ball. Yet is is genuinely unclear—even to those who commission it—what this activity is for. Ask a businessman what he would do, if he were given a completely accurate prediction of what his profits would be in 1999. It relieves the task of management hardly at all. If we knew everything about the future,

[2] Edited extract from *Economic Journal*, 101/404 (Jan. 1991).

that would relieve the task of management, but only because the task of management would already have been done. As 'Back to the Future' films demonstrate, there is a problem about the role of an individual in a future which is already determined.

The question to which the businessman or woman wants an answer is not 'what does the future hold?' but 'how will my actions affect the future?' It has not been well understood that answering the first is not an essential preliminary to answering the second, and, moreover, that a model developed to answer the first is not necessarily well adapted to answering the second.

I could establish how braking affects the motion of my car by inviting a motor engineer to predict the position of the car with and without the application of force to the brake pedal. But it is not a very good way of arriving at the answer. It does not give it very precisely and it does not clarify the distinction between applying the brakes and making a hole in the petrol tank, each of which may have very similar short-term effects on the position of the car. The better approach is not to model the car, but to try to understand the braking system—to focus on the element of interest, not to describe the structure as a whole.

The analogy makes the point seem obvious, but it seems to be not at all obvious. The usual purpose of modelling is not to make predictions, but to enhance our understanding of complex systems. The most useful model—and the test of such a model is utility, not truth or falsehood—is the minimal model necessary to capture the essence of the problem. Such approach is quite alien to the professional modeller who objects that the minimal model leaves many things out. How can you model the brake system, he asks, without also modelling the accelerator? If you want to predict what will happen to the car, the objection is well founded. If you want to understand the brake system, it is a red herring. The purpose of modelling complex structures such as firms is not to predict the future—in which neither group of models are much use—but to illuminate the structure of the problem, and here the model that has an analytic solution wins every time against the model which needs three hours of mainframe time for every simulation. It does appear that economists have acquired the most sophisticated understanding of how models can, and cannot, be deployed in the social sciences: it also appears that they have kept that understanding firmly to themselves.

4

....

Uses and Abuses of Economics

The first part of this chapter was written in response to the Chancellor of the Exchequer's appointment of the panel of independent forecasters—the so-called 'Seven Wise Men'. Its thesis—that resources were better deployed towards the microeconomic questions to which economists had answers, and which were not necessarily less important—was eventually accepted when the Treasury created not just one, but several, microeconomic panels.

The second part of this chapter responds to a number of attacks on economics and economists by Paul Ormerod, former director of Henley Centre for Forecasting, which culminated in the publication of a book entitled The Death of Economics *(Ormerod 1994).*

TAXIS OR TAXES?

It would be churlish for economists not to welcome the appointment of the Seven Wise Men to deliberate and give economic advice to the Chancellor of the Exchequer.[1] Certainly they can hardly make things worse. Yet the exercise reinforces the world's misunderstanding of what it is that economics is really about.

So the Wise Men appear before the Budget just as a motley band of soothsayers used to appear before a Greek or Roman general went to war. Some of them inspect the entrails, paying careful attention to M0, or to M3. Others have their black boxes, the econometric forecasting models. Still others hear voices in the air. And the sage Wynne Godley is doyen of them all, proclaiming disaster as he has before every battle that anyone can remember, and mostly proving to be right.

This ritual accomplished, the Chancellor can put on his armour and enter budget purdah. As with the soothsayers, no one really believes it all but no one dares to disregard it either: and the shrewd forecaster, like the Delphic

[1] *Daily Telegraph* (13 Jan. 1993).

oracle, assures sufficient ambiguity in his prediction to be vindicated by events, whatever events may be.

And the operation of the Wise Men is also designed to support the prejudice that economists always disagree. Indeed—to change the analogy, though not to make it more flattering—it is as if the zookeeper has deliberately put all the most quarrelsome monkeys in the same cage, so that the public can stand safely behind the bars and chortle as they throw insults and banana skins at each other. Yet the truth of the matter is that economists do not disagree very much about economics. What they do disagree about is politics.

It was Keynes who expressed the hope that one day economists would simply be regarded as technicians like dentists, and I share his hope. The thought came home particularly forcefully the other day while waiting in the rain for a taxi. I offer two empirical laws about the behaviour of taxis. The first is that there are no taxis when it is raining. The second law, and the less widely appreciated, is that where there is one vacant taxi, there is another. London taxi drivers are mostly sharp-eyed, but if one does fail to see you flag him down it rarely matters. If an empty cab passes you by, another will come soon.

Now a simple understanding of the economic theory of supply and demand explains why these two fundamental laws of taxi availability holds good. London taxi fares are fixed by (for some bizarre reason) the Home Secretary. But demand for taxis varies enormously, from time to time and place to place. Sometimes the Home Secretary's fare is too low to equate supply and demand (as when it is raining) and then there are no taxis to be had. More often, the Home Secretary's fare is too high and there are many vacant taxis in the locality.

Perhaps you think that economic insight obvious. Try telling the taxi driver that London taxi fares are too high. He will tell you they are certainly not too high and that business is terrible. He will blame the Chancellor, and not the Home Secretary.

To investigate the taxi issue further, go to Heathrow. You will see that in the peripheral area there are almost as many black cabs waiting as there are cars in the long-term car park. The reason for that is that the cab fare to and from Heathrow is much too high.

It is much too high because the Home Secretary, in a not very successful attempt to encourage black cabs to take you with a smile from London to Streatham, has decreed a higher fare per mile for long journeys than for short ones. But with Heathrow, in contrast to Streatham, you can get there quickly and there are lots of passengers waiting to come back.

The result is that cab drivers are willing to queue for an hour or two to secure one lucrative Heathrow fare. If the fare was £1,000 not £30 there would be an even longer queue of cabs and an even shorter queue of passengers. One result of the recession is that minicab fares to Heathrow, which are fixed by supply and demand, have come down while black cab fares, which are fixed by the Home Secretary, have gone up. That is why many black cabs now have notices demanding that the Home Secretary's baleful jurisdiction should be extended to minicabs.

Now I am willing to bet that if the Wise Men had been asked to discuss the Heathrow cab problem rather than the future of the pound they would have quickly diagnosed the problem, and agreed the solution: which is not the one recommended by cab drivers.[2] That discussion would have had a purpose and a useful outcome, which is more than could be said for the one which took place.

The cab driver, who sees only the outlook from his cab, knows only that he could not survive at a lower fare if other things remained unchanged. The economists, who view the market, can see that other things would in fact change and that , with lower fares, taxi drivers, as well as everyone else, would be better off.

But surely the Wise Men were addressing more important problems, even if less tractable ones? There, most of all, I disagree. The functioning of markets is far more important than the differences between M0 and M3. The London taxi market is a microcosm of the failure of the Eastern European economies, the Common Agricultural Policy, and the attempts to develop a European industrial strategy.

The surplus or shortage of taxis precisely mirrors the surplus or shortages in Gum, the Moscow department store, and the queue of black cabs at Heathrow, like the butter mountain, exemplifies the waste of resources which results when the system establishes perverse incentives.

We know that forty years of substituting wise men for market forces reduced incomes in East Germany to less than half of what they were in the West, and no amount of macroeconomic mismanagement has yet achieved that degree of devastation. Whether we reach an accord on the General Agreement on Tariffs and Trade is enormously more important than when or whether we rejoin the European Monetary System, and if the latter decision is more controversial it is mainly because by comparison, it does not matter very much either way.

THE DEATH OF ECONOMICS?

Paul Ormerod confirms everyone's suspicions of economists.[3] They know nothing of the real world. They will never give you a straight answer. There are as many different opinions as there are economists. At last a professional economist has confirmed it.

Ormerod lists apparently compelling examples to prove his case. Suppose the rate of VAT were to be reduced. What would be the effect on prices? If you

---

[2] This was confirmed a few days later when a cab driver recognised me as the author of this article.

[3] *Daily Telegraph* (4 Sept. 1992; 21 Mar. 1994), edited.

ask that question of the six leading macroeconomic forecasting models, two of them say that prices would go down, three that they would go up, and one that they would stay the same. What use is that to chancellors of the Exchequer or practical businessmen?

Or look at the application of the most fundamental of economic principles: the law of supply and demand. Price is determined by the balance of supply and demand, or so economists have claimed for more than a century. Yet, Ormerod points out, a bond trader at Salomon Brothers is paid many times more than a teacher of children with learning disabilities. Is that the law of supply and demand? Hardly; there are innumerable candidates for every vacancy at Salomons, and few good applicants for jobs teaching disadvantaged children.

Ormerod's problem is that he shares the popular misconception that economics is about foretelling the future, rather than trying to understand better how the economy works. Since economists are no better than anyone else at foretelling the future (though perhaps no worse), their failure discredits the whole profession. It is perhaps not surprising that Ormerod thinks that, since he used to run a centre for forecasting. But most economics, and almost all the economics that is of any value, is not about forecasting at all.

So if economics is not about forecasting, what is it about? What use is economics, people ask indignantly, if economists cannot tell what is going to happen to the economy? But economics is not about foretelling the future, any more than physics, chemistry, or biology is about foretelling the future, and if people thought that physicists, chemists, or biologists ought to be judged by their clairvoyant skills no doubt they would conclude that physicists, chemists, and biologists were not much use either. What physics, chemistry, and biology are really about is understanding the world. Similarly economics is about understanding the economy, and although we do not know all, or anything like enough, about how the economic world works we do know quite a lot.

Before you can explain, you have to measure, and a lot of what serious economists do is exactly that. It is not just economists, but ordinary people, who talk every day about inflation, or economic growth. But what does it mean to say that inflation is at 4 per cent, or that growth was 2 per cent, and how do we know? There is no great mystery about either of these things, but unless you understand how an index number is compiled, or what is meant by gross domestic product, you can talk about these concepts only in the rather loose and general way that laymen talk about heat, or momentum, or the difference between solids and liquids. All science begins from making concepts precise and going on to define their meaning and their implications.

But science must move on, as natural science did five centuries ago, from description to understanding and explanation. It is worth looking at Ormerod's examples more carefully, because what they illustrate is not quite what he suggests. Rather the examples show the ways in which economics can be used, and the ways in which it can be abused, and Ormerod's ignorance of the difference.

Begin with the issue of what a change in the rate of VAT will do to inflation. A policy of this kind has two distinct effects. One effect, which is short run and immediate, is that shops have to pay less VAT on what they sell and will therefore be able to charge lower prices to their customers. The second effect, which is long run and indirect, is that lower VAT increases everyone's spending power. In turn, that raises demand for goods and services, and the consequences are inflationary. The overall effect depends on the balance between that initial impact and that subsequent consequence.

Now what that balance will turn out to be in practice depends on the general structure of the economy and on specific economic conditions. If there is not much competition between retailers, then little of the benefit of lower VAT will go to consumers and so the first effect will be comparatively small. If the economy is in recession, the inflationary impact of increased demand is not likely to be great and so the second effect will be comparatively small. In an uncompetitive economy in a boom, reducing VAT will probably raise prices. In a deregulated environment in slump—as now—it is more likely that prices will fall.

So there is nothing to be ashamed of in the answer, 'It all depends.' If you ask a physicist whether a glass window will break if you throw a ball at it, the sensible response will be, 'It all depends.' It all depends on whether it is a tennis ball or a cricket ball, whether you throw it hard or gently, whether the glass is toughened or not. The answer, 'It all depends,' accompanied by an outline of what it depends on, is more accurate—and of more practical value—than a simple yes or no.

And what of the paradox of pay at Salomon Brothers? Far from refuting the laws of supply and demand, Salomon Brothers illustrates them in all too vigorous action. The reason there is a queue to work there is that bond traders at Salomons are paid a lot, and the reason there are not enough good teachers is that teachers are not paid very much. The truly interesting question is why this is so, since most people's intuition is that teaching is really a lot more useful than bond trading.

There is a clear and coherent economic explanation. It rests on the difference between the market for bonds on the one hand and that for classes for those with learning disabilities on the other. Identifying small divergences in bond prices is very lucrative. There is a fault in the way markets work which means that seeing that something priced at £1 is really worth £2 is every bit as profitable as making something which was worth £1 into something which is now worth £2. These arbitrage gains are the sources of the profits of Salomon Brothers and its clients. Since Salomon Brothers is competing with other bond trading firms, it bids up the wages of people whom it thinks will be good at spotting these discrepancies.

But there is only one possible employer of teachers of children with learning disabilities, and that is the government. The government is more interested in keeping down costs than in ensuring the highest standards. Bluntly, Salomon Brothers has to compete and government does not. So Salomon

Brothers takes the cream of British graduates, and teaching is left to those who cannot get jobs at Salomons, or do not want them. Economic analysis explains why this anomaly exists, and also helps to indicate what, if you feel concerned, you might be able to do about it.

Examples could go on. Most of what we really know about the economy is to do with microeconomics—about the behaviour of markets, firms, consumers, and industries—rather than about the macroeconomic issues of growth, unemployment, and inflation. Many economists now think that real progress in economic knowledge will come from building from the bottom up rather than from the top down. The day of huge economic models, in which some people imagined that the economy could be perfectly controlled and managed by sufficiently large computers, has gone—gone with the Berlin Wall and the ideal but hopeless central planning systems of Eastern Europe.

It is curious that so many people who affect to disparage macroeconomic modelling remain in thrall to it, and 'this has been tested on the Treasury model' is still regarded as a seal of approval. Macroeconomic models are—and have always been—a way of organizing thought about the economy, not a crystal ball, and what you get out of one is a direct reflection of the analysis, the perception, and the judgements that you put in. Naïve forecasting is to economics as astrology is to astronomy, and although astrology is bunk it does not follow that we can learn nothing from the stars.

5

··

Can There Be a Science of Business?

This chapter is concerned with whether there can be such a thing as a science of management. It begins with an exchange with an Economist *reviewer, and goes on to exemplify some of the issues involved in turning management from a subject based on the assertions of gurus to one which reproduces the structure of concepts, hypotheses, and empirical tests which is characteristic of the natural sciences. 'Good food costs less at Sainsbury's' is based on a much longer article, written with Michael Cronshaw and Evan Davis, which was published in the* British Journal of Management *(Cronshaw, Davis, and Kay 1994).*

QUACKS AND GURUS

For centuries, the subject of medicine was mostly nonsense.[1] Doctors applied fashionable nostrums, sometimes bleeding their patients, sometimes starving them. Generally these remedies were useless, sometimes they were fortuitously beneficial, at other times unintentionally harmful. States of health were defined by reference to ascientific categorization, such as the humours or the elements. The prestige of a doctor rested more on the status of his patients and the confidence of his assertions than on the evidence of his cures.

The parallels with management are obvious, if not exact, and the reasons for the parallels are obvious too. Both medicine and management deal with urgent and pressing problems. The demand for a cure is so pressing that critical faculties are suspended. The quack who promises relief often receives a warmer welcome than the practitioner who recognizes the limitations of his own knowledge, and since it is difficult to measure the effectiveness of treatment, this impression may persist even after it is over.

But in the last fifty years, the application of scientific method to medical

[1] Kay (1993: 362–3).

subjects, and the development and adoption of knowledge gained in physics, chemistry, and biology, has transformed their effectiveness. Medicine remains a practical subject. The experience and judgement of a good doctor is as important as the extent of his knowledge and the quality of his training.

Untrained individuals continue to express opinions on medical matters, not all of which are wrong. But few of us would now wish to put ourselves in the hands of doctors who had no such knowledge or training, or who professed to despise it.

GALILEO'S TELESCOPE

A critical reviewer for *The Economist* focused on this analogy. He asserted that the complexity, and pace of change, of management processes was such that no scientific management would ever be possible; managers would always be forced to rely on human intuition and judgement. I wrote the following reply, which was published in *The Economist*.[2]

The Inquisitors who visited Galileo refused to look through his telescope since what he claimed to see could not be there. In similar style, you dismiss on a priori grounds the possibility that management might be the subject of scientific inquiry.

As you rightly say, 'Dealing with those you know best is one of the oldest rules of business, and even that rule should sometimes be broken.' But when should it be broken? 'Some firms have damaged themselves by ignoring long term relationships' while others 'like Philips or IBM are suffering because of them'. How are we to know whether we are in one situation or the other? You do not know, or at least you do not tell us. That is why checklists for managers are so often misleading—'always deal with those you know'—or vacuous—'always deal with those you know except when it is better not to'.

The objective of putting science into management is to offer answers to such questions—to know when best to develop long-term trust relationships, and when to drive the hardest bargain available. You argue, as the Inquisition argued of the mysteries of the universe, that the business world is so complex that such knowledge is unattainable. Actually, understanding why IBM is failing is easier than explaining the motion of the planets. Yet you deny that management might even aspire to the status of medicine. 'Human bodies are similar enough to be the proper subject of scientific study. The differences between companies are far greater.' If you believe that, you do not know many people. 'Unlike the human body, companies change rapidly.' If you believe that, you do not know many companies, or any children.

2 *The Economist* (Apr. 1993).

So why are many professors and practical business executives, as well as journalists, so vehement that management cannot be the subject of scientific inquiry? The world in which everything is either well known or unknowable is a comfortable one. There is little to be learnt. One commonplace opinion is as good as any other, and the masters of the unknowable, whether the Church or Tom Peters, have unchallengeable authority. It is these attitudes which blocked progress for millennia.

A scientific proposition, in the Popperian tradition, is a generalization based on theory or experience, which constitutes a potentially falsifiable statement about the world. Here are five examples, drawn from hundreds in my book, *Foundations of Corporate Success*, to which you will have to refer for underlying theory and evidence.

- *Two competitors in an industry adopt similar pricing and positioning strategies. With more than two, strategies diverge.*
  Cellnet and Vodafone have had virtually identical services and price structures, but are changing them as new entrant is in prospect.
- *Joint ventures with a common objective succeed more often than those which offer mutual, but individual, benefits.*
  Joint marketing arrangements succeed more often than agreements to share information technology.
- *Diversification into related industries is much more often successful than diversification into related markets.*
  Attempts by oil companies to move into 'the energy business' by buying coal-mines failed, and Rank and Bass did not define a 'leisure business'.
- *Competitive advantages based on market positioning rarely last long.*
  Which is why Next and Ratners enjoyed only transitory success.
- *The size of the installed base and the credibility of the supplier matter more to the success of a standard than the technical quality of the product.*
  So Sky Television defeated BSB and IBM's unimaginative PC conquered the market.

So when should you 'deal with those you know best' and when 'should that rule be broken'? This really needs its own article, but relational contracts are most valuable where business relationships benefit from a continuing exchange of information. These form the basis of competitive advantage in fashion, media, and financial services but in property, energy, and commodities it is better to drive a hard bargain.

Failure to understand these propositions has cost companies involved hundreds of millions of pounds. Yet you are correct to say that none of them amounts to 'compelling advice'. That is to misunderstand their purpose. No medical text ends with a list of recommended operations; when you visit a doctor, you hope that her knowledge is for all time but her advice is specific to your situation. Analysing business problems should reflect the same approach. The recurrent theme of my book—that the achievement of successful companies owes more to differences between them than similarities—

has profound implications for business behaviour, but these need to be assessed in the context of each individual company, not encapsulated as tips for busy managers. Gurus who offer universal prescriptions—raise quality, go global—are exact analogues of pre-scientific doctors who peddled all-purpose remedies because they knew no better.

Worse still, you suggest that there can be no general principles of good management, and that corporate success depends on identifying the next fad ahead of the competition. It is hard to imagine more misconceived advice. To believe that the systematic study of business is impossible, you must not only refute all the propositions above, but assert that none like them will ever be established. That requires the arrogant confidence of the Inquisition, or *The Economist*. And even the Inquisition eventually gave way to the power of Galileo's telescope.

GOOD FOOD COSTS LESS AT SAINSBURY'S

One of the first tricks a management guru learns is the art of the 'shifting concept'.[3] The following exchange will give you the idea. The business school professor tells the class that successful firms must establish high market share. 'What about BMW?', asks the smart alec student in the front row, who knows that BMW have a far smaller share of the world car market than many less successful companies. 'Ah,' the professor replies triumphantly, 'BMW have a high market share in the luxury saloon segment.'

Take another example: the claim widespread a few years ago, that quality is free: higher quality invariably leads to higher profits. It only requires a second's thought to see that this claim is quite absurd, although a second is a long time in the world of management gurus. Harrods makes less profit than Wal-Mart, the Savoy was not as good an investment as Forte Travelodges, and Anita Brookner receives lower advances than Jeffrey Archer. Not many people need, or will pay for, the level of quality which Harrods, the Savoy, and Ms Brookner provide.

I expect that several management consultants have already switched on their laptops and modems to communicate with the Editor. They will write that I have completely misunderstood what is meant by quality. Other people would say that the Waterside Inn at Bray provides better-quality meals than McDonald's. That is how the Michelin guide assesses quality when it awards three stars to the Waterside Inn and does not trouble to list McDonald's at all. It is also what ordinary people mean by quality, and is why your partner will be more appreciative if you celebrate your wedding anniversary at the Waterside than at McDonald's.

But that ordinary meaning of quality is not what business gurus mean

---

[3] *Financial Times* (10 May 1996).

by quality. What they mean is quality relative to customer expectations, or quality relative to what you set out to achieve. By these standards, McDonald's quality is outstanding, and that is why McDonald's is such a successful company. There is a sense in which this is right. But the price a guru pays for this kind of infallibility is very high. Since there is no observation which could ever refute his claim, his maxim gives you no practical guidance.

So does the pursuit of quality mean these firms should change what they do? Should McDonald's offer duck à l'orange, or the Waterside Inn offer even more exquisite morsels at even more elevated prices? I do not know and nor does he. And the injunction creates confusion among simple people who thought that quality meant what it usually means. It had precisely that effect on British Home Stores, which though it had to move up market, only to discover that Marks & Spencer customers were happy at Marks & Spencer and British Home Stores customers did not want to pay the extra.

One of the most famous propositions in business strategy is Michael Porter's injunction not to be 'stuck in the middle'. 'The worst strategic error is to be stuck in the middle, or to try simultaneously to pursue all the strategies. This is a recipe for strategic mediocrity and below-average performance, because pursuing all the strategies simultaneously means that a firm is not able to achieve any of them because of their inherent contradictions' (Porter 1990: 5). 'A classic example is Laker Airways, which began with a clear cost focus. Over time, Laker began adding frills, new services and new routes. The consequences were disastrous' (Porter 1985: 17).

The trouble with this proposition is that it is just not true. Porter is wrong in his account of why Laker failed, and many successful firms are stuck in the middle. Every Sainsbury van has 'good food costs less at Sainsbury's' painted on the side. Is Sainsbury's problem today that it is stuck in the middle?

No: Sainsbury's is not alone. Table 5.1, drawn from the PIMS database, shows how return on investment relates to strategic position. The stuck in the middle position—medium cost, medium quality—in fact does slightly better than the clearly focused choices.

So what does a guru do when faced with the prospect of an own goal? You shift the posts. Perhaps do not be stuck in the middle means not that you

Table 5.1. Return on investment, by strategic position (%)

Cost relative to competitors	Quality relative to competitors		
	Low	Medium	High
Low	11.7	14.2	19.7
Medium	6.8	13.9	17.9
High	3.4	4.8	13.8

Source: Cronshaw, Davis, and Kay (1994).

must choose one or the other, but that if you do not succeed at something you will fail. Confronted by the Sainsbury van on British television, Porter argued that since Sainsbury was not a delicatessen, it must be a low-cost competitior. Yet if 'good food costs less' is not a strategic position which is stuck in the middle, it is hard to know what is.

Perhaps all 'do not be stuck in the middle' means is that it is good to be good at something. You can find support for that version from Porter as well. 'The firm failing to develop its strategy in at least one of three directions—a firm that is stuck in the middle—is in an extremely poor strategic situation' (Porter, 1980, p. 41). That, at least, is true. If you look at Table 5.1, you see that firms which have high cost/low quality do not do very well, and indeed that the best situation to be in is to achieve high quality at low cost. But while it is always useful to have one's intuitions confirmed, I think I already knew that.

The version of stuck in the middle that is true—you will not succeed if you are not good at something—is so nearly tautological as hardly to be worth enunciating. The version of it that has major content—that you cannot pursue both cost reduction and product differentiation—is clearly false. There are obvious dangers in confusing one with the other.

That is why clarity of terms and precision of concepts are essential precursors to worthwhile knowledge on any subject, including management. Dr Joad was not simply pedantic when he argued that it all depends what you mean by market share, quality, or being stuck in the middle. It does.

II

COMPETITIVE ADVANTAGE

At the end of Part I, I used the analogy of pre-scientific medicine to describe the weaknesses and the potential of management theory today. There is a cycle of fads and fashions, in which business buzzwords rapidly succeed each other. Yesterday it was 'total quality management', today 'business process re-engineering', with numerous texts on each making their inevitable way from the airport bookstalls to the remainder stores. In this world, each new guru emphasizes—often rightly—the irrelevance of all that has gone before, in a way which operates to his (or her, but usually his) commercial advantage but which precludes the development of the structured, progressive body of knowledge and analysis of the kind which is characteristic of any established intellectual discipline.

But there is an exciting contrast to this depressing picture. The development of what is called the 'resource-based theory of strategy' provides, for the first time in the study of the strategic issues of the firm, a substantial paradigm of the kinds which have been developed for physics, for economics, and for medicine as these subjects moved out of their pre-scientific phases into the age of modern rationalism. The resource-based theory unifies most of what is substantial and significant in our existing knowledge of business behaviour. I believe it is increasingly the case, as it is with dominant paradigms in other subjects, that serious contributions to strategic management can now be made only by people who have mastered this tradition and relate their analysis to it. The measure of a scientific paradigm is that those who work outside it are either geniuses or cranks (and overwhelmingly cranks).

The main elements of the resource-based theory may be summarized as follows:

- firms are essentially collections of capabilities;
- the effectiveness of a firm depends on the match between these capabilities and the market it serves;

- the growth, and appropriate boundaries, of a firm are limited by its capabilities;
- some of these capabilities can be purchased or created and are available to all firms;
- others are irreproducible, or reproducible only with substantial difficulty, by other firms, and it is on these that competitive advantage depends;
- such capabilities are generally irreproducible because they are a product of the history of the firm or by virtue of uncertainty (even within the firm itself) about their nature.

The term 'resource-based theory' appears to be due to Wernerfelt (1984; 1989; see Conner 1991); but its origins are probably most appropriately traced to Penrose (1959) and Richardson (1972). The best recent survey is probably Montgomery (1995). Some of the key contributing elements are:

- capabilities as contracts (Alchian and Demsetz 1972) or assets (Grossman and Hart 1986; Hart 1988);
- uncertain imitability (Lippman and Rumelt 1982);
- the identification of inimitable resources and capabilities (Dierckx and Cool 1989);
- an understanding of the relationship between resources and the evolution of the firm (Nelson and Winter 1982; Teece *et al* 1994);
- an emphasis on path-dependency (David 1986).

My own understanding of the resource-based theory is set out in Chapter 6, 'The Structure of Strategy'. Chapters 7 and 8 are designed to explore the relationship between that resource-based theory and conventional measures of firm performance, developing the central role of economic rent (or added value).

Those two chapters develop the theme that added value is created by competitive advantage based on distinctive capabilities: Chapter 9, 'No Free Lunches', is intended to emphasize that there are, in the long run, no other ways in which firms can successfully add value. Chapter 10 applies the resource-based theory of strategy to the competitive advantage, not of firms, but of nations.

6

The Structure of Strategy

In 1986 I was offered the opportunity, and substantial resources, to answer the question, 'What are the origins of industrial success?'[1] There are, perhaps, more important questions, but not many, and that was certainly the most important question I felt in any way equipped to try to answer. So I accepted the challenge.

It was obvious that there was no shortage of data. Every corporation is required to file detailed returns of its activities. In all Western economies there are several journals which track the performance and activities of leading companies. Case studies, business histories, and business biographies describe how decisions were made and problems overcome. I began to understand that what was needed was not to collect new information, but to establish a framework for understanding what was already known.

There were those who told me that the task I had set myself could not be done, or was not worth doing. Business problems were too complex to be susceptible to the use of analytic techniques. Every situation was unique and there could be no valid generalizations. It had even been argued by some (as in Abernathy and Hayes 1980) that the attempt to apply analytic methods to business issues is at the heart of Western economic decline.

It might be true that there can be no valid generalizations about business, and that there can be no general theories of the origins of corporate success or failure. But it does not seem very likely that it is true. It is not just that similar observations were made ahead of much greater leaps in scientific knowledge. How could we hope to understand something so complex, and so subject to change, as the motion of the planets or the make-up of genetic material?

The strategy of the firm is the match between its internal capabilities and its external relationships. It describes how it responds to its suppliers, its customers, its competitors, and the social and economic environment within which it operates. These aspects of management activity are the subject of strategy. Did it make sense for Benetton, an Italian knitwear manufacturer, to

---

[1] *Business Strategy Review* (Summer 1993), edited.

move into retailing, and was it right to decide to franchise most of its shops to individual entrepreneurs? Should Saatchi & Saatchi have attempted to build a global advertising business? What segment of the car market was most appropriate for BMW? These are typical issues of corporate strategy. Corporate strategy is concerned with the firm's choice of business, markets, and activities.

Should Eurotunnel offer a premium service or use its low operating costs to cut prices? How should Honda have approached the US motor cycle market? Faced with three different standards for high-definition television, and a market potentially worth tens of billions of pounds, what stance should a television manufacturer adopt? What will be the future of European airlines as deregulation progresses? These are typical issues of business, or competitive, strategy. Competitive strategy is concerned with the firm's position relative to its competitors in the markets which it has chosen.

On the face of it, these are issues which respond to analytic tools, and if analysis has failed to offer at least partial answers it is because it is bad analysis, not because the objective is misconceived. The analysis of strategy uses our experience of the past to develop concepts, tools, data, and models which will illuminate these decisions in future. Taking corporate and business strategy together, we learn why some firms succeed and others fail. Why did EMI fail to profit from its body scanner while Glaxo succeeded brilliantly in marketing its anti-ulcer drug, Zantac? Why has Philips earned so little from its record of innovation? Why has Marks & Spencer gone from strength to strength when so many other retailers have enjoyed spectacular, but purely transitory, success? What are the origins of corporate success?

What is success?

One paradox was immediately apparent in my pursuit of the origins of corporate success. If I asked what was meant by corporate success, many different answers were proposed. Some people emphasized size and market share, others stressed profitability and returns to shareholders. Some people looked to technical efficiency and innovative capability. Others stressed the reputation that companies enjoyed among their customers and employees, and in the wider business community.

Yet this disagreement was hardly reflected at all in disagreement about which companies were successful. Whatever their criteria of success, everyone seemed to point to the same companies—to Matsushita and to Hewlett-Packard, to Glaxo and to Benetton, to BMW and to Marks & Spencer. I formed the view that the achievement of any company is measured by its ability to add value—to create an output which is worth more than the cost of the inputs which it uses. These different opinions on how success should be measured were partly the result of disagreement about how added value was created, but rather more the product of different views as to how, once created, added value should be used. Successful companies, and successful economies, vary in the relative emphasis to be given to returns to shareholders, the maximization of profits, and the development of the business. Different firms, and different business cultures, gave different weights to these purposes. But the underlying objective of adding value was common to all.

I began by asking the managers of successful companies to explain the sources of their success. They told me that success depended on producing the right product at the right price at the right time. It was essential to know the market, to motivate employees, to demand high standards of suppliers and distributors. I recognized that all these things were true, but those who emphasized them were describing their success, not explaining it. There was much that had been written on strategic management. But stripped of rhetoric, most strategy texts offered checklists of issues that senior executives needed to address in considering the future of their business. That literature posed questions but yielded few answers.

Economists had studied the functioning of industry, but their concerns were mostly with public policy, not business policy, and I was sure that industrial success was founded on the behaviour of firms, not on the decisions of governments. Sociologists had studied the functioning of organizations, but only a few had matched the characteristics of the firm to the economic environment that determined its competitive performance.

I came to see that it was the match between the capabilities of the organization and the challenges it faced which was the most important issue in understanding corporate success and corporate failure. There are no recipes and generic strategies for corporate success. There cannot be, because if there were their general adoption would eliminate any competitive advantage which might be derived. The foundations of corporate success are unique to each successful company.

That uniqueness is a product of the firm's contracts and relationships. I see the firm as a set of relationships between its various stakeholders—employees, customers, investors, shareholders. The successful firm is one which creates a distinctive character in these relationships and which operates in an environment which maximizes the value of that distinctiveness.

BMW

Few who drive a BMW car know what the initials stand for, or realize that the distinctive blue and white propeller badge reproduces the colours of the state flag of the State of Bavaria. The Bayerische Motoren Werke were established during the First World War. They specialized in the manufacture of engines. The company subsequently diversified into what are now its two principal product ranges: automobiles and motor cycles. Today BMW is one of Germany's largest and most successful companies.

BMW cars are not the most powerful, or the most reliable, or the most luxurious on the market, although they score well against all these criteria. No one has ever suggested that they are cheap, even for the high level of specification that most models offer. Although BMW rightly emphasizes the quality and advanced nature of its technology, its products are not exceptionally innovative. The design of the company's cars is conventional and the styling of its models is decidedly traditional.

The achievements of BMW are built on two closely associated factors. The company achieves a higher quality of engineering than is usual in production cars. While most car assembly has now been taken over by robots or workers from low-wage economies, BMW maintains a skilled German labour force. The company benefits, as many German firms do, from an educational system which gives basic technical skills to an unusually high proportion of the population. Its reputation has followed from these substantial achievements. In this, BMW is representative of much of German manufacturing industry.

Yet BMW's success was neither easy nor certain (Mönnich 1989; Bastow 1991). In 1945 the company was Germany's leading manufacturer of aero-engines. Its primary market and its capital equipment were both in ruins. Its principal factory at Eisenach was across the border in the Soviet occupation zone. While German recovery through the 1950s occurred at a pace which attracted the title of economic miracle, BMW did not prosper. Uncertain of its future, the company emphasized automobiles but its products ranged from tiny bubble cars, manufactured under licence, to limousines. In 1959 the firm faced bankruptcy and a rescue by Mercedes seemed its only hope of survival.

Instead, BMW found a powerful shareholder—Herbert Quandt—who perceived the company's inherent strengths. The turning point came when the firm identified a market which most effectively exploited its capabilities—the market for high-performance saloon cars, which has since become almost synonymous with BMW. The BMW 1500, launched in 1961, established a reputation for engineering quality in the BMW automobile brand. The brand in turn acquired a distinctive identity as a symbol for young, affluent European professionals. That combination—a system of production which gives the company a particular advantage in its chosen market segment, a world-wide reputation for product quality, and a brand which immediately identifies the aims and aspirations of its customers—continues to make BMW one of the most profitable automobile manufacturers in the world.

Today, the BMW business is structured to maximize these advantages. Retail margins on BMW cars are relatively high. The company maintains tight control over its distribution network. This control supports the brand image and also aids market segmentation. BMW cars are positioned differently and priced very differently in the various national markets. The same tight control is reflected in BMW's relationships with suppliers, who mostly have continuing long associations with the company. BMW's activities are focused almost exclusively on two product ranges—high-performance saloon cars and motor bikes which reflect its competitive strengths. The company also uses the brand to support a range of motoring accessories.

BMW is a company with a well-executed strategy. It is a company which came—after several false starts—to recognize its distinctive capabilities and chose the market, and subsequent markets, which realized its full potential. Its dealings with its suppliers and distributors, its pricing approach, its branding and advertising strategies, are all built around that recognition and these choices. There was no master plan, no single vision which took BMW from where it was in 1959 to where it is today. There was a group within the company which believed strongly that a model like the 1500 was the firm's main hope of survival. There were other views, other options. No one had more than partial insight into what the future would hold. But BMW's success was no accident either.

Honda

Honda's redefinition of the US motor cycle market is a classic case in corporate strategy (Harvard Business School). Motor bikes in the USA in the 1950s were associated with a subculture now best recalled through movies, leather jackets, the smell of oil, and teenage rebellion. In 1964, five years after its entry into the United States, one in three motor cycles sold there was a Honda. The best-selling product was a 50cc supercub, marketed under the slogan, 'You meet the nicest people on a Honda.'

There are two views of this achievement. In one, Honda's strategy was an archetype of Japanese penetration of Western markets. The aggressive pursuit of domestic volume established a low-cost base for expansion overseas. This was the conclusion of a Boston Consulting Group study for the British government (Boston Consulting Group 1975). A rather different account was given by Richard Pascale, who went to Tokyo to interview the elderly Japanese who had brought the first Honda machines to the United States. As they recalled it, Honda had aimed to secure a modest share of the established US motor cycle market. 'Mr Honda was especially confident of the 250 cc and 305 cc machines. The shape of the handlebar on these larger machines looked like the eyebrows of Buddha, which he felt was a strong selling point' (Pascale 1982: 54). These hopes were not realized. The eyebrows of Buddha had little attraction for the leather-jacketed Marlon Brando.

'We dropped in on motor cycle dealers who treated us discourteously and, in addition, gave the general impression of being motor cycle enthusiasts who, secondarily, were in business' (Pascale 1982: 54). The first supercubs exported to the United States were used by Honda employees for their own personal transport around the concrete wastes of Los Angeles. It was only when these caught the attention of a Sears buyer, and the larger machines started to show reliability problems, that Honda put its efforts behind the

50cc machines. The 'nicest people' slogan was invented by a University of California undergraduate.

Neither of these accounts is entirely convincing. The BCG account is an expression of the near paranoia created for many Westerners by Japanese achievement. But Pascale's suggestion that Honda's success was simply the result of good fortune would be more persuasive if the company had not been blessed by such good fortune quite so often in the course of its spectacular rise. The 'eyebrows of Buddha' are all too reminiscent of the South Sea island girls who teased Margaret Mead with ever more extravagant accounts of their sexual exploits.

We shall never know the extent to which Honda's success was truly the result of chance or rational calculation. But while knowing may be important to the business historian, it is of little significance to the corporate strategist. Quinn, Mintzberg, and James (1988)—in what is perhaps the best of recent strategy texts—pose for their readers the question (p. 81), 'Ask yourself while reading these accounts, how the strategic behaviour of the British motor cycle manufacturers who received the BCG report might have differed if they had instead received Pascale's second story.' The correct answer, of course, is 'Not at all.' Suppose it were shown conclusively that Honda's success was the result of purest chance. It would not then follow that the right approach for British firms was to wait for similar good fortune to fall on them. This was what they in fact did, with notable lack of success.

Honda effected a brilliantly successful market entry. Like all successful strategies, it was based on a mixture of calculation and opportunism, of vision and experiment. Like all successful corporate strategies, it was centred on Honda's distinctive capability—an established capacity to produce an innovative but simple, low-cost product. Its realization depended on a successful competitive strategy, which made full use of segmentation and involved the creation of a distinctive distribution network which bypassed the traditional retail outlets of the enthusiasts. The lessons we can learn from that strategy are much the same whether Honda conceived it by grand design or stumbled on it by accident.

The nature of strategy

The issues that BMW and Honda handled so successfully are the central questions of strategy. BMW and Honda had to consider what markets to enter, how to position their products within these markets, how to build relationships with dealers and component manufacturers. The subject of strategy analyses the firm's relationships with its environment, and a business strategy is a scheme for handling these relationships. Such a scheme may be articulated, or implicit, pre-programmed, or emergent. A strategy—like that of BMW or Honda—is a sequence of united events which amounts to a coherent pattern of business behaviour.

If the subject of business strategy focuses on the relationship between the firm and its environment, there are many key management issues which it does not address. Strategy is not principally concerned with employee motivation, or with finance, or with accounting, or with production scheduling and inventory control, although these may influence the firm's strategy and be influenced by it. In the last two decades, the pretensions and prestige of the subject of strategy have been such that strategists have stressed not only the central importance of the issues with which they deal but also the relevance of strategy to all aspects of business behaviour. For the same reasons, everyone involved in business—from the personnel manager to the public relations consultant—has asserted a right to contribute to the strategy process.

But strategy is not simply another word for important. There are many aspects to good management, and to say that strategy and operations management are distinct facets of it is not to disparage either. Yet there is a difference between strategy and these other elements of management practice which illuminates the nature of strategy itself and may partly explain its supposed primacy. In most industries, there are many firms which have their finance and accounting right, their human relations right, their information technology adapted to their needs. For one firm to succeed in these areas does not damage others. In implementing finance and accounting, human relations and information technology, it is right, and normal, to look to the best practice in other firms.

But strategy is not like that. Honda and BMW did not establish their market positions by methods which built on the best practice of their competitors. For both companies attempts to match their rivals' strategies failed. BMW's bubble cars were not as well regarded as Innocenti's, and its limousines were inferior to those of Mercedes. Honda was able to sell powerful motor bikes in the USA only after its success with quite different products had destroyed its competitors' finances and established its own reputation. Successful strategy is rarely copycat strategy. It is based on doing well what rivals cannot do or cannot do readily, not what they can do, or are already doing.

Groupe Bull

Despite its current well-publicized problems, IBM has been, for the last three decades, perhaps the most successful corporation in the world. It has dominated a large, rapidly growing, and profitable market and its products have changed every aspect of business behaviour. IBM is a high-tech. company but its strength is not simply derived from its technology, where it has often chosen to follow rather than to lead. IBM's most famous advertising slogan— 'No one ever got fired for choosing IBM'—was not devised or used by the company, but by its customers. It reflects the company's true distinctive capability—its ability to deliver not just hardware but solutions to its clients' problems, and its reputation for having that ability.

European politicians and businessmen have long dreamt of creating a European IBM. The British government promoted ICL, the Germans Nixdorf and Siemens, the Italians supported Olivetti. These companies have succeeded only in subsectors of the computer market. The European government most determined to resist IBM's hegemony across the full range of computers has been the French, and the European company most determined to resist it has been Groupe Bull.

Bull is, curiously, named after a Norwegian whose patented punch card system proved popular with French banks before the Second World War. But Bull's greatest success came when its gamma sixty range offered perhaps the most advanced and innovative machines available as the computer age dawned in the 1960s. That gave the company a world-wide name, and marketing capability, but the ninety range which followed failed to live up to specifications. The company recognized that it lacked the technical capacity to challenge IBM alone and that the USA would be by far the largest geographic market for computers. It looked for a US partner, and found a strong one in General Electric. De Gaulle, outraged by the dilution of the vision of a French world leader in computing, first blocked the deal. When it eventually went ahead, the irate President established a state-owned, and wholly French, competitor, Cii. Cii was less successful than Bull and in 1976 the two companies merged. The firm soon reverted to its original name but the French state now had a majority stake.

General Electric came to an early conclusion that the computer market was IBM's, and quit it completely. Bull found a new American partner in Honeywell. The company enjoyed a captive market in the French public sector, and did well more generally in francophone countries, but elsewhere the gap between IBM and either Honeywell or Bull continued to widen. Through the 1980s Bull struggled, surviving only on the continued support of its indulgent principal shareholder. Eventually Honeywell too gave up the chase, and Bull bought out its partner.

In 1989 Groupe Bull acquired a new chief executive, Francis Lorentz, who reasserted the company's primary objective—'To become the major European supplier of global information systems.'[2] The emphasis had shifted slightly from a French to a European base, but the central message remained the same. But by now even IBM was faltering. IBM's distinctive capabilities remained strong, but markets had changed. A computer had become a commodity, not a mystery, and there could be one on every manager's desk. In 1990 Bull posted large losses, and 1991 was a worse year still. Early in 1992 Bull announced an alliance with IBM, and Lorentz left the company soon after.

For thirty years Groupe Bull has been a company driven not by an assessment of what it was but by a vision of what it would like to be. Throughout it has lacked the distinctive capabilities which would enable it to realize that

[2] *Financial Times* (30 June 1989), 29.

vision. Bull—and the other attempts at European clones of IBM—epitomize wish-driven strategy, based on aspiration, not capability. Effective strategy, like that of BMW or Honda, starts from what the company is distinctively good at, not from what it would like to be good at, and is adaptive and opportunistic in exploiting what is distinctive in these capabilities.

Creating strategy

There is nothing new in saying that strategies should be adaptive and opportunistic, or that planning should start with an assessment of the firm's distinctive capabilities. Yet these observations are often misinterpreted. Adaptive strategy is contrasted—quite mistakenly—with analytical approaches to strategy, while the real contrast is with the vision, the mission, and the wish-driven strategy, about which there is nothing analytical at all. To say that we cannot forecast where our organizations will be in five years' time is not to say that we cannot plan for the future. To say that successful businesses and successful entrepreneurs are opportunistic, like Honda, is not to say that firms and managers should, like the British motor cycle industry, wait to see what turns up.

When strategists talk of distinctive capabilities they quickly turn to talk of how to build them. This is evidently important, and most distinctive capabilities have, in some sense or other, been created by the firms which hold them today. Yet the attempt to establish distinctive capabilities confronts its own version of wish-driven strategy. Building distinctive capabilities must be a task of exceptional difficulty because, if it were not, the capability would soon cease to be distinctive. The story of Komatsu's conquest of Caterpillar—how a small Japanese company took on the world's largest producer of earth-moving equipment, and won—has become the business equivalent of 'from log cabin to White House' (HBS 1985; 1990). But, like the epic of Abraham Lincoln, it is often misinterpreted .[3] The lesson of Lincoln's success is not that anyone can become president of the United States if they try hard enough, but that in an open society exceptional talent can thrive however humble its origins. The lesson of Komatsu is that the internationalization of modern business creates commercial opportunities as wide-ranging as the political opportunities offered by the democratization of the United States. Komatsu succeeded because of the quality and competitive price of its products. Its achievement was the product of its competitive advantage, not the strength of its will.

---

[3] And, like much written abut Lincoln, largely apocryphal. Komatsu entered the US market with a very aggressive pricing strategy, and imposed massive losses on Caterpillar, which was unwilling to cede market share, and ready to cut prices to retain it. Komatsu's price policy proved difficult for the Japanese company itself to sustain, and in the end it allowed prices to drift upwards and has settled for a modest share of the US market (Kotler 1991: 13).

So firms should generally look to define and identify distinctive capabilities rather than create them. Although it is possible to create distinctive capabilities, success is more often based on exploitation of those capabilities which the firm already enjoys. These may derive from its history or from its location, or they may be capabilities which it has already established in related markets or industries. Strategy begins with an understanding of what these distinctive capabilities are.

Saatchi & Saatchi

Saatchi & Saatchi was, for a time, the best-known advertising agency in the world. An advertisement devised to promote birth control, which showed a picture of a pregnant man, created a mixture of controversy and envy which promoted a small agency controlled by Charles and Maurice Saatchi to national fame. The agency's contribution to Margaret Thatcher's first successful election campaign in 1979 turned that domestic reputation into an international one.

But international recognition was not enough. The Saatchis determined to create an international business. In 1983, it is reported (by Fallon 1988: 203), Maurice Saatchi read a famous article in the *Harvard Business Review* on the development of global markets (Levitt 1983). Inspired by the vision it held out, he flew the Atlantic to learn the full details of the new doctrine. These transatlantic flights were to become more frequent as the operating companies within Saatchi & Saatchi came to span not just Britain and the United States but other continents and other markets.

By the end of the decade, Saatchi & Saatchi was, as the brothers had intended, the world's first truly international, interdisciplinary, marketing and consultancy organization. It was also in serious financial difficulty. Under pressure from bankers and stockholders, the Saatchis relinquished executive control and a new management team set to work dismantling the empire which the brothers' vision had put together.

Saatchi & Saatchi began with a reputation that was unmatched in its business, and a creative team that was almost equally admired. These are characteristic assets of the highly successful professional service firm. The firms it bought were firms which had precisely these assets themselves. Its largest acquisition, Ted Bates, was itself one of the largest and most respected advertising agencies in the United States and had no need of the Saatchi label. It already enjoyed an equivalent reputation in its own market and there was never any suggestion that it would trade under the Saatchi name. International customers did not bring their business to the new merged agency. They took it away, fearing conflicts of interest as the enlarged concern was often already handling the accounts of their competitors. Ted Bates was worth less to Saatchi & Saatchi than to almost any other purchaser. Saatchi already had those things which made Bates valuable and they were worth less, not more, under Saatchi ownership.

But in the grip of the strategic objective of internationalization, Saatchi paid a large premium to gain control of that and other businesses. For a time, the inherent weaknesses of the strategy were concealed by the growth in the underlying earnings of the businesses, and the capacity of the Saatchi share price to drift ever upwards on a cushion of hot air. Eventually, earnings faltered and the hot air escaped. The company was left with a mountain of debt and a collection of businesses that, while sound in themselves, were not worth the prices that had been paid for them.

Wish-driven strategy failed for Groupe Bull because the goal was unattainable. Wish-driven strategy failed for Saatchi & Saatchi because the goal, although attainable and attained, was not a sensible one for that particular company to pursue. Wish-driven strategy emphasizes the importance of the corporate vision, frequently starts with an assertion of the mission statement, and creates a company driven by a view of what it would like to be. The Saatchi strategy was based on a dream, rather than an analysis of the competitive strengths of the business, and the company adapted to market realities only when corporate collapse was staring it in the face.

Sustainability and appropriability

A capability can only be distinctive if it is derived from a characteristic which other firms lack. Yet it is not enough for that characteristic to be distinctive. It is necessary also for it to be *sustainable* and *appropriable*. A distinctive capability is sustainable only if it persists over time. Honda's achievement was not only to redefine the US motor cycle market, but to remain leaders in that market. A distinctive capability is appropriable only if it exclusively or principally benefits the company which holds it. Often the benefits of a distinctive capability are appropriated instead by employees, by customers, or by competitors. There are relatively few types of distinctive capability which meet these conditions of sustainability and appropriability. There are three which recur in analysis of the performance of successful companies. *Innovation* is an obvious source of distinctive capability, but it is less often a sustainable or appropriable source because successful innovation quickly attracts imitation. Maintaining an advantage is most easily possible for those few innovations for which patent production is effective. There are others where process secrecy or other characteristics make it difficult for other firms to follow. More often, turning an innovation into a competitive advantage requires the development of a powerful range of supporting strategies.

What appears to be competitive advantage derived from innovation is frequently, in fact, the return to a system of organization capable of producing a series of innovations. This is an example of a second distinctive capability which I call architecture. *Architecture* is a system of relationships within the firm, or between the firm and its suppliers and customers, or both. Generally, the system is a complex one and the content of the relationships implicit rather than explicit. The structure relies on continued mutual commitment to monitor and enforce its terms. A firm with distinctive architecture gains strength from the ability to transfer firm product and market-specific information within the organization and to its customers and suppliers. It can also respond quickly and flexibly to changing circumstances. It has often been through their greater ability to develop such architecture that Japanese firms have established competitive advantages over their American rivals.

A third distinctive capability is *reputation*. Reputation is, in a sense, a type of architecture, but it is so widespread and so important that it is best to treat it as a distinct source of competitive advantage. Easier to maintain than to create, reputation meets the essential conditions for sustainability. Indeed, an important element of the strategy of many successful firms has been the transformation of an initial distinctive capability based on innovation or architecture, to a more enduring one derived from reputation.

From capabilities to competitive advantages

A distinctive capability becomes a competitive advantage when it is *applied to an industry* and *brought to a market*. The market and the industry have both product and geographic dimensions. Sometimes the choice of market follows immediately from the nature of the distinctive capability. An innovation will usually suggest its own market. Pilkington discovered the float glass process, a system by which thin sheets of glass were formed on a bed of molten tin, which made the traditional grinding and polishing of plate glass unnecessary. Little need be said about the industry and markets where such an innovation is to be applied and it is other aspects of strategy that are critical. There are few geographical boundaries to innovation. While most innovating firms will begin in their home markets, successful innovation is rarely inhibited by national boundaries. The appropriate product market for an innovation is not always obvious, and identifying precisely what it is can be crucial. The demand for video cassette recorders turned out to be based on pre-recorded films rather than home movies. That required a playing time of three hours rather than one. JVC saw that small difference more quickly than Sony, and that was one key influence on success and failure in that particular market. The liquid crystal display, a scientific curiosity when it was introduced, was an innovation waiting decades for an application.

Other firms have distinctive capabilities based on their architecture, and the same architecture advantage can often be employed in a wide range of industries and markets. For BMW, the choice of industry and market segment was by no means obvious, but was ultimately crucial. For Honda, the choice of market segment did seem obvious. In the wide open spaces of the United States, they anticipated little demand for the small machines which were popular in congested Japan. But this view was doubly wrong. The market for large bikes which they had chosen was one in which Honda had no competitive advantage. Success came only from a very different product positioning. The market segments these companies selected, high-performance saloons for BMW, lightweight, low-powered motor cycles for Honda, were both innovative but well suited to their underlying distinctive capabilities.

Reputations are created in specific markets. A reputation necessarily relates to a product or a group of products. It is bounded geographically, too. Many reputations are very local in nature. The good plumber or doctor neither has nor needs a reputation outside a tightly defined area. Retailing reputations are mostly national. But an increasing number of producers of manufactured goods, from Coca-Cola to Sony, have established reputations world-wide, and branding has enabled international reputations to be created and exploited for locally delivered services in industries as diverse as accountancy and car hire.

A firm can only enjoy a competitive advantage relative to another firm in the same industry. So BMW may enjoy a competitive advantage over Nissan, but be at a competitive disadvantage to Mercedes. As this example illustrates, a competitive advantage is a feature of a particular market. These three firms compete in several different markets, or market segments, and the pattern of relative competitive advantages and disadvantages is different in each one. The value of a competitive advantage will depend on the strength of the firm's distinctive capability, the size of the market, and the overall profitability of the industry.

It is easier to sustain a distinctive capability in a narrow market than a wide one, more profitable to hold it in a wide market than a narrow one. And the profitability of a firm depends both on the competitive advantage the firm holds relative to other firms in the industry, and on the profitability of the industry itself. If there is excess capacity in the industry—as in automobiles— then even a large competitive advantage may not yield substantial profits

But if entry to an industry is difficult, then a firm without any competitive advantage may nevertheless earn very large returns. There is little reason to think that the large monopolistic utilities which control many parts of the European energy, transport, and communications industries have strong distinctive capabilities of the kind that characterize BMW, or Honda, or IBM. Their market dominance has not been built on doing things that others could not do as well, but on doing things that others were not permitted to do at all. Yet many of these firms are very profitable. There can be no greater competitive advantage than the absence of competitors. Profits come not only from distinctive capabilities but from possession of *strategic assets*—competitive advantages which arise from the structure of the market rather than from the specific attributes of firms within that market.

Glaxo and EMI

Corporate strategy is concerned with matching markets to distinctive capabilities. Business strategy looks at the relationship between the firm and its competitors, suppliers, and customers in the markets which it has chosen.

In the 1970s two British firms, Glaxo and EMI, developed important innovations. Both depended critically on their sales in the US medical services market (dell'Osso 1990). Glaxo had found an effective anti-ulcer drug, Zantac. EMI's scanner was the most important advance in radiology since the discovery of X-rays. Glaxo transformed itself from a medium-ranking drug company with an uncertain future, to Europe's leading pharmaceutical producer. EMI, crippled by losses on its scanner business, ceased to exist as an independent company and is no longer involved in medical electronics. EMI's capability was much the more distinctive. The scanner won the Nobel Prize for Physics for its inventor, Geoffrey Houndsfield. The market for anti-ulcerants has long been recognized as a potentially lucrative target—ulcers are common, persistent, and rarely fatal. An effective therapy emerged from the research of a British scientist, Sir James Black, but it was a US company, SmithKline, which developed Tagamet, the first commercial product based on it. Zantac was discovered after Glaxo refocused its research programme following the publication of Dr Black's results.

For both Glaxo and EMI, the choice of markets was not a difficult issue. Their markets were suggested by the nature of their innovation. (Although this was less obvious at an earlier stage of development in the scanner. EMI had a defence-based technology seeking an application, and it was a lateral leap by Houndsfield which took the company into medical electronics. For Glaxo, however, the innovation followed the market and the market the innovation.)

The key questions for both companies were issues of business strategy. The choice of market identified suppliers, customers, and competitors. Relationships with suppliers were not of special importance to either company, but relationships with customers and competitors most certainly were. EMI attempted to create its own US distribution network and to price at a level designed to recoup development costs. President Carter, concerned about spiralling medical bills, imposed a 'certificate of need' requirement on publicly funded hospitals. This delayed sales while General Electric developed its own version of the scanner. Although EMI had little experience of any manufacturing in this field, far less overseas, the company established a US manufacturing plant, which ran into serious output and quality problems. When GE entered the market, EMI was rapidly swept away and the rump of the business was sold to its larger competitor.

Patent protection—which had not proved sufficiently effective either for SmithKline or EMI—served Glaxo well, and helped ensure that its competitive advantage was sustainable. Glaxo began to market its drugs in the USA through Hoffmann-La Roche, whose sales of Librium and Valium had made the firm by far the most effective European pharmaceutical company in the US market. Glaxo entered Japan through a joint venture with a Japanese partner. In Britain and Italy, where Glaxo had a strong established market reputation, Glaxo skilfully exploited concern about possible Tagamet side effects, and priced Zantac at premia to Tagamet which reflected the company's own variable relative strength in different markets. By the mid-1980s, Zantac had become the world's best-selling drug, and over the decade the company earned about £4 billion in profits from its sale. By any standards, Glaxo is an outstandingly successful European company.

7

....

Competitive Advantage

In Chapter 5, I emphasized that clarity of concepts and quantification were essential to the provision of any scientific basis for the analysis of business issues. Here I attempt to establish definition and quantification for the most widely used term in business strategy—competitive advantage.[1]

The sources of competitive advantage

The profits a firm earns depend partly on the industry it is in and partly on its relative performance within that industry. Most of the evidence we have suggests that relative performance is much the more important of the two. The best survey of this issue is by Richard Rumelt, who was able to use a unique dataset which disaggregated the returns of a large sample of American firms by reference to their profitability in different industries. Rumelt's findings are shown in Table 7.1. One factor that seems to matter hardly at all is corporate ownership. The company headquarters makes almost no difference to the performance of its operating divisions. It does not matter much whether a business unit belongs to ICI or DuPont, to ITT or British Telecom. That raises fundamental questions about the rationale of diversification and of conglomerates—questions, indeed, which company executives have increasingly asked themselves.

Table 7.1. **Contributions to the variance of profits across business units (%)**

Corporate ownership	0.8
Industry effects	8.3
Cyclical effect	7.8
Business unit-specific effects	46.4
Unexplained factors	36.7

Source: Rumelt (1991).

[1] *Economics and Business Education*, 1/1/2 (Summer 1993), edited.

Rumelt goes on to show that what industry you are in does make a difference, but that a lot of this is explained by what he calls cyclical effects. At the moment, most contracting and construction firms are reporting low profits, but that is not because construction is intrinsically a bad business to be in (or not necessarily), but because this particular recession, created by high interest rates, has hit all the firms in that industry. But by far the largest contributor to explaining differences in profits is business unit-specific effects. There are no systematically successful firms, there are no systematically successful industries—but there are systematically successful business units, which outperform their competitors year by year. These are businesses that enjoy competitive advantages.

Firm performance and competitive advantage

One confusing thing about looking at the profits of a firm is that economists and accountants mean different things when they talk about profit. Accountants are concerned to establish what has been earned for the company's shareholders. The economist, however, wants to deduct the cost of the capital services the company buys—including those the shareholders provide—in order to arrive at the supernormal profit, or economic rent, which the firm earns.

I prefer to call this 'added value' because most businessmen dislike the term supernormal profit and think that rent is what you pay your landlord. Added value should not, however, be confused with the 'value added' of the firm, which is the sum of the operating profit and the wages and salaries the firm pays. This is the basis for measuring its value added tax liability and its contribution to national income; added value is what is left of value added when you have subtracted both labour costs and the cost of capital from it.

Table 7.2 shows how this works for two companies. One is Glaxo, which added more value than any other European company in the 1980s, by virtue of the enormous success of its anti-ulcer drug Zantac. The other is Philips, the Dutch electronics giant whose repeated failure to translate its innovative

Table 7.2. Success and failure in adding value, 1990 (m. ECUS)

	Glaxo	Philips
Revenues	3,985	24,247
Less: material costs	1,528	15,716
Value added	2,457	8,531
Less: wages and salaries	901	7,666
Less: capital costs	437	2,932
'Added value'	1,120	–2,067

record into commercial success means that it subtracted value rather than added it.

One forceful way of expressing this is to say that each pound of net output that Glaxo created cost it 54p to produce, whereas the comparable figure for Philips was 124p. Assessing different companies in this way leads directly to the measurement of competitive advantage which, after all, rests directly on producing the same output with less input, or greater output with the same input, than your competitors. Figure 7.1 makes that comparison for the six leading British supermarket chains.

Competitive advantages are always relative. A firm has a competitive advantage—or not—over another firm which serves the same market, or over another firm in the same industry. In Figure 7.1, Sainsbury has a very slight competitive advantage over Tesco. These firms serve very similar markets and they see themselves as members of the same strategic group. The battle for leadership in UK food retailing is fought between these two firms and there is a skirmish in that battle at every new supermarket location.

Does Kwik Save have a competitive advantage over Sainsbury? There is a sense in which it does. £1 of output costs Sainsbury 91p and Kwik Save only 82p. But Sainsbury and Kwik Save are not really in the same market. Each would see the other as a peripheral, rather than a direct, competitor. Sainsbury focuses its attention on Tesco, Kwik Save on new entrants such as Aldi and Food Giant. The comparison only makes any sort of sense because Sainsbury and Kwik Save are part of the same industry—they are members of the same trade association, they are grouped together when official statistics are compiled.

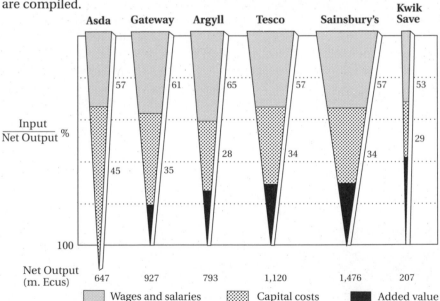

Fig. 7.1. The Value of Competitive Advantage
Source: Kay (1993).

If Kwik Save has a large competitive advantage, it is because its market niche is small and it has few rivals. Sainsbury has a lesser competitive advantage in a broader and more competitive market segment. So although Kwik Save adds more value per unit of input, Sainsbury adds more value overall. This is a trade-off which every firm faces. The markets where a company has the greatest competitive advantage are usually—and certainly ought to be— the markets which the firm is already in. As it expands into new product and geographical markets, its competitive advantage, relative to firms which are already serving these markets, is likely to be less. But so long as it has *some* competitive advantage over a firm which is profitably serving these markets, it should enter, even at the cost of reducing its overall competitive advantage. That is what has been happening, and will continue to happen, to Kwik Save. Initially, it chose the best stores in the best locations for its style of business, situations in which it faced the least competition from its rivals. As its business grows, its overall competitive advantage diminishes but, so long as it handles that expansion correctly, the total added value the company creates will nevertheless increase.

Asda—as the weakest of the major firms in the food-retailing industry and the weakest in the mainline market segment—provides a possible baseline for the performance of the others. Asda is not a bad or a badly managed firm. Its stores are modern, clean, and well stocked with products that are good value for money. Asda has survived in a period when many weaker chains and very many independent grocers have failed. Asda has a competitive advantage over these firms, but that is no longer relevant since these firms no longer compete. In British food retailing, which is a competitive market and one in which overall standards are high, you need to be as good as Asda in order to survive. Strategy and competitive advantage are what distinguish the best companies from the ordinary, not what distinguish the good from the bad.

A natural way to measure the competitive advantage of Sainsbury and Tesco, of Kwik Save and Argyll, is in relation to Asda. Both Sainsbury and Tesco are firms with competitive advantage, but Sainsbury's competitive advantage is greater than Tesco's. *Where no explicit comparator is stated, the relevant benchmark is the marginal firm in the industry. The weakest firm which still finds it worthwhile to serve the market provides the baseline against which the competitive advantage of all other firms can be set. In this way, it is possible to measure the size of a competitive advantage.* Sainsbury's competitive advantage over Asda is 10 per cent of net output and 1.7 per cent of gross output, implying that a unit of net output costs it only 90 per cent of what it costs Asda and that a unit of gross sales is achieved with 1.7 per cent fewer total inputs. The value of that competitive advantage over Asda is around £100 million per year, given that Sainsbury has gross output of nearly £5 billion and net output of around £1 billion. That is a measure of the difference in the value created by a highly successful firm, with strong distinctive capabilities, over that achieved by the merely competent.

The definition of that benchmark provides an immediate link from competitive advantage to added value. In a contestable industry, one in which entry and exit are relatively free and not very costly, marginal firms—the Asdas of their particular markets—will neither add value nor subtract it. They will not add value because if they did, others would be attracted to enter the industry. Either returns to everyone would be bid down or the marginal firm would be joined by another, yet more marginal firm, over which the original firm had a competitive advantage. Nor in a contestable industry will the marginal firm continue to subtract value by earning less from its assets than it would if they were sold and the resources used elsewhere. If that were true, it should quit the industry. Some other firm would then become the marginal firm, and that would be the new baseline for competitive advantage.

Food retailing is close to being a contestable industry. Small-scale entry is not too difficult. Capital requirements are modest and there are few regulatory restrictions. Stores can be used for other purposes, so that leaving the industry, or reducing capacity in it, is less costly than in many areas of business (although the growth of specialist superstores is changing this). No market is perfectly contestable, but this one is workably so and several firms have entered and left. If others are discouraged from entry, it is from a perception of the strength of the competitive advantages of the incumbents. In a contestable market, as in food retailing, the added value earned by firms reflects the value of their competitive advantage.

The sources of competitive advantage

So where do firms—like Glaxo, Sainsbury, or Kwik Save—derive their competitive advantage? A firm can be defined as a set of contracts and relationships. Added value is created by its success in putting these contracts and relationships together, so it is the quality and distinctiveness of these contracts that promote added value. The distinctiveness is at least as important as the goodness. The reason is that in an efficient market there are few opportunities to make good contracts.

The term 'efficient market' is most frequently used in financial markets. An efficient market is simply one in which there are no bargains, because what is to be known about the item being sold is already reflected in its price. The advice 'Buy Glaxo shares because Glaxo is a well-managed company with outstanding products' is worthless, even if it is a type of advice that is often given, because these facts about Glaxo are well known and fully incorporated in the value of its shares. In broader business terms, the more general implications of market efficiency are much the same. Opportunities that are available to everyone will not be profitable for everyone or perhaps anyone; what other people can equally see and do is unlikely to be a sustained source of added value.

Thus the efficient market hypothesis relates directly to the finding—

described above—that there is no such thing as an attractive or unattractive industry. It will not remain attractive or unattractive for long because entry and exit will deal with that. But another implication of the efficient market hypothesis is that value cannot be added on a sustained basis simply by making better contracts than other people since these opportunities are unlikely to be available for long. Value is added by developing a set of relationships which others are unable to make. A firm can achieve added value only on the basis of some distinctive capability—some feature of its relationships which other firms lack and cannot readily reproduce.

The firm may make a new contract or arrangement of contracts. This might be for a new type of good or service, as with ordinary product or process innovations. Or the innovation might lie in the form of the contract itself, as is often the case in financial services. The difficulty in establishing competitive advantage from this source is rapidly apparent. Most innovation can be quickly replicated. Sustained competitive advantage depends on the ability to protect the innovation, through legal restriction (as for Glaxo and Zantac) or through strategy.

Added value can be achieved if customers or suppliers are systematically willing to undertake relationships on terms which they would not make available to other people. Most usually, this is the result of the supplier's reputation. International car hire firms offer the same models of car on the same terms as local firms, but at higher prices. They attract customers not because the quality or reliability of the service is necessarily any better, but because these customers believe the reputation of the franchisor provides them with an assurance of that quality and reliability. Reputation is often—as in this case—associated with a brand name.

The distinctiveness of a firm's relationships may rest in the group of contracts taken as a whole. While any part of it can be reproduced the complexity of the set defies imitation. Typically, this requires that many contracts should have implicit, or relational, terms. If you can write a contract down, others can make the same contract. This architecture is a major part of what distinguishes Sainsbury, both in its internal architecture—its relationships with employees—and in its external architecture—its relationships with suppliers.

A firm with no distinctive capability may still achieve competitive advantage if it holds a strategic asset. A concession to exploit a resource, or an exclusive right to supply, is a strategic asset. In other markets, being first, or being the incumbent firm, may in itself confer advantages over any potential entrant. Some companies are no better—perhaps worse—than other firms would be at the activities they perform; but they enjoy the strategic asset that they already perform them.

In my research, I have identified the ten European firms which added most value in the 1980s (Table 7.3). They illustrate all these sources of competitive advantage—innovation, reputation, architecture, and strategic assets. Glaxo's competitive position is built around innovation, principally Zantac. Benetton gains from its architecture—the distinctive structure of its subcontracting and

Table 7.3. Sources of competitive advantage

Position	Company	Distinctive capability or strategic asset
1	Glaxo	Innovation (principally Zantac)
2	Benetton	Architecture (subcontracting and franchise arrangements) and retail brand
3	Reuters	Incumbency advantages, reputation
4	Petrofina	Control of oil resources and dominant position in Belgian supply markets
5	Kwik Save	Market positioning
6	LVMH	Brands
7	Guinness	Brands
8	Cable & Wireless	Licences in regulated markets, incumbency advantages
9	BTR	Architecture (control systems between centre and operating business)
10	Marks & Spencer	Architecture (subcontracting and employee relationships), reputation

Source: Kay (1993).

franchising arrangements—and from its brand. Marks & Spencer enjoys similar strengths. Petrofina and Cable & Wireless hold strategic assets and may also gain competitive advantage from architecture. LVMH and Guinness exemplify competitive advantages built around brands. Reuters' position is based largely on strategic assets—incumbents have substantial advantages in information services, although reputation also plays its part. BTR is a company with a powerful, and distinctive, architecture. Kwik Save does not fall easily into any of these categories; its competitive advantage seems to be in occupying a market position that its rivals have abandoned and it is interesting that that positioning has recently come under attack from new entrants. Kwik Save was perhaps a beneficiary of the 'quality is free' preoccupation of the 1980s; quality was not free for Gateway and Asda, whose up-market moves were not successful.

8

Adding Value

The object of business is to create, maximize, and defend economic rent. Rent is what is left over after all the factors of production employed in a business or activity—including the providers of equity capital—have been paid. The term 'profit' includes both the cost of equity and the added value which the firm creates. That is responsible for many of the ways in which profit is a misleading indicator of company performance—as, for example, when firms increase profit but subtract value by reinvesting at less than the cost of capital, or enhance earnings per share without adding value by acquiring firms on less elevated price-earnings multiples.

Economists talk about rent because the central analytic concept dates from David Ricardo, who lived almost two centuries ago in an environment in which the cultivation of agricultural land was the principal commercial activity. The analogue between Ricardo's approach and the assessment of the competitive advantage of firms remains an instructive one (Fig. 8.1).

Today, unfortunately, the term 'rent' has inappropriate connotations. Some economic texts use the phrase 'supernormal profit' to describe economic rent, but this, if anything, aggravates the terminological problem: what business readily admits to making 'supernormal profits' still less to having them as its objective? I have preferred the phrase added value. This essay describes the relationships between competitive advantage, added value, and various conventional measures of firm performance. Coincidentally, it establishes links between the resource-based theory of strategy and my own earlier work on the relationship between economic concepts and accounting profitability (Kay 1976; Edwards, Kay, and Mayer 1987).

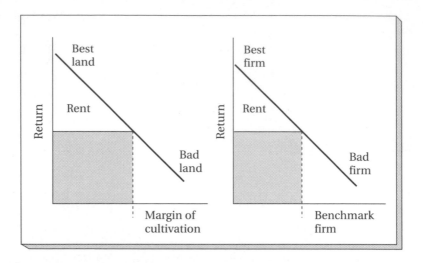

Fig. 8.1. Ricardian Rent v. Firm Rent

In measuring the financial health of a business, different people focus on different things—earnings, profits, cash flow, or competitive advantage.[1] However, these signs do not point in different directions. Underlying all of them is the ability to sustain a positive margin between input costs and output value.

In the long run, the marginal firm in an industry will be one for which £1 of output costs exactly £1. A company that does worse than this will not survive indefinitely while if £1 can be earned for less than £1, new businesses will be attracted to the industry. When a competitive market is in equilibrium in this way, the added value created by any firm will be exactly equal to the size of its competitive advantage over the marginal, or weakest, firm in the same industry.

That proposition establishes a fundamental link. It is competitive advantage, moderated by market conditions, that creates added value. In a market with over-capacity, where marginal firms are losing money, even companies with a competitive advantage may not succeed in adding much value. On the other hand, in industries where entry is difficult—perhaps because of regulation, perhaps because demand has grown more rapidly than expected—firms may seem to add value even if they hold no advantage.

But there is an ambiguity that needs to be resolved if added value is to be an operational concept for the corporate strategist or the finance director. Added value is calculated after comprehensive accounting for the costs of inputs. In particular, it differs from operating margin or profit because it includes a full

---

[1] *Financial Director* (Apr. 1993).

allowance for the capital costs of operating assets. But how are these capital costs to be calculated?

There are four different ways of measuring them, and each relates to a different perspective on corporate behaviour and a different view of the measuring of corporate success (Table 8.1). The economic perspective, based on cash flow, and the accounting perspective, which emphasizes historic cost, are both familiar. The strategic perspective is less so. Why is current cost accounting the most relevant way of assessing competitive advantage? The answer is that the replacement cost of assets tells you what it would cost a new firm to set up in that industry now. A company that cannot add value relative to this benchmark has competitive advantage in that market and should not be in it in the long term. A firm that does add value relative to the benchmark has correctly identified a market in which it has competitive advantage.

Table 8.1. Four perspectives on corporate success

Whose perspectives?	How they measure capital cost	What they measure
Economist/banker	Expensing	Cash flow
Accountant	Historic cost	Historic cost earnings
Strategist	Current cost	Current cost earnings
Investor	Market value	Shareholder value

The fourth perspective is that of the investor. Here the concern is with shareholder value, that fashionable concept of the 1980s. In this approach, the capital resources used in the business are measured by reference to their market value, and the assets of the firm have depreciated when the value of the firm has increased by less than the magnitude of its retained profits.

Fig. 8.2 shows how these relate to each other for a typical investment project. The cash-flow impact occurs at the beginning; historic cost accounting spreads expenditure over the useful life of the asset. Under current cost principles, asset depreciation in the early years is largely offset by holding gains. But as asset life increases, these holding gains diminish and the depreciation charge itself rises. The market value measure sometimes lags behind cash flow, sometimes anticipates benefits yet to come.

There are four perspectives on corporate performance and four ways of measuring capital costs. But over time, the area under each of these curves is the same. In the long run, all these ways of measuring financial performance are equivalent. The different vantage points differ only in their timing. That result can be proved mathematically. but the clearest way of demonstrating the equivalence is by example.

Eurotunnel is an unusual company. It was formed to undertake a single

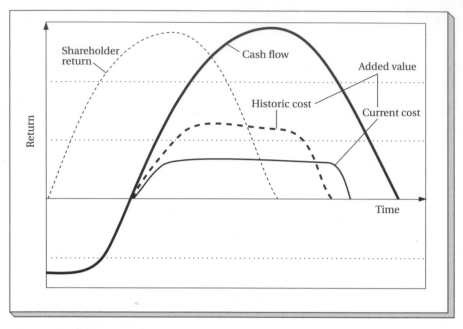

Fig. 8.2. Four Approaches to the Performance of an Activity

activity—the building of a tunnel between Britain and France. The estimates of costs, revenues, and other operating data used here are drawn from the prospectus issued when the company was floated on the London Stock Exchange and the Paris Bourse in November 1987. Estimates of the market value of Eurotunnel at various dates are based on estimates made contemporaneously by Warburg Securities. All these have been overtaken by events, but since updated information and estimates are not available in equally comprehensive form, I use the 1987 figures.

Table 8.2 shows the anticipated cash flow from the tunnel in various years. It follows broadly the pattern of Fig. 8.2. During the construction phase, cash

Table 8.2. Cash flows: Eurotunnel (£m.)

	Operating revenue	Capital expenditure	Cash flow
1990	0	728	−728
1995	642	0	642
2003	920	108	812
2020	2,598	0	2,598
2040	8,186	0	8,186

Source: Derived from Eurotunnel PLC prospectus.

flow is negative. It turns around when the tunnel comes into operation. There are some subsequent capital expenditures, but these are small and cash flow grows (in money terms) until the expiry of the firm's concession in 2042, when ownership of the tunnel is due to revert to the French and British governments.

Table 8.3 looks at the added value created by Eurotunnel in historic cost terms. As capital employed in the tunnel diminishes (because depreciation charges have repaid most of the initial construction costs), added value rises.

Table 8.3. Added value: Eurotunnel (£m.)

	Operating revenue	Capital expenditure	Capital cost	Added value
1990	0	3,170	244	−244
1995	642	3,936	554	88
2003	920	2,755	438	471
2020	2,598	−494	184	2,413
2040	8,186	−4,510	−123	8,309

Source: Own calculations based on prospectus estimate.

Table 8.4 shows the evolution of shareholder returns. Excess returns to investors are, in this projection, greatest as the tunnel approaches completion and begins operations. Once the tunnel is established it becomes a rather dull utility stock offering relatively poor shareholder returns, and there are large capital losses to shareholders as the concession expires.

Table 8.4. Shareholder returns: Eurotunnel (£m.)

	Market value	Capital gain	Net dividend	Excess return
1990	39,945	878	—	479
1995	8,136	811	126	123
2003	16,125	1,273	565	−116
2020	41,562	1,422	1,777	−857
2040	24,996	14,998	6,277	−8,720

Source: Own calculations based on prospectus and Warburg Securities' estimates.

There is something paradoxical about the concept of predicted excess returns. These projections should be seen as a view of what shareholders will receive if certain events transpire—the tunnel is completed to time and budget, and the concession expires worthless. The tunnel will not have been completed to time and budget, so shareholders are earning less than this projection allowed.

Table 8.5. Eurotunnel's performance (£m.)

	Cash flow	Added value	Excess return
1990	−728	−244	−479
1995	642	88	123
2003	812	471	−116
2020	2,598	2,413	−857
Present value over life of concession	2,316	2,316	2,316

Table 8.5 brings together the three measures of performance described above. Although the three columns display completely different patterns of returns, they have the same present value. Cash flows, added value, and shareholder returns are all equivalent in the long term. Each provides a valid measure of the value, over time, of a firm's competitive advantages and strategic assets.

Profits and earnings per share remain by far the most widely used measures of performance, and despite challenges accountants retain a dominant grip on the manner in which corporate financial statements are presented. There is a tradition in which advocates of alternative measures shower scorn on each other and, particularly, accountants. For some strategists, it is pre-occupation with accounting numbers that is at the root of the decline of Western economies. For many economists, accounting information is mean-ingless mumbo-jumbo. The shareholder value movement has argued that

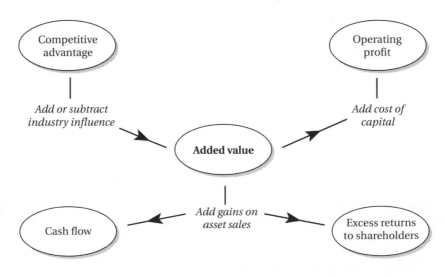

Fig. 8.3. The Equivalence of Measures of Financial Performance

accounting profits are not related to investor returns, and proposes a return to a cash-flow basis of assessment.

But this disagreement is exaggerated and unnecessary. Cash flow, profits, shareholder returns, and competitive advantage are not different things but different ways of measuring the same thing and the different interest groups concerned with a company's performance are not pulling it in radically opposed directions but adopting different perspectives on the same phenomenon. And the full exploitation of a firm's competitive advantage serves the interests of every observer and enhances every measure of corporate performance. As Fig. 8.3 shows, the concept of added value underpins them all.

9

No Free Lunches

Chapters 7 and 8 set the ground for one version of the maxim that 'there is no such thing as a free lunch'. The profitability of business, its real cash flow, and the returns it generates for shareholders are ultimately entirely dependent on the competitive advantages of the firm's operating businesses. This chapter develops that theme.

THE IRRELEVANCE OF FINANCE

Mikhail Gorbachev's colleagues are said to have observed sardonically that the Nobel Prize he won was not the prize for economics.[1] Less attention was given to those who did get the prize for economics. The £364,000 went to a clutch of three American finance professors—Harry Markowitz, Merton Miller, and William Sharpe.

Just as Gorbachev's prize did not go down well in his natural constituency, Markowitz, Miller, and Sharpe also found themselves lacking honour in their own country. Thursday's *Telegraph* reported the contemptuous reaction of Wall Street bankers. The work of the three professors was damned as a set of elegant ideas which might go down well in the classroom but not in the real world. Actually, this is a case where theory is closer to the real world than is Wall Street.

It is easy to understand why Miller is not so popular with investment bankers (which is not to say that he has not generated a consulting income sufficient to ensure that the Nobel Prize will not make a fundamental difference to his lifestyle). Miller's most famous discovery is the proposition that corporate finance is, fundamentally, irrelevant.

Like many good ideas, the argument is one that seems obvious after it has been explained. For centuries, financiers have devised more and more complex instruments to meet the needs of the companies they serve. That inge-

---

[1] *Daily Telegraph* (22 Oct. 1990).

nuity has grown beyond bounds in the 1980s, with caps, collars, swaps, drop-locks, and all the other paraphernalia of modern corporate finance. Miller demonstrated, in a rather sophisticated way, that unless these instruments exploit distortions in the tax system, they are unlikely to do you any good.

In the end, the underlying reality of the fundamental uncertainties associated with the business will come through. The reason is that by changing the risk profile associated with one part of your financing structure, you alter the risk pattern which attaches to the rest. If you raise your gearing, you reduce the quality of your equity—and by an amount which exactly offsets the apparent savings you make from the lower cost of debt. If you give some option to holders of one class of your debt, that cost will be borne by the holder of your other securities. Sooner or later—and probably sooner rather than later—the prices of these other securities will adjust.

And that, of course, is precisely what has happened. It seemed clever at the time to substitute cheap borrowings for expensive shares through leveraged buy-outs, until the price of both the debt and the shares fell to reflect the much greater risks to which they were subject. Since the prices of shares in companies like Next and Saatchi were certain to go on rising, there seemed to be no cost to giving holders of their convertible securities an option to demand repayment of their principal. But there was a cost, and it was the shareholders of these companies who eventually had to pay it. Miller's basic insight—you cannot make a business better by creative financing—would hardly seem worth a Nobel Prize if there had not been quite so many bankers and company treasurers who thought they knew better. But hard experience has borne out academic theory.

The second part of the revolution in the theory of corporate finance centres around what is called the capital asset pricing model. The CAPM—as it is known to *aficionados*—emphasizes that risk is something to be measured by reference to the characteristics of a whole portfolio, rather than an individual security. Some applications of this seem very obvious. An insurance company can assume the risk that your house will burn down—while you will not—because it takes on many such risks and spreads them over many shareholders who, in turn, have many other assets. The outcome of an evening's gambling depends on all the hands the gambler plays, not on the fall of a single card. There are many things which are individually risky but add little to the risk of a portfolio. Indeed, they may actually reduce it if they hedge a risk which it already contains. Commodity prices are speculative, but for people who expect to need a commodity in future that speculation is one they may positively wish to assume. Understanding that risk is a part of a portfolio which has led to the creation of modern derivative markets in options and futures. In these, risky assets are artificially created because the additional risk may actually reduce the total uncertainty about the returns from a portfolio taken as a whole.

The principal achievement of modern portfolio theory has been to demonstrate how wide-ranging the application of that principle can be. Many activities that are commonly thought of as speculative can have their risks much diminished through appropriate diversification. These specific risks—like oil exploration or pharmaceutical development—can be quite easily and cheaply dealt with in modern capital markets, and returns to them have been bid down correspondingly.

The type of risk that cannot be diversified is the general market risk associated with overall economic conditions; and in this view it is cyclical stocks, not specialist stocks, which should command premium earnings or dividend yields to the market. As with most insights on management subjects, the contribution of the capital asset pricing model is partly to explain what, rather imperfectly, we always thought we knew; it is also to explain why other things we thought we knew are wrong. Mark Twain observed that ignorance was not so much what folks didn't know as what folks did know that ain't so. Professors Markowitz, Miller, and Sharpe pointed to a good deal of market lore that ain't so.

FATHER CHRISTMAS DOES NOT EXIST

Every year, millions of children believe that Father Christmas comes down the chimney to deliver presents, in return for nothing more than a glass of warm milk.[2] Every year, some of these millions of children suffer a rude shock. They learn that Father Christmas does not exist, and the men with red robes and white beards whom they see in the week before Christmas are all impostors.

Something similar is true in business. There is no Father Christmas there either, and those who wear his clothes are either deceivers or themselves deceived. Yet there are many who believe otherwise, and each year some of them, ruefully, discover their mistake.

So Christmas 1994 was the last of childhood illusion for Peter Baring and his colleagues. It was remarkably easy, he had assured the Bank of England, to make profits by arcane arbitrage trades in derivatives in Far East markets. He did not know exactly how Father Christmas got down the chimney, but, regular as clockwork, the present arrived. Until Father Christmas took a plane ticket to prison.

There is only one way in which firms make profits on a sustained and sustainable basis, which is to add value for their customers and to do so in ways that other people cannot. That simple and obvious truth is easily forgotten by those who would like to believe that, at least for them, Christmas has come round early.

Investors, who may know very little about the businesses to which they commit their funds, are the most readily taken in. They believed that Polly

---

[2] *Financial Times* (28 Dec. 1995).

Peck could build a £2 billion company out of putting north Cyprus fruit into cardboard boxes. And they were attracted to the excess of loss syndicates in Lloyd's of London, or to providing mortgage indemnity guarantees. After all, what could be a better investment than an insurance business that took premiums but had never had to pay anything out?

These examples seem easy enough to see through, though they were not easy enough to see through for those investors, by no means all of them unsophisticated, who lost money in the activities concerned. But they do illustrate the two fundamental questions which anyone is business should ask when they think they have met Father Christmas. Does this activity add value to customers that corresponds, at least roughly, to the profits which are earned from it? And if this is such a rewarding business, is there a reason why the opportunity is specifically available to me? If you cannot answer yes to both these questions, then the story you are being told either is not true, or will not last.

You do not, for long, make more money than you add value. Take GPA, the aircraft leasing company which, from a small office in Shannon, borrowed money from the world's major banks to lend to the world's major airlines. I do not know how you can add value of hundreds of millions of pounds a year doing that, and nor, when it came to the point, did the investors who were asked to take shares in the company's flotation. Indeed it is hard to see how you can ever add much value as financial intermediary between large companies or governments. With hundreds of banks trying to do just that, this may be the reason why it yields them prestige and expands their balance sheets while doing nothing for their profitability.

The fallacy is to think that by simply interposing yourself in a transaction you can collect a return, like those usherettes in French cinemas who must be tipped before they will get out of your way. Yet people in business go on thinking that by vertical integration they can acquire the 'manufacturer's profit' or the 'retailer's turn', or that they will do better to 'cut out the middleman'. Or that they will make more money if they cross-sell, or offer a one-stop shop.

But in a competitive market, what manufacturers, retailers, and middlemen earn is exactly equal to both the cost and the value of the services they provide. It follows that restructuring the value chain will give you nothing unless you either enhance that value, or there is some specific and particular reason why you can provide these same services at lower cost. Or, of course, you may not be operating in a competitive market.

So regional electricity companies still have their 'supply business', and argue with their regulator about the return they should earn on it. When you have a monopoly, you can charge for 'supply', but once you are in a competitive market – which they will face from 1998 – there is no margin for supply because there is no value-adding activity. You can earn a return for generating electricity, or sending it through your wires; you can recover the cost of sending a bill; but there is no per cent margin for supply. And there is no longer 15 per cent for helping a householder fill in an insurance proposal form. Direct writers have shown that traditional retail broking is as valuable as the French usherette.

So when you tell your children that there is no Father Christmas in Lapland, tell them that there is none in commerce either. And when someone describes the projected returns from a business to you, measure it in close relation to the value which you yourself will add.

10

The Competitive Advantage of Nations

This chapter was delivered in 1994 as the annual lecture of the Economic and Social Research Council. It explores how the application of the resource-based theory of strategy can be extended from the competitive advantage of firms to the competitive advantage of countries.

Our dissatisfaction with Britain's industrial performance begins when we compare ourselves with our principal competitors. The quality of our manufactured goods is lower than that of Japan. Our record of innovation cannot match that of the United States. The skills of our designers are often outstripped by those of Italy. Our levels of scientific and technical education are lower than those of Germany. The job of research is to find out why these things are so; the job of government is to put them right.

Tonight I want to propose a rather different perspective. When I view my own personal performance, I find the outlook equally depressing. I cannot bat as well as Brian Lara. I cannot write as felicitously as Tom Stoppard. I am not as handsome as Hugh Grant. You may feel that I should spend more time in the nets, improve my writing style, and spruce up my image, and indeed I should perhaps do all these things. But the solution I have found is a rather different one. I know I cannot match Lara's cover drive, but when it comes to calculating a demand elasticity I know that I can beat Lara ninety-nine times out of a hundred. Let Lara face the bowling, while I deal with the economics.

Competitive advantage is based, not on doing what others already do well, but on doing what others cannot do as well. We know that this is true for us as individuals. We can see—with greater difficulty—that this is true for firms; that real corporate success is based on distinctive capabilities, not on imitating the successful. What I wish to argue tonight is that the same is true for countries. It follows that the focus of industrial policy should not be on what we do worse than other people but on what we do better.

Is there a competitive advantage of nations?

In a question that echoes Mrs Thatcher's assertion that there is no such thing as society, we might ask whether there is such a thing as a national economy, or national competitiveness. Can there be a competitive advantage of nations, as distinct from a competitive advantage of individuals or firms?

The evidence that there is indeed a competitive advantage of nations seems all around us. The camera you use and the audio equipment you listen to were almost certainly made in Japan. The aeroplane in which you fly is far more likely to have been built in the United States than in any other country, and the same is true of the software you use and the movies you watch. The largest world insurance market is in London, and if you go behind the scenes at a Grand Prix you will discover that the skills that put Formula One motor cars on the track are mostly British. I have a German kitchen and an Italian bathroom, and I bet that so do many of you.

A striking feature of all these industries is that I can predict the country of origin with much more certainty than the manufacturer. Japan dominates sales of cameras, but there are many Japanese camera manufacturers. The software industry is fiercely competitive, but most of these competitors are US firms. When you buy your German kitchen, Poggenpohl and Bulthaup will eagerly seek your custom. Competitive advantages in these industries seem to be as much with countries as with firms.

Now the theory of international trade we learn in beginning economics did indeed focus on the nation as the unit. Portugal was sunny and England wet, so the former country sold its wine for the latter's textiles. But the theory of comparative advantage, in which world trade reflects these differential endowments of natural resources, seems almost irrelevant in the context of twentieth-century trade. While comparative advantage still explains Saudi oil and Colombian coffee, most trade today is in manufactured goods between countries whose resource endowments are apparently similar. It is not clear what natural resources are necessary, or useful, in writing software or building kitchens. The Heckscher-Ohlin theory sought to revive the theory of comparative advantage by emphasizing differences in the availability of capital and labour. Capital-rich countries would sell capital-intensive goods in return for labour-intensive ones. But does writing an insurance policy use more or less capital than making a camera? It depends on how you write the policy or make the camera, and successful firms in the same country do so in a range of different ways.

Modern trade theory is rather different. It stresses the imperfection of competition and the ubiquity of scale economies. But these factors, at best, explain the fact of trade rather than its structure. Why does Japan export cameras and the United States aeroplanes, and not the other way around? Home market bias, the design of products to meet particular national preferences, is part of that story—Germany makes a recognizable style of limousine because these are cars that Germans aspire to drive. Japanese tourists do like to take photographs, and the British are prone to worry about unanticipated events. But there is more to Japanese strength in optics and Britain's leadership in insurance than that.

Who are us?

There is a more fundamental problem if national competitive advantage is to be explained by scale economies. Most scale economies arise at the level of the individual firm. America's leading position in aircraft manufacture is in large measure the product of the leading position of Boeing, and that position is in turn the product of that firm's economies of scale and experience. These are the competitive advantages of Boeing. The Coca-Cola corporation earns considerable returns from the exploitation of its powerful brand. It is based in Atlanta, its shareholders are mostly American, and it pays substantial taxes to the US government. In these ways it makes a major contribution to the wealth and welfare of the United States. Yet it is stretching language to call Coca-Cola an American competitive advantage.

This distinction between those competitive advantages which appear to belong to a particular firm—such as those of Boeing or Coca-Cola or Reuters or Glaxo—and those which seem to be characteristic of many firms in the same location—such as those of German kitchen manufacturers, Japanese optical companies, or Italian tie makers—has a variety of important implications. It does seem that the competitive strengths we associate with the United States and Britain are often the assets of particular firms, while those of countries such as Germany, Italy, or Japan are more often recognizable as national competitive advantages. I shall suggest later why this may be so. It may also be one reason why the profitability of American and British firms is very much higher than those of Japanese or German firms even though the competitive performance of Japan or Germany may be superior. Anglo-American competitive advantages earn returns for British and American firms; Japanese and German competitive advantages earn returns for whole economies.

This relationship between national and firm competitive advantage raises another fundamental issue. If the City of London retains a pre-eminent position in the world financial services market, but many of its firms are foreign owned, is the competitive advantage ours, or theirs? Should we care if a new British motor car industry, under Japanese ownership, rises from the ashes of the old; or if British Aerospace exploits its technical capabilities by manufacturing in Taiwan? In a world of multinational firms and multinational production, where is competitive advantage located? Robert Reich, now President Clinton's Labor Secretary, posed the question for Americans in the stark, if ungrammatical, phrase, 'Who are us?' Reich's question deserves an answer; it is important in itself and also bears directly on the definition of national competitive advantage.

The answer is that we own those factors from which we earn and we earn from those factors which we own. If firms in London locate, and pay, to exploit the skills they find there, we need not care whether they trade as Morgan Grenfell or Deutsche Bank, as Brown Shipley or as Goldman Sachs. We should judge Japanese car manufacturers in direct proportion to the value they add in the UK. And if offshore manufacturing maximizes the value of British Aerospace's research capabilities, then that is what 'us' should do. In each case, the question is how much economic rent, or added value, is established here.

Sources of competitive advantage

A strictly national competitive advantage would be derived from a scarce factor whose availability coincided with the boundaries of a nation. There are some, but few, economically important resources which are exactly aligned with national borders. Language frontiers broadly follow political frontiers, so the English language helps Britain and America to have competitive advantage in broadcasting, films, publishing, and a range of associated industries, such as graphic design and sound-mixing equipment. Time zones are national, and that gives Europe some advantages in financial services. Legal systems, fiscal rules, and regulatory regimes also coincide with national boundaries. Britain and the United States derive competitive advantage from the widespread adoption of their legal jurisdictions. Some small countries— Panama in shipping, Monaco in gaming, Switzerland in banking—derive competitive advantage through attractive regulation (regulation which is attractive, in the main, for its absence). But all these factors are minor in relation to the aggregate of world trade. What we recognize as national competitive advantages are mostly not advantages of countries as such. They are the product of factors which are located within particular countries. The observation is not that firms necessarily gain competitive advantage in fitted kitchens by locating in Germany; it is that many German firms in that industry appear to have competitive advantages.

That theory of comparative advantage explained trade by reference to the physical location of scarce natural resources. But the most successful economies of the post-war era, like Germany and Japan, are countries singularly devoid of any natural resources at all. Indeed, the belief that these countries could only prosper if they secured access to natural resources proved perhaps the most costly and damaging misconception in world history. If we are here tonight to justify the role of analysis, research, and education in the social sciences, then we need do no more than observe that two world wars were substantially the product of elementary misunderstanding of the relationships between physical resources and economic power. But if popular discourse is not yet free of that misunderstanding, it is a misunderstanding which is much less prevalent than it was.

Historically, the concentration of industry in particular locations was often explained by access to natural resources. What is interesting is not just that these natural resources have become very much less significant elements in production, but that geographical concentration has often long outlasted the natural resources concerned. Firms located in the Ruhr to access its coal and steel; the coal and steel are no longer there but the firms are. Film studios went to Los Angeles in the 1920s to benefit from the natural light of southern California. This no longer matters, and few films are now shot in California, but Hollywood is still the centre of the world film industry. And London is still the world's shipping market even though we no longer have a great navy or a substantial merchant marine.

Now there is something surprising at work here. Where geographical concentration is not the result of shared access to physical resources, it might instead have been the product of the costs of transport and communication. Once, physical proximity was critical to supplier relationships. The Fisher body plant was located on the opposite side of the road to the Morris assembly line even though it was owned by a separate company. But as obstacles to trade and transport costs have fallen, and data transmission has become cheap and instantaneous, location would seem to matter less and less. Today we take it for granted that cars will be put together from components manufactured in different locations around the world. It was once true that a strong national firm in one industry would confer competitive advantages on many related businesses within the same country. With a great merchant marine went a strong shipbuilding industry and a powerful position in steel production. Italian success in domestic appliances was associated with Fiat's achievements in small motors. With firms increasingly free to seek preferred partners on a global basis these sources of national competitive advantage are steadily eroding.

Yet geographical concentration remains important. One recent study of the evolution of financial services wrote of 'the end of geography', suggesting that location had become irrelevant. Appropriately enough, he was the chief economist of American Express Bank. Yet the more striking observation is that geography has not ended. Traders now operate on screens, rather than in a physical market; but the screens are mostly to be found within a few hundred yards of each other. Financial information can be sent immediately around the world, and is; yet the financial services industry remains concentrated in tiny areas of east London and lower Manhattan.

Relationships and networking

And the same is true of manufacturing. Observers of the rise of Toyota from second-line manufacturer of sewing machines to dominance of the world automobile industry in a period of forty years have emphasized the role of Toyota's keiretsu—the integrated but nevertheless independent group of suppliers which underpins Toyota's exceptional reputation for reliability—their pioneering of just-in-time inventory management, and their shortening of the traditional model cycle. Most of the firms involved are not only based in Japan; they are located close to Toyota's main assembly plant in Nagoya. But this need for physical proximity is not directed at reducing transport costs. Ford of Europe makes bodies in one country and engines in another without suffering any serious cost penalty. So what is the purpose of this continuing geographical concentration? Its purpose is to cement the relationship between Toyota management and the executives of other members of the keiretsu. That keiretsu involves a complex structure of implicit contracts—long-lasting understandings whose context is not, and cannot be, written down. The nature of these relationships enables Toyota to be confident in the quality of its suppliers' parts, unconcerned about its potential vulnerability to component shortages, and ready to share proprietary knowledge in order to accelerate design and retooling.

Toyota illustrates well why some competitive advantages will continue to be associated with particular geographical locations. Despite the internationalization of markets, despite air travel, despite information technology, there are still things that are done best by people who find themselves frequently in the same room. The most important of these are the transfer of skills and knowledge and the development of trust between individuals. It is on success in creating networks which facilitate these exchanges that many competitive advantages in today's world depend.

Why learning and trust require physical proximity is a matter for psychologists rather than economists. Yet it remains true that distance learning—even for material that has been completely mastered and communicated many times before—is but a shadow of a classroom experience, and that video conferencing has made a negligible dent on the market for world air travel. Effective communication depends on non-verbal, possibly even non-visual, cues. The barely perceptible hesitation introduced by a satellite link invites misunderstanding when we are used to interpreting hesitation in other ways. Shared experiences and values are a central element in developing trust. The linking of social and commercial relationships increases the penalties for opportunistic behaviour. That is why the lunch room is a central facility of the City of London and extensive entertainment an integral part of Japanese business culture.

Tacit knowledge and flexible response

Locally concentrated networks are characteristic features of the Italian industrial organization of northern Italy—the knitwear producers of Carpi, the shoemakers of Varese, the metalworkers of Lumezzane. Although these groupings are based on small firms, with production facilities sometimes still attached to houses, they are not cottage industries in any pejorative sense of that term. Their technology is as advanced as any in the world, and levels of investment are high. The competitive strength of each firm within the network derives from the knowledge base to which all contribute and have access—'The mysteries of the trade are in the air', as Marshall noted of similar concentrations a century ago. Their competitive performance also benefits from the capacity of flexible structures, based on trust, to respond more rapidly and more effectively to changing conditions than can either monolithic corporations or individual proprietors. For those who equate competitive advantage with size and scale and see these as the prerogative of multinational companies, the structure of Italian industry, in which its large firms are subsidized by the more vibrant small business sector of the economy, provides a powerful antidote.

In financial services the competitive advantage of London has long rested on access to shared knowledge and on trust relationships between participants. Trading floors, and the Room at Lloyd's, are physical manifestations of the advantages of casual proximity in developing tacit knowledge. The traders who chose 'My word is my bond' as the motto of the Stock Exchange clearly thought they were making an important statement about London's competitive position. This was supported by the homogeneity of background and the rigid values established by the English class system and the English school system.

Tacit knowledge need not be industry-specific. Italian—and to a degree European—pre-eminence in design rests ultimately on a skill base that dates back to the Renaissance. It is a casual—but undeniable—observation that quite average French or Italian women have a sense of style in dress that the typical American tourist on the Rue du Faubourg-Saint-Honoré or the Via Veneto conspicuously lacks. The mechanisms by which that style is acquired are complex—they are 'in the air'—but the fact has consequences for the competitive position of French and Italian firms that extends well beyond the field of *haute couture*.

The most important of such non-specific skill bases lies in scientific and technical training. The levels of scientific education and achievement in British universities are as high as any in the world, and this is reflected in the success of British firms in industries that depend on élite science, like pharmaceuticals and certain areas of defence electronics. Once the product is designed it has, for practical purposes, been made. Britain's dominance of technical support for Formula One motor racing stands in stark contrast to its competitive failure in volume car production. Where—particularly—Germany and Japan stand out is in the technical capabilities of workers further down the ability spectrum. The manufacture of fitted kitchens, precision optical equipment, or computer-aided machine tools requires little in the way of the kind of science that wins Nobel Prizes, but it does require a production line work-force with quantitative skills.

National culture and competitive advantage

Social institutions which support trust relationships and the development of tacit knowledge have major advantages. But this is not a wholly one-sided story. Although the advantages of collaborative and co-operative activities are obvious, tacit knowledge can often be conservative and constraining, and networks of relationships nepotistic and corrupt. What makes Italian and Japanese business strong is not so different from what makes Italian and Japanese politics rotten. The most striking comparison is that between Japan and the United States. In one country, business emphasizes consensus and shared knowledge; in the other information is an individual property and bargains are struck, enforced, and disputed in precise legal form.

The United States is a country founded by immigrants, many of whom were throwing off the constraints imposed by the values and social structures of the countries from which they came. (That tourist with ill-fitting pants is probably of European descent.) That history has contributed to its strongly individualistic ethos and helped to lay the foundations for the most innovative and entrepreneurial society the world has known. These attributes are translated into the competitive advantages of US firms. It is this capacity for innovation and individual entrepreneurship which explains why the United States dominates in pharmaceuticals and in computer software.

Even in industries where market leadership has subsequently been ceded to firms in other countries, like semiconductors or VCRs, the product is often based on an initial American innovation. The difficulty of appropriating innovations fully for the benefit of innovating firms is a problem for the US economy, but the innovative environment which these spillovers foster is the most important of American competitive advantages.

Societies which rely less on trust relationships between individuals have greater need of public forms of quality certification. So most of the world's great brands originate in the United States, and they help to sell products as different as hamburgers and legal and accounting services around the world. It is a direct result of the different nature of the two societies that the competitive strength of the individualistic United States is substantially founded on the competitive advantage of American firms while the competitive strengths of Japanese firms are substantially founded on the competitive advantage of the collectivist Japanese nation.

So political and cultural history exerts a continuing influence on economic performance. A clearer appreciation of that might make us more cautious in the models of reform we urge on the countries of Eastern Europe. The most unbridled forms of individualism—as in Nigeria—are not a recipe for economic success, and individualism in the United States is mediated by a complex collectivism reflected in intense patriotism and an unusually rich variety of voluntarist institutions from churches to charities to country clubs. There are dangers in the breakdown of established structures of relationships, however debased, in conditions where there is nothing to take their place.

It is easier to destroy trust relationships than to create them. So whatever the commercial advantages of these structures, they are under constant pressure from those who identify immediate gains from more opportunistic behaviour. In the banking industry, for example, many established relationships were fractured in pursuit of the supposed advantages of a more performance-oriented, transaction-driven, culture. Even if the mistakes are now evident, the pieces cannot easily be put together again. Is it possible, then, that the competitive advantages of the Far East nations are essentially transitory? Do we see today a short interval in which the institutions of contemporary capitalism coincide with the collectivist values of more traditional feudal systems, before one inevitably drives out the other?

It certainly is possible that this is what we see, and the rigid conventions of Japanese firm structure and labour markets are under increasing pressure. Yet we can look to the successful maintenance of relationship structures over decades if not centuries in Switzerland and in parts of Italy and Germany as evidence that such national competitive advantages can be sustained.

Patterns of trade and competitiveness

A country's international competitiveness depends, therefore, on three things. The first is the strength of the competitive advantage of its individual firms. This is the benefit the United States derives from the fact that Coca-Cola, Merck, and Microsoft—all among the most profitable firms in the world—are American owned and managed, and have a bias, although by no means an overwhelming one, in favour of conducting their business within the United States, and pay tax there.

Second, international competitiveness may be derived from access to scarce resources which are available within a country, but not to those outside it. Once, as we have seen, these were natural resources. Today, I have suggested, such strategic assets are more likely to be intangible; the English language, the European time zone. Such national competitive advantages exist—although they matter much only for small countries like Switzerland, Saudi Arabia, or Singapore.

But mostly, national competitive advantages lie in supportive networks of firms and activities, and are based on those things which such networks typically facilitate—speed and flexibility of response, and the construction of a base of tacit knowledge, which may be industry-specific—Japanese capabilities in optics—or more general—German craft skills.

I believe an appreciation of these trends largely explains why it is that the growth of international trade among developed countries has led ultimately to widening income differentials and to higher levels of unemployment everywhere. Widening markets increases the rewards for those—individuals, firms, or groups of individuals or firms within nations—who have truly distinctive capabilities. Pavarotti, Microsoft, Italian knitwear producers earn more by displaying their talents on a wider stage; while widening markets equally bids down the earnings of those—individuals, firms, or groups of firms—who have nothing distinctive to offer.

The history of the last forty years has been one characterized at first by attempts to resist these changes. Governments tried vainly to arrest the decline of firms which had no competitive advantages—indeed, often whole industries in which no firms had any marked competitive advantages, such as steel, automobiles, or airlines. They absorbed low-skilled workers into the public sector. Ultimately, unwilling or unable to bear the costs of these policies, they allowed unemployment to be the consequence.

Establishing national competitive advantages

This account of the dependence of competitive advantage on history makes clear that establishing national competitive advantages is no easy task. Indeed, it is self-evident that the process of creation must be hard, since if it were otherwise there could be no enduring source of *competitive* advantage. There can be no general recipes for competitive success—for individuals, firms, or countries—since if there were their general adoption would defeat their object. It is almost impossible to implant trust where it does not already exist. The process of developing skills and shared knowledge is inhibited by the limitations on the ability of individuals to communicate, or teach, more than they themselves already know. The unflattering comparison of British and German technical education is hardly new, for example; but to recognize the problem is, as history has shown, only the smallest of steps towards a solution.

Yet it is not impossible to build national competitive advantages. The evolution of Singapore as a financial services centre has illustrated the creation of trust through austere communal discipline and the stimulation of shared knowledge through a powerful collective ethos. Korean industry has been encouraged to develop in ways that mimic the networking structures of Japan. Policies can change the skill bases of populations, but there is no escaping the slowness of the process.

Let me now turn to some policy implications of what I have been saying. If there is one issue in industrial policy on which everyone is in agreement, it is that governments should not pick winners, and that attempts to do so are responsible for many of our past failures. You will understand by now that I completely disagree; I think that picking winners is exactly what the government should do. The past problem was not that we picked winners—no one could describe an industrial policy focused on Leyland and on expanding steel output, on Magnox reactors and on Concorde, as one of picking winners. We picked things that were losers but that we would have liked to be winners.

Next, we should not focus our attention on those areas of economic activity which others already do well. There is a complex series of issues here. The trade liberalization of recent decades has been heavily focused on semi-sophisticated manufactured goods. So much so, in fact, that we have come to take for granted that this is what trade and competitiveness is about; cameras and textile machinery, cars and audio equipment. Now these are, as it happens, areas in which Britain and British firms have relatively few competitive advantages. We are much further from free trade in basic manufactures, where protectionism and subsidy is rife, or at the most sophisticated levels, where public purchasing dominates; in agriculture, where we have retreated from free trade when liberalization has been happening elsewhere; and, most importantly for Britain, in business and financial services, where different national standards are entrenched and where entry barriers and cartels abound.

We supported a world trading order which directed liberalization at areas in which we enjoyed no particular competitive advantage, and joined a European Union with essentially the same characteristics. The results were massively beneficial to British consumers, but not at all beneficial to British producers. One response is, indeed, to focus on improving our performance in those areas where others enjoy these competitive advantages. But, for the reasons I have explained, this strategy is not likely to be successful nor likely to be rewarding if it were successful.

An alternative is to focus on those areas in which Britain and British firms have real competitive advantages. Let me give some examples. I have already noted that Britain's greatest strategic asset is the English language. It feeds directly into British competitive advantages in publishing—traditional and electronic, all kinds of audio-visual media, and tertiary education. I find it difficult to see that considerations of international competitiveness have played any role in policy for these areas; certainly a negligible one relative to more important concerns, such as anti-intellectualism, cost minimization, and a belief that the BBC is insufficiently deferential to politicians.

Let us take pharmaceuticals. This is another industry of undoubted British competitive advantage. Two of the principal members of the European Union—France and Italy—have clear policies of promoting indigenous clones of established products and buying international drugs only at low prices. If we are to make ourselves unpopular with our European partners, I would rather do it on this issue than by being rude about the Belgian Prime Minister.

Britain has the best located of the world's international airports, and an airline which is a few years ahead of others in realizing that it is almost as important to please passengers as to please politicians. Yet it is only within the last few months that British Airways has been able to make any flights which do not start or end in the UK, and that represents a tiny fraction of its business. Contrast that with the trade liberalization we have seen for manufactured goods.

In all these areas, government is not creating competitive advantage; it is promoting opportunities to exploit competitive advantages that already exist. My account of the origins of national competitive advantages, which emphasizes the importance of history and the role of supportive relationships between firms and the creation of collective knowledge bases, makes clear how a government role in the development of competitive advantage can only be marginal, indirect, and long term. But it can exist.

Take insurance, for example. If there is any British industry where government intervention and support would have been justified it is not, in my judgement, steel or shipbuilding or cars or biotechnology; it is insurance. We have real competitive advantages here; yet they have been seriously eroded by a combination of weak management and personal aggrandizement. I am not just talking about Lloyd's, although the problems of Lloyd's have made the issues particularly visible. The industry is starting to get its act together, with more effective management and improving standards of training and competence; these are precisely the sorts of issues with which a sympathetically critical government can help.

Or look at retailing. This is again a British winner; it is not, however, yet an international industry, and it will become one only slowly. Once we understand how national competitive advantages are created, we can see a role for government in encouraging the sharing of the costs of learning and the results of experience; precisely the role, in fact, that the Japanese government has played in relation to many Japanese export industries.

I have argued tonight that there are such things as national competitive advantages, which are based in the specific and unique business histories of individual countries; and that for these reasons attempts to imitate the competitive advantages of others are doomed to failure. I have argued that the past failure of British industrial policy was not that we tried to pick winners, but that we did not; that our measures were based on a vision of what we would like to be rather than an analysis of what we are. I have attempted to describe a real and constructive role of industrial policy.

There is not much comfort in my analysis for those individuals who have few distinctive capabilities to offer in the labour market, or those firms which have few distinctive capabilities to offer their customers. We should not have expected that a policy aimed at enhancing competitiveness would.

III

CORPORATE PERSONALITY: SHAREHOLDERS AND STAKEHOLDERS

The theme of Part II was that firms are best seen as a collection of capabilities, and the chapters in it examined some business implications.

I came to see that this perspective had implications not just for the management of firms themselves, but for the role of the corporation in society, and ultimately for the system of market organization itself. These are the themes of this part of the book.

Chapters 11 and 12 explore the concept of corporate personality. That concept denies some of the perspectives of the firm which are common in economics texts. The firm is not a black box or production function which produces predictable outputs from defined inputs. Nor is the firm a structure of principal–agent relationships, in which busy and numerous shareholders hire professional managers to communicate their wishes to their many employees. Both the technological and the financial description leave out what is in reality most important about the firm. Companies can only add value if they achieve something more than these descriptions include: if they develop capabilities which are uniquely characteristic of the firm itself.

But if that is so, our firms consist of assets which could not by owned by anyone. You cannot own a structure of relationships between people, or own their shared knowledge, or own the routines and modes of behaviour they have established, at least in the sense in which we normally use the word 'own'. It follows that this approach to the firm has major implications for the way we think about corporate governance. These issues are pursued in Chapters 13 and 14.

The 'stakeholding' approach which this implies leads in turn to a variety of radical perspectives on how markets function and on macroeconomic management itself. Chapter 15 develops that broader context.

11

Relationships and Commitments

The three essays in this chapter are all written around the theme of trust and commitment in business and personal relationships. They illustrate, in different ways, the severe limitations of what can be achieved by contracts that we can write down and by instructions to pursue predetermined objectives.

TRUST OR CONTRACT?

I have in front of me an American marriage contract.[1] There are no lofty platitudes here about sickness and health, for richer for poorer. The loving couple's attorneys have an entirely down-to-earth approach. The contract does not just demand sexual fidelity. It divides up the housework—not equally, in this example—Jill is responsible for it in three weeks of the month and Jack only in one. Jack is allowed to go out with his own friends from time to time, but not in excess of a prescribed frequency. And so it goes on.

The British courts would, thank goodness, decline to enforce such a document. The American courts might be willing to do so. Given the lengths to which the US legal system stretches, one can all too readily envisage the sheriff handcuffing Jill to the vacuum cleaner or a court awarding $1 million damages against Jack for one night too many on the town. Our own legal system is not yet out of control. But the outcomes of the Guinness and Blue Arrow cases can have left very few people thinking that we have got these areas of commercial law right. It is a good moment to consider what role the law can play in governing business relations, and when—as in marriage—it should leave well alone.

Reflect for a moment on *why* that marriage contract is so absurd. Either there is trust between the parties to a marriage, a free flow of information, and flexibility on both sides, and the contract is completely unnecessary. Or

---

[1] *Daily Telegraph* (24 Feb. 1992), edited.

else there is not, in which case the relationship will not work satisfactorily in any event and the contract is completely useless. The English legal position—which says that if you want to end the relationship we will provide a forum in which you can sort things out, but otherwise you must settle who cleans the house when between yourselves—gets things precisely right.

Now this is not only true of private life; it is often true in business as well. There may be a legal contract—your lawyers will almost certainly insist you have one—but if you need to look at it that suggests that the commercial relationship is already in deep trouble. In a good business arrangement, you respond flexibly, you share information, you recognize each other's needs and objectives. The real contract between you—often very different from the one the lawyers have drawn up—is largely implicit and it is enforced, not by reference to the courts, but by the need the parties have to go on doing business with each other.

If you wish to look for a structure of business relationships which relies heavily on these devices, turn to Japan. There are few commercial lawyers in Japan, and Japanese commercial contracts are often informal and framed in general terms. Japanese business is characterized by keiretsu—networks of subcontractors who are willing to make long-term supply commitments—and kigyo-shudan—groups of companies ranged across different industries which share common trading and banking relationships and often have reciprocal shareholdings in each other. These types of arrangements—designed to enforce performance by establishing stability in commercial relationships—have given Japanese industry a capacity to ensure product quality, exchange information, and respond effectively to changing market information which the tightest of legal contracts has failed to achieve for these firms' US competitors.

The role the law can play in business is a strictly limited one, and legal processes can never effectively enforce rules of good conduct or ensure the smooth running of continuing relationships

The extravagant entertainment associated with Japanese business, designed to solidify commercial relationships by binding them with social ones, is hardly less expensive than protracted meetings with Wall Street attorneys. It might even be more fun.

CHARACTERISTICS AND POLICIES

When you go to Sainsbury or Marks & Spencer, you expect that you will be well treated and given value for money.[2] You believe these things because you know that this is the sort of business they are. You believe that this is the way these companies behave, rather than that the management of these companies has decided that value for money is a profitable trading strategy.

---

[2] *Daily Telegraph* (20 Feb. 1995).

That is a subtle difference, but it is a very important one. There is the same difference between a man who thinks that honesty is the best policy, and an honest man. When you deal with the man who thinks that honesty is the best policy, you are constantly afraid that this might be the occasion on which he has concluded that honesty is *not* the best policy. So you keep your hand firmly on your wallet. The key difference is the one between a policy and a characteristic. You can easily change your policy, but only with great difficulty change your characteristic.

There is a similar difference between the policy of a company and the characteristic of a business. Value for money is not just a policy for Sainsbury or Marks & Spencer. It is a characteristic of the way they do business. It is immensely more valuable to them because of that. If their trading style were just a policy, then everyone else would adopt it too. The reason others find it so hard to emulate is that it is not just a policy, but something rooted in the nature of these organizations.

If the characteristics of a business are hard to emulate, they are also hard to change. If the board of Sainsbury or Marks & Spencer was to decide that in today's difficult trading environment it had to cut more corners and take a more robust line on customer complaints, it would find that policy extremely difficult to implement. It is very likely, in fact, that the organization would simply reject the new policy and the management which sought to impose it. Our knowledge as customers that these attitudes are deeply embedded in the organization is an important part of the confidence we have in them.

Little of this is understood by those who emphasize that the purpose of companies is to maximize shareholder value or to implement the vision of their chief executives. If it were better understood, we might appreciate better what is one of the great paradoxes of modern business; why it is that German and Japanese companies, which show very little regard for the interests of their shareholders, are often more successful—even in terms of what they deliver to their shareholders—than their English and American counterparts.

No British company has talked more about shareholder value in the last decade than Lloyds Bank. Yet when I visited a Lloyds branch recently, the notepad on the manager's desk did not say 'think shareholder', it said 'think customer'. That was wise. If I had thought that what the manager was doing was 'thinking shareholder', I should have been much less inclined to do business with him. And, in fact, it is because many people now *do* believe that what the bank manager is doing is 'thinking shareholder' that the reputation of banks has fallen so low—and with it their profitability.

Now it is possible that what Lloyds Bank was doing was purely cynical. The reason that its senior executives had told their employees to 'think customer' was not that they had any concern for their customers' interests as such, but that they believed that such an attitude would make more money for the shareholders in the long run. Possibly their policy is as cynical as that; but, if so, it is not very likely to work.

When cabin staff go to a British Airways training school, they are not told, 'the shareholders have instructed me to tell you to smile at the passengers'. They are told that British Airways aspires to be the world's favourite airline, that building a successful airline depends on satisfying customers, and that a successful airline will deliver benefits for employees, passengers, and shareholders alike. And they are not told these things by cynical, hard-nosed managers with one eye on the clock and another on the bottom line, whose real interests are with the shareholders, and who would like to put across the first message but believe that the other will get a better reception. They are told these things by people who genuinely believe that the second message is true.

The businessman whose concern is to build a good business will be more successful than the businessman whose concern is to create shareholder value, and will often be more successful in creating shareholder value. That sounds contradictory, but it is not. The doctor whose motivation is to make as much money as possible will not be a good doctor, and may well make less money than an able doctor whose motivation is the welfare of his patients. A good business is not measured by the amount of profit it makes, any more than a good doctor is measured by the amount of money he makes, and what we mean by a good business is as multi-faceted as what we mean by a good doctor. In spite of that, good doctors and good businesses generally make more money than bad doctors and bad businesses. And there is no inconsistency in general, although there often is in relation to specific actions, between being a good doctor or business and making money.

We have often failed to understand these issues in the last decade. We see deals that supposedly enhance shareholder value, but are not related to the development of better operating businesses. We see greedy executives who fail to appreciate that good business involves community responsibilities. We see managers of electricity companies who do not see how sharing the benefits of selling the National Grid with customers can be in the interests of the company. We have a take-over mechanism that encourages a focus on immediate gains to shareholders at the expense of other stockholder groups.

And yet we compete with a country—Japan—which has united investors, workers, managers, and suppliers in a single-minded focus on the growth and development of good business. They have created on that basis the most successful industrial machine the world has ever seen. And it is not their shareholders who are complaining about the consequences.

OBJECTIVES AND OUTCOMES

Is the purpose of a large public company to maximize its profits?[3] Or to develop its business, in the interests of customers, employees, suppliers, investors, and the wider community? Like most people, I think the right

[3] *Daily Telegraph* (11 Sept. 1995).

answer is the second, but when I said so a few weeks ago institutions like the Institute of Directors denounced the prescription as wet, woolly, and vacuous.

It is a tribute to the influence of irrelevant economic theory. Most economists believe that people maximize things. Firms maximize their profits. Individuals maximize their incomes, or their utility. Left-wing economists think governments maximize social welfare. Right-wing economists think government maximize their size, or their chances of re-election.

But real people and real institutions mostly do not maximize anything. Do they try to get the greatest possible satisfaction from their job, or to find fulfilment in their personal lives? They do both, of course. And what do they do when these things make opposing demands on them, as they sometimes do? Sensible, healthy people try to strike a balance. They do not try to maximize one thing, or the other.

So does a good teacher try to attract the interest and excitement of his or her class, or to impart information? A good teacher tries to do both. And how does a good teacher strike a balance between one objective and the other? It is knowing how to do that that makes a teacher good.

Similarly, John Major aspires to be a good prime minister. But is a good PM one who gets inflation down, or who reduces unemployment, or one who increases Britain's standing in the world? He has to do them all. But which of these objectives takes priority? That is up to him. It is no use Mr Major complaining that an ungrateful electorate is not rewarding him for reducing the rate of inflation. Deciding what it is we really want, and distinguishing it from what we say we want, is part of his job; and his low opinion poll ratings are the result of his failure in that.

Sophisticated economists have an answer to all this. They rely on a theorem in mathematical logic which says that anyone who behaves consistently acts as if he were maximizing something. I maximize my utility. So why do I give money to charity? Because that increases my utility. The trouble with this theory is that all it says is that people do what they do, and that must have been the right thing for them, otherwise they would not have done it. The logic of the theory is preserved, but all its content is removed.

It is simpler if we can pursue a single clear objective. But that is the world of sportsmen and soldiers, not of business and politics. You can tell athletes to run as fast as they can. You can tell soldiers to kill the enemy. You can apply the same approach to rather simple, menial jobs; get the floor as clean as possible, stop any unauthorized person coming into the building. But as soon as you get to any job that involves observation, analysis, or flexibility of response, you have to acknowledge that there are multiple objectives and allow discretion as to which is to be adopted. There is nothing wet or woolly or vacuous about that. Balancing interests and objectives is what people live their lives for and earn their salaries for.

So does a good parent put the interests of the children before the interests of the parents, or vice versa? Does he or she put the first child first, or the second child first? A good parent is concerned with all these interests. What does a good parent do when the interests of different members of the family come into conflict? A good parent makes a judgement. That is what being a good parent, and creating a happy family, involves.

And is a good prime minister one who pursues the welfare of pensioners, or children? Does he favour the weak and disabled or those who produce wealth? Again, a good prime minister is concerned for all these interests, and one of the deepest of his responsibilities is to make these choices when choices have to be made.

Now the fact objectives are multiple and complex does not mean that we should not hold people responsible for achieving them. It is a ridiculous argument to say that because it is difficult to define what is meant by a good teacher—which is true—and that because there are many dimensions to good teaching—which is also true—we should therefore not try to distinguish good teachers from bad. Or that we should not vote bad prime ministers out, and elect people whom we think will be good ones. When objectives are multiple and complex, it is easier to find excuses for bad performance. The class does not know anything because I was trying to arouse their interest in the subject—the economy did not prosper because I was more concerned with social justice. Or vice versa. But we do not need to let people get away with these claims. In practice, students, colleagues, and parents rarely have much difficulty agreeing which teachers are good and which are bad, and we do not really find it very hard to distinguish good and bad prime ministers either.

So why are we reluctant to say that a good butcher is one who is concerned both for the freshness of his meat and for the cleanliness of his premises? He wants to earn a decent income but also to serve his customers. Or to accept that a good company is one which tries to find new products, and also to improve the quality of old ones, to seek to grow and yet to be profitable, which aims to meet the needs of customers and also the requirements of shareholders. An effective manager is one who successfully balances all these things, and he should be judged against all these criteria. We all know that this is how companies really behave, and that it is how we would want them to behave. So why are so many people anxious to deny it? Keynes wrote that practical men, who thought themselves free of any intellectual influence, were usually the slaves of some defunct economist. Perhaps, yet again, he was right.

12

Contracts or relationships

This chapter, which draws extensively on chapter 5 of Foundations of Corporate Success, *explains how the structure of—often implied— relationships within and between firms, which I call architecture, provides the basis of competitive advantage for many companies.*

How history conditions current behaviour

Some companies—like IBM or Marks & Spencer—have a powerful and identifiable corporate culture.[1] The term 'culture' has been widely used, and abused, in business over the last few years, often to refer to rather superficial aspects of corporate organization. But with these firms everyone knows what is meant. Although admiration for their products and their achievements in the market-place is virtually universal, their culture is not to everyone's taste. Employees are, in the main, fiercely loyal, and those who find the organization uncongenial leave.

The legacy of the architect of the modern company—Thomas Watson for IBM, Michael Marks in Marks & Spencer—is strong in both firms. But the myths which surround these figures draw attention away from central current reality: how little either organization depends on any individual or group of individuals. Each company has established a structure, a style, a set of routines, which operates to get the best out of relatively ordinary employees, and these routines have continued to produce exceptional corporate results over many years and through many changes in the economic environment.

Other styles of management are also distinctive and also successful. In the last twenty years, Japanese firms have dominated the consumer electronics industry and become market leaders in automobiles. Initially, their output was exported from Japan, but in the face of the rise in the value of the yen and protectionist reactions in both Europe and the United States, they have

---

[1] *European Business Journal* 5/1 (Jan. 1993).

shifted production to the West. Nissan now builds cars in the north of England, and Akai makes video equipment in Normandy. In Western environments, these firms have pursued Japanese styles of relationships with subcontractors and employees and have achieved impressive levels of quality and productivity. They have succeeded in avoiding the alienation and abrasive labour relations seen in large-scale assembly activities in most Western countries, and have built demanding but productive associations with their suppliers.

These facts are well known, most of all to the Western competitors of these Japanese firms. But the successful implementation of these Japanese models in the West has been undertaken by Japanese companies. Those competitors which have responded most forcefully, such as Ford and Caterpillar, have done so by the more effective implementation of a traditional Western management style. It is only a slight exaggeration to suppose that, by the end of the century, Britain will again be a major locus in automobiles and Europe in consumer electronics, by virtue of largely closing down the indigenous industry and replacing it by greenfield operations, with new workers and new management systems, under Japanese ownership and control. The structure of commercial relationships is fundamentally, and permanently, influenced by the past experience of these relationships.

The power of shared knowledge and established routines does not only benefit large companies. The Lumezzane valley in Brescia in northern Italy is not on many tourist itineraries. Although its natural scenery is attractive, its calm is shattered by the noise from hundreds of small metalworking establishments, which often continues late into the night. In parts of the valley it seems as though almost every house has a small factory attached. Casual tourists would probably be surprised that this style of economic organization had lasted so long. They might plan to revisit Lumezzane in a few years' time when these industries had finally been swept away by the forces of international competition, reinforced by global marketing and the research and development and quality control resources which only large firms can command.

That judgement could hardly be more wrong. Far from threatening Lumezzane, the opening of international markets has brought unparalleled prosperity. Most of the output of the valley is exported and the region is one of the richest in Italy. Nor does it rely simply on traditional craft skills. Lumezzane is a market leader in a range of sophisticated metal-manufacturing products including valves, taps, and the customized machine tools used in their production. The structure of relationships between the small firms of the Lumezzane valley, often specialized in a single component of the final product, which gives each access to the knowledge, abilities, and resources of the whole, has given Lumezzane a continuing competitive advantage in its markets. That competitive advantage has endured and grown.

Competitive advantage based on architecture

There are strong common elements in these very different stories of organizational design and evolution—the corporate cultures of IBM and Marks & Spencer, the style of Japanese management, the networks of Lumezzane. In each, there is a pattern of relationships variously within firms, around firms, and between firms which is complex, subtle, and hard to define precisely or to replicate. That pattern is the product of history, and is almost impossible to reproduce in the absence of that history. It is also a pattern of relationships which can yield substantial competitive advantage for those firms or groups of firms. Their competitive advantage typically arises through the acquisition of organizational knowledge, the establishment of organizational routines, and the development of a co-operative ethic. This allows flexible response, the sharing of information, and a process in which the monitoring of quality is such a natural characteristic of the organization that it is often barely necessary to make it explicit.

What is common to all these examples is a structure of what legal theorists have come to call relational contracting (Macneil 1980). This is a framework within which the key terms of a contract are implicit rather than explicit, are not written down and often cannot be written down, and in which the 'contract' is enforced not by a legal process but by the need the parties have to go on doing business with each other. That framework is one which I call architecture, because its effectiveness rests on the framework as a whole, not on individual elements; yet while modern buildings, at least, are built to architectural drawings powerful business architecture, like great buildings, cannot easily be reproduced because important elements of it cannot be written down. Relational contracting is necessarily the product of a specific history, and a specific culture, because it is entirely dependent on knowledge of what others have done in the past and expectations of what they will do in the future.

Architecture plays a minor role in the business environment of the United States, where dealings are normally based on conventional contracts with legal terms and formal enforcement proceedings. That is appropriate in an individualistic culture with little history of relational contracting and low penalties for opportunistic behaviour. In Japan, by contrast, lawyers play a much less significant role in corporate life, and relational contracting both within organizations and between organizations is central to business behaviour. American automobile firms normally own the plants which provide them with specialist subcomponents, or make them in-house; Japanese firms feel confident in externalizing these relationships through their keiretsu. There is no clear superiority of one form of business organization over another. The individualism of the American approach facilitates experiment and innovation, while that of the Japanese fosters co-operation and flexibility of response.

European culture, and European business, lies somewhere in between. We find Italy closest to the Japanese end of the spectrum, and Lumezzane is representative of many similar networks in different sectors of Italian business. Britain is perhaps closest to the American position. As Europe develops more common approaches to management, and draws on both American and Japanese models, it may hope to gain the best of both worlds, or risk importing the worst of each. To understand these choices, it is necessary to begin by understanding more fully what architecture is, and how it creates competitive advantage.

Architecture as a characteristic of the organization

In every field of human activity, and in every century of human history, there have been organizations whose structure others have tried, and failed, to replicate successfully—the democracies of classical Greece, the armies of ancient Rome, the city states of medieval Italy, the administration of British India. In the twentieth century these exceptional organizations are often corporations. So *In Search of Excellence*, a survey of 'America's most admired corporations', became a best-seller of the 1980s (Peters and Waterman 1982). But excellence is not the same as architecture. Excellence is often founded on the abilities of individuals, while architecture is the achievement of an organization. The men who ran British India were, in the main, of mediocre talent. The achievement of the Raj was to create a system within which a small number of these undistinguished people could administer, tolerably well, one of the largest and most diverse nations of the world. Architecture does not create extraordinary organizations by collecting extraordinary people. It does so by enabling very ordinary people to perform in extraordinary ways.

Contrast this with a professional service firm or a university. The achievements of Price Waterhouse rest principally on the talents of its partners, and those of London University on its professors, and without the expertise of these partners or professors neither institution would have much to offer its customers. The organization may add value to these talents through a reputation which attracts other talented partners and professors as well as clients, customers, and students. And it may be that there are further gains to be realized through the pooling of the skills and knowledge which are to be found in the institution. But no one doubts that the excellence of the institution is based primarily on the excellence of its individual members.

This distinction between the attributes of the corporation itself and the attributes of the individuals within it has a commercial as well as a sociological significance. It is central to the distribution of the added value earned by the organization as a whole. If the exceptional performance of the organization rests solely on the exceptional talents of the individuals within it, then the rewards of that performance will accrue to these individual talents, rather than to the organization. We see this happening in professional or financial service firms where the high fees charged to clients are largely translated into the high earnings of members of the firm. An investment bank will be very profitable only if it can add value of its own to the abilities of its employees. Sometimes it can do this through reputation. Or the bank may dominate the channels by which these individuals can exploit their abilities. It can then demand a share of the value which they add. In these cases, the true competitive advantage arises from a reputation or a strategic asset.

But architecture is something different. An organization with distinctive architecture, like Marks & Spencer or IBM, will often emphasize its dependence on its people. But that dependence is to be interpreted in a particular way. The organization is dependent on them taken as a whole, because the product of the organization is the product of the collectivity. But it is not dependent on any particular one. Every individual with the organization is readily replaceable. It is only in these circumstances that added value can be appropriated for the organization itself.

Liverpool Football Club

Over the last two decades,[2] Liverpool has been the most successful football club in England by a considerable margin and one of the most consistently successful clubs in Europe. What is particularly interesting about Liverpool's performance is not just that the club has done well; it has done better than could be expected from the quality of its players. That suggests that Liverpool is deriving competitive advantage from its architecture.

There are various ways of demonstrating that point. The most commercial of them is shown in Fig. 12.1. This measures club performance against expenditure on playing staff including both wages and transfer fees spent on acquiring players from other teams. Liverpool players rank more or less equally with those of Manchester United, but Liverpool's playing performance is decidedly better. For league clubs taken as a whole, there is a strong relationship between spending on players and competitive success, with a few outliers. Liverpool is the most marked of the outliers.

Much has been written about Liverpool's achievements, most of it not of a very scholarly nature. Two factors seem to be critical. Liverpool has built up a detailed intelligence on other clubs, other grounds, other players. The experience of each game is carefully reviewed and used to enhance that information base. Apparently, there are secret books in which that intelligence is inscribed, but there is more to this activity than is contained in the books—if Manchester United could overtake Liverpool by means of simple burglary, there would be no shortage of skilled volunteers to do the job. Rather, the books are a measure of Liverpool's commitment to the maintenance of its distinctive knowledge base.

Liverpool illustrates the principal ways in which architecture can form the

---

[2] This was written in 1992.

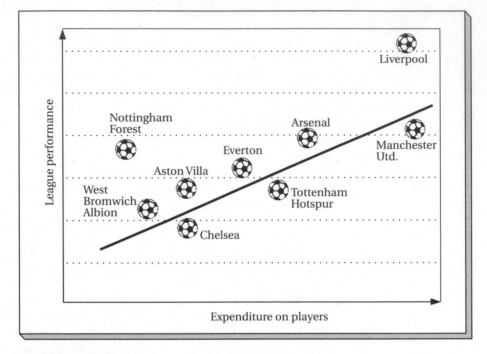

Fig. 12.1. Performance of Football League Clubs
Source: derived from dell'Osso and Szymanski (1991).

basis of a distinctive capability. The club has created an intangible asset—the organizational knowledge of the club which, although it is derived from the contributions of individual members, belongs to the firm and not to the individual members, and cannot be appropriated by them. There are organizational routines—complex manœuvres, perfected through repeated trial, in which each player fulfils his own role without needing, or necessarily having, a picture of the whole. And there is the 'passing game', the co-operative ethic, in which the player's instinct is to maximize the number of goals the club scores rather than the number of goals he scores. Each of these sources of sporting success has its precise business analogies.

The co-operative ethic or the passing game

Most firms hope to establish a co-operative ethic. But the essential question here is how to establish consummate, rather than perfunctory, co-operation. While consummate co-operation is often achieved in small groups, it is rarely attainable across large organizations, where strategic bargaining between units is generally inevitable. Still less often is it accomplished between firms or within groups of firms. Perfunctory co-operation marks the limit of what can be prescribed in a spot or classical contract. Consummate co-operation demands a deeper relationship.

The sporting metaphor illustrates the distinction well. If football were a more predictable game than it is, the club manager could define a set of instructions which would describe when players should hold the ball, when they should pass, and when they should shoot. He could monitor the players' adherence to his instructions, and reward or punish them accordingly. This would be the analogue of running a business by a comprehensive system of classical contracts. It is how some football coaches—rarely the best—try to run their clubs and it is also how some managers—rarely the best—try to run their businesses.

The reasons such a structure would not work in football are clear enough. Football moves too fast and unpredictably for the instructions to be able to deal with the almost infinite variety of situations which might occur. This might not matter if the coach were always in a position to shout orders from the touch-line—another common characteristic of bad coaches and bad managers—but the coach is simply not in a position to obtain, or to assimilate sufficiently quickly, the range of information which is held by the eleven players on the field. The need for rapid response, and for quick absorption and exchange of information, means that the passing game can only be implemented by the players themselves. It cannot be imposed. The maintenance of a co-operative ethic relies on the underlying structure of relational contracts—the unwritten rules, the tacit understandings, the common purpose which is sustained by the expectation of all parties that these will be part of continuing relationships.

These structures are of particular value—and here the football analogy is again helpful—where the nature of the business requires flexible responses and ready exchange of information. Fashion businesses, or film and television production, are striking cases. Sometimes the architecture is internal—the key co-operative ethic is that within the firm itself, as it is for Liverpool. Sometimes it is external—the passing game is played between the firm and its customers or suppliers, or among a group of co-operating firms in the same industry. Often both characteristics are found in combination.

Organizational knowledge

All firms possess organizational knowledge, in the sense that an insurance company knows about insurance and an automobile manufacturer knows about automobiles. But what an insurance company knows about insurance is, as a rule, what its employees know about insurance, and is much the same as what other insurance companies know about insurance. Organizational knowledge is distinctive to the firm, is more than the sum of the expertise of those who work in the firm, and is not available to other firms. If an insurance company builds up data and skills in the assessment of a particular category of risk, and if those data and these skills are truly those of the company and not those of a small group of employees, then it has created organizational knowledge. That organizational knowledge gives it a distinctive capability and may yield a competitive advantage in the market for that risk category. The purest form of organizational knowledge is where each employee knows one digit of the code which opens the safe; such information is of value only when combined with the information held by all the others. The analogy makes clear, too, why the issue is important; any individual who knows the whole code has access to the safe.

For some firms—professional service firms and many small companies in high-tech. industries, technical knowledge is the business. But if the company is to add value, it needs to create organizational knowledge from the skills of its members. This is achieved when the combined skills of two experts increases the value of each. The problems the organization faces are, first, those of securing this exchange of knowledge and, secondly, those of preventing that knowledge, and the rewards associated with it, being captured by one or both of the individuals concerned. Both issues have been evident in the major accountancy firms where the supposed synergies between audit and consultancy have increasingly turned into tension for precisely these reasons.

Organizational knowledge is more easily captured by the firm when it results from the specific application of generally available technology. Most of an automobile company's knowledge base is derived from technical skills that are general to the industry, but the very large investment now involved in the development of individual models leads to the creation of organizational knowledge which is specific to that design. The application of information systems in a bank raises similar issues. The requirement here is to turn individual expertise into business know-how. The problem of re-appropriation hardly arises in such a case. The difficulty is that of capturing the expertise in the first place. In passing on expertise, experts give up precisely what creates their value to the organization, and this can only be a rational strategy in the context of a relational contract and a repeated game. This is strikingly true of consultants, for whom the build-up of skills within the client organization is a threat to their continued role. Organizational knowledge is often distinctive only at the price of being applicable to a narrowly defined market. Large competitive advantages come when the organizational knowledge is unique, appropriable to the firm, and relevant to a market which is large or a range of markets which is wide. This does not happen often. It was, perhaps, achieved by IBM, but eroded even there as the knowledge base became diffused and the market more fragmented.

In other cases, organizational knowledge may take the form of organizational systems and routines. This is very much a key part of the effectiveness of strong retailers—and, indeed, it was the power of routines which lay behind the ability of British India to turn inexperienced youths into administrators of large tracts of territory. The transcription of individual expertise into organizational routine is a means by which some professional service firms—

particularly management consultants such as McKinsey or Bain—seek to create added value which arises from, and adheres to, the organization and not just to the able individuals within it.

An internal control system is a different form of organizational routine. These tight financial reporting systems are most appropriate where uncertainties are limited—so that the link from performance to outcome is tight—and in businesses which require little long-term investment whose success cannot equally be monitored within the control framework. Within these limitations, increased margins and reduced costs have generally been achieved. The success of these companies, like BTR and Hanson, has spawned imitative 'miniconglomerates', often managed by former employees of the original conglomerates. This replication of the systems has limited the competitive advantage of the originators and has forced the original proponents into ever larger acquisitions in order to maintain their distinctive capabilities.

The sources of architecture

Liverpool's achievements are the product of a structure of relational contracts. The relationships between players are rich and complex, but implicit. They rest on repetition and reciprocation. There is no room for team spirit in a world of formal contracts. There are two reasons why distinctive capabilities in organizational design must rest on relational contracting. One is the problem of achieving the 'passing game', with sharing of information and flexibility in response. It is in everyone's collective interest to do these things, but in no one's individual interest. You can only benefit from a co-operative ethic, or the knowledge and expertise of others, in a context of reiteration and reciprocation.

This is apparent in organizations which have successfully established a strong architecture. There is an expectation of long-term relationships both within the firm and between its members, a commitment to a sharing of the rewards of collective achievement, and a high but structured degree of informality. This informality is sometimes mistaken for disorganization—in popular discussion of chaos, entrepreneurship, or adhocracy as conditions for innovation—but truly chaotic organizations rarely perform well, and a system of relational contracts substitutes an extensive set of unwritten rules and expectations of behaviour for the formal obligations of the classical contract.

If we look at the historical examples of immensely powerful organizational architecture—ancient Greece and Rome, medieval Italy, British India—we see all of them characterized by unwritten codes of behaviour, of great strength and considerable complexity. Indeed, many of the tragic heroes of literature are individuals who, for apparently good reasons, broke these codes and were destroyed by them.

But there is a closely related issue of imitability. If the structure of relationships which underpins corporate architecture could be formalized, it could also be imitated and would at that point cease to be a source of competitive advantage. Many books have been written which purport to describe IBM and Marks & Spencer. These books are available in any public library. They have been avidly read by would-be imitators of IBM and Marks & Spencer. Many employees have left Marks & Spencer and IBM and are available for other firms to hire. Their competitors have done that too. Yet attempts to replicate the architecture of these organizations have not been at all comparably successful. Clearly, there is more to the architecture than these books contain; more to the architecture than any individual employee, or group of employees, knows. Neither reading the book nor recruiting the employees is sufficient to allow reproduction of the IBM or Marks & Spencer architecture.

Internal architecture

Internal architecture is a structure of relational contracts between the firm and its employees, and among the members themselves. Some features of the formal structure of the firm follow immediately from that definition. There is a high degree of job security; if the labour contract is a spot contract it cannot be a relational one. This stability of employment needs to be mutual; it is not just that the firm rarely terminates the contract, but the employee rarely chooses to leave. There is a flat remuneration structure, or at least one in which differentials reflect seniority as well as merit, and performance is measured by reference to intangible as well as tangible criteria. If the labour contract is a classical contract it cannot be a relational one.

Relational contracting offers scope for opportunism. In the main, the firm will be concerned for its own reputation in future relational contracts, and this is sufficient deterrent to its own opportunism. But it needs to protect itself against such behaviour by its employees. Remuneration may be deferred, through seniority-related payment structures or generous pension arrangements. Opportunism among employees is inhibited by linking social and business life. Geographical concentration, or domination of a town by a single company, often helps. So does the recruitment of employees of similar background or homogeneous personality type.

The objective is to stimulate collective rather than individualistic behaviour. The suppression of individuality is a serious objective of army training, for very necessary reasons. If soldiers thought of themselves as individuals, rather than as part of a collectivity, the irrationality of sacrificing the individual for the collectivity would be immediately apparent. British India thrived on the limitations of those whom it recruited and, as E. M. Forster eloquently demonstrated, less limited people rendered the structure untenable.

All of this has disadvantages as well as benefits. For most people, working for the company is never quite such a powerful motivation as working for oneself. Since firms with strong internal architecture tend to restrict individuality and to recruit employees of characteristic, and familiar, type, inflexibility is a potential weakness of such a structure. It is easier to keep a supertanker on course than a flotilla of small ships. And the supertanker is more effective at ploughing through choppy seas. But changing the course of the supertanker may be a more demanding process, and organizations with distinctive architecture, including successful ones like IBM and Marks & Spencer, have often proved monothematic or rigid.

Competitive advantages may accrue from structures that are so distinctive that others find them hard to reproduce—or, conceivably, may not wish to reproduce them. Such cultures are powerful weapons, as the continued success of Procter & Gamble, IBM, or a number of Japanese corporations demonstrates; but, like many powerful weapons, they are also dangerous ones. Dangerous to themselves—many of the most potent corporate cultures of the past are associated with organizations which no longer exist, or have been forced to abandon these cultures to survive (Krupps, the Great Western Railway, the shipyards of Clydebank, the Ford Motor Company). And such strong cultures have at times appeared more widely threatening.

While most firms with strong internal architecture—whether Liverpool Football Club, Marks & Spencer, or IBM—would be described as firms with strong corporate cultures, architecture and corporate culture are not the same thing. Drexel Burnham Lambert had a strong, if deeply unattractive, corporate culture built around highly individualistic behaviour. The elaborate rituals which surround the marketing activities of life insurance companies may be classed as corporate culture, if culture is defined as patterns of collective behaviour, but are in no sense internal architecture. In these companies, strengthening individual motivation is all. Co-operative behaviour is not necessary or expected, organizational knowledge is minimal, and organizational routines are purely administrative.

If the passing game creates problems as well as solving them, then the same is true of organizational knowledge. We are all familiar with companies in which organizational knowledge is of the kind, 'We don't do things that way here' or 'We tried that in 1970 and it didn't work'. Organizational routines may be pursued for their own sake long after their purpose has vanished. Such structures can have negative value—the whole is less than the sum of the parts, the organization produces less than the sum of the talents of individual members.

External architecture and networks

External architecture is found where firms share knowledge, or establish fast response times, on the basis of a series of relational contracts between or among them. Marks & Spencer pioneered a method of retailing, first for clothing and subsequently for a wider range of commodities—particularly food. The retailer was to engage in detailed product design. These products were then to be manufactured by a limited range of selected suppliers whose activities were closely monitored. These suppliers often commit a major portion of their output to Marks & Spencer and many of them have been suppliers to the company for decades, although there are no formal long-term agreements between them. These are very clear and very potent examples of relational contracts.

The merit of such relational contracts is that they facilitate the sharing of product knowledge and encourage flexibility of response. These advantages are important in businesses, such as fashion retailing, where customer requirements may change rapidly and where there is strategic posturing by both parties. These arrangements again expose both sides to the risks of opportunistic behaviour. Typically, this is inhibited by the reputation of the firms involved in relational contracting and by the investment which both sides make in the relationship.

Networks are groups of firms which make relational contracts with each other. The metalworkers of Lumezzane were described above. Many other Italian products, from tiles to ties, are also manufactured by geographically concentrated groupings of small firms. Typically, these firms share, draw on, and contribute to a common knowledge and skill base, make spare capacity available to each other, and implicitly and explicitly monitor each other's quality while retaining a speed of response and a degree of motivation that large firms find difficult to emulate. Although Italy has developed this form of organization particularly far, analogous networks are to be found everywhere, from Silicon Valley to the diamond traders of Antwerp.

Such networks are of particular importance in financial services, and explain the continued pre-eminence of traditional financial centres in New York and London even as economic power seems to have moved elsewhere. These networks create distinctive capabilities both for firms and for groups of firms.

The 'pulling power' of stockbrokers Cazenove is based on the strength of its list of corporate and institutional clients and enabled that firm to emerge, independent, as one of the most successful in the City of London's Big Bang. Competitive advantage in broking generally, or in lead banking, rests on similar factors. The competitive strength of Lloyd's of London in the world insurance market is largely due to the ability of many underwriters gathered in a single room to exchange information relevant to risk assessment.

Some firms have obtained competitive advantage through the development of distinctive supply networks, often in areas of the world which others have found difficult to penetrate. Such architecture has been a traditional strength for many firms in Britain and in the Netherlands, Europe's two strongest trading nations. A section of the London Stock Exchange's official list was, until recently, headed 'Overseas Traders'. Multinational Unilever was formed by the unlikely conjunction of soap and margarine manufacturers in these two countries, bound together by the common requirements of sourcing raw material from West Africa. United States companies, such as United Brands, developed somewhat similar networks in Central and South America. The

Japanese sogo shosha, trading companies at the centre of the zaibatsu, were for long at the core of Japanese economic development. Lonrho has based a similar competitive advantage on its networks in Africa (based, in turn, on the distinctive capabilities of its dominant chief executive).

As with all other types of competitive advantage, the profitability of this type of architecture rests on the inability of others to replicate it. In advanced economies no company can expect to achieve the sort of position which a firm like United Brands enjoys in the countries in which it operates. Even so, in small countries a dominant local firm may develop a unique network of contacts and interrelationships. In Belgium, Société Générale has achieved that position, with interests across much of Belgian industry and finance. When the Italian Carlo de Benedetti saw a take-over of the somewhat sleepy Société as a means of enhancing his pan-European ambitions, the political strength of the company, on top of its economic interests, enabled it to survive his attack.

Architecture in Japan

It is Japanese industry which has been most successful in creating distinctive capabilities through architecture. In Japan we can identify the power of internal architecture, external architecture, and networks.

The 'three pillars' of the internal labour market in Japanese firms are lifetime employment, the seniority system, and enterprise unionism. The lifetime employment system emphasizes the long-term relationship between the employee and the company. Even Japanese companies, particularly small ones, cannot completely predict their labour requirements, and fluctuations are dealt with by employing part-time or irregular workers on spot contracts without detriment to the basic lifetime employment system. Although lifetime employment is particularly associated with Japanese companies, the reality of employment relationships in large continental European firms is not so different. The stark contrast is between Japan and the USA and, to a lesser degree, the United Kingdom.

The seniority system in wage determination and in promotion, heavy investment in on-the-job training which is company-specific, and an emphasis on enterprise unionism are similarly designed to support relational contracting. The industrially based structure of Western unionism is designed to increase the union's negotiating power by diluting the common interests of firm and worker. The Japanese system is intended to reinforce that identity of interest. As in any relational contract, these concerns are reciprocated in the emphasis which Japanese managers place on employee interests over those of shareholders.

Continuity and stability in supplier–assembler relationships is a well-known feature of Japanese business, and firms such as Toyota and NEC are surrounded by their keiretsu, or supplier group. Just-in-time inventory management, as developed by Toyota, is a striking example of a structure possible only under relational contracting. The urgent demand requires the urgent willing response of the partner in a long-term relationship, not the hard-nosed spot contract which can be achieved when the opposing party is most vulnerable.

Japan has a long tradition of co-operative groupings of companies, originating in the zaibatsu which were dissolved by the Allies after the Second World War. Today's networks are looser associations of companies. These groups typically include one company in each main industrial sector, including a bank and a trading company. There are commonly reciprocal shareholdings among members of the group.

Although there is some presumption in favour of inter-group trading among these networks, members of them also trade extensively with Japanese companies outside the group. The power of the network seems to rest partly in the exchange of information through it (hence the emphasis on 'one-set-ism', the requirement that the group contains precisely one company in each sector), and on the ready ability of the group to support transactions which benefit from relational contracting, such as financing, overseas distribution, and joint venture.

The social context of architecture

The Japanese experience, and the contrast between Japan and the United States, illustrates the degree to which relational contracting and architecture are the product of the broader commercial and social environment. Geographical proximity is important to networking, although the role it plays is not entirely obvious. Since transporting ties is neither slow nor expensive, why are most Italian ties produced in a single small region? At first sight it seems absurd that at a time when capital markets have become international and world-wide communication of data, funds, and information has become instantaneous, the financial institutions of the world should be concentrated in tiny and fabulously expensive areas of lower Manhattan and eastern London.

What lies behind this is the need to establish trust and penalize opportunism in a network of relational contracts, which is facilitated if business relationships are supported by a corresponding network of social relationships. We are all more inclined to trust people we know; a view which is based partly on instinct and emotion, partly on our capacity to make our own judgements (we are also inclined to mistrust some people we know), and partly on a rational calculation that people are less likely to cheat us if by doing so they sacrifice a social reputation as well as a commercial one.

It may be no accident that the City of London's pre-eminence rested on the homogeneity of background and values created by the English class system and the English school system. These factors may also explain why conscious attempts to emulate the competitive advantages of networking through replication are rarely successful.

It follows that some social environments are more conducive to the development of competitive advantage through architecture than others. Since the essence of architecture is that organizations or groups of organizations have values—social and economic—distinct from those of their members, there is a direct conflict between individualism and the creation of architecture. This conflict is reinforced by the absence of powerful sanctions against opportunistic behaviour in an individualistic environment. Competitive strengths based on these architectures are therefore relatively rare in those environments where the prevailing ethos is strongly individualistic. Where they exist—as in the financial sector, in networking activities in less developed countries, and in the performance of companies with a very distinctive corporate ethos—the activities concerned are commonly viewed by outsiders with a degree of hostility and suspicion. Nepotism is a term of abuse, contact networks are corrupt, and the organization man is regarded with uneasy laughter.

Our reaction is the same when we hear of Japanese workers gathering to sing the company song. But our incomprehension of this cultural divide applies also in countries where the difference is less apparent. Networking within Italian communities resurfaced in the United States in the form of criminal conspiracies and political corruption (as it does in Italy also) and we feel relieved when it is stamped out; but we also observe it in Italy itself as a potent form of commercial organization.

In all this, European business lies, as it often does, in an intermediate position. Britain's financial markets, and systems of corporate governance, are close to those of the United States. Italy, in which a large part of effective business is conducted in smaller firms in which proprietorial influences are dominant, occupies rather different ground, while France and Germany pursue the 'Rhine model' described by Michel Albert (1991), in which the firm is perceived as operating within a wider social context.

How is the need for stability and continuity in relationships to be reconciled with the equal need for change and flexibility which confronts every organization in business today? If there is a single central lesson from the success of Japanese manufacturing industry, it is that the stability of relationships and the capacity to respond to change are mutually supportive, not mutually exclusive, requirements. It is within the context of long-term relationships, and often only within that context, that the development of organizational knowledge, the free exchange of information, and a readiness to respond quickly and flexibly can be sustained.

So the most important challenge for European business is to maintain, and enhance, those competitive advantages which are based on architecture. Of the three major economic areas of the world, one—North America—has developed a business culture which offers little support for structures of relational contracts, and the competitive advantages of US firms are mostly to be found elsewhere. Firms in Japan and the Far East have made much of the sources of competitive strength which I have identified with architecture. Yet the pressures on European companies are principally to move in a transatlantic direction. This is reflected in an increasing pace of merger and acquisition activity, a more American approach to corporate strategy, and a more aggressive business environment characterized by tighter financial controls, more specific monitoring of performance, and less emphasis on long-term relationships with contractors or with employees. In public policy, and in business policy, the potential losses from these developments far outweigh the potential gains.

13

Corporate Governance

This chapter, written with Aubrey Silberston, explores some of the policy implications of the view that the large, successful corporation is a social institution rather than the creation of private contract, embodying a corporate personality and incapable of being 'owned' by any one.

It is better that property should be private, but that man should make it common in use. . . . It is the task of the legislator to see that the citizens become like that.

(Aristotle)

Introduction

The issue has existed for as long as there have been social institutions; yet two decades ago the term 'corporate governance' had not been coined.[1] The matters involved were of concern only as an esoteric branch of commercial law. Today, the subject is a central political and economic issue in Britain and the United States.

There are several reasons. One is corporate fraud and corporate collapse on a previously unimagined scale. Economic history records many instances of the collision of greed and *naïveté*—the South Sea Bubble was only the most memorable of many ill-fated trading ventures. The Companies Acts of 1844 and 1856 established the limited liability corporation, and many contemporary commentators expected an explosion of fraud and irresponsibility. They were wrong. There were inevitable scandals and crashes, but the majority of corporations—which still controlled only a modest proportion of economic activity—were run with prudence and integrity.

The record of recent decades—in which the corporation has come to dominate business—has been a more chequered one.[2] Names as famous and as unquestioned as Rolls Royce and Barings have collapsed. Robert Maxwell,

---

[1] *National Institute Economic Review* (Aug. 1995).

[2] Although it is open to argument whether fraud and mismanagement have become more prevalent, or whether modern institutions are better at detecting them.

declared by DTI inspectors to be unfit to act as director of a public company, went on to plunder the assets of several more. Polly Peck, an FT-SE 100 company founded on little more than hot air, collapsed amongst allegations of false accounting and vanished assets. The grandly named Bank of Credit and Commerce International turned out to be a web of fraud and deception. In the last recession a number of sound operating businesses were damaged or destroyed by inappropriate financial structures assembled around them in the speculative excesses of the 1980s.

These events have dictated a public policy agenda, and a variety of reforms. In the last decade, we have had a new Insolvency Act, a Cadbury Code on corporate governance, and a Greenbury Code on executive remuneration. What should be the rules for corporate bankruptcy and liquidation? How should directors of public companies be selected, reappointed, and disqualified? What should they be paid? Who should define accounting standards? Or the relationship between investors and company management? What are the responsibilities of auditors? These questions have gained attention far outside the narrow circle of professionals who once debated them.

But the issue that has made corporate governance a subject for tabloid headlines is greedy bosses. The salaries of senior managers have risen far faster than earnings generally (Conyon, Gregg, and Machin 1995). Their pay has been enhanced by share option packages, which allow senior executives to buy shares in the company at a future date for a figure around the current price. Over a decade in which share prices generally rose substantially, share options proved very valuable. The result is that many salaried managers have become personally very rich in a way which was simply unknown in earlier decades. While security of employment for most workers has been reduced, service contracts for senior managers ensure that even the unsuccessful leave with generous pay-offs.

No British companies have yet matched the excesses of some American corporations: the chief executive of RJR Nabisco notoriously used a corporate jet to fetch his dog (Burrough and Helyar 1990), and Steven Ross of Time Warner managed to earn, or at least receive, the best part of $1 billion for his services to his company (Crystal 1991). But even in Britain the only restraint on executive pay and perks appears to be the modesty of executives themselves, and that is a commodity in increasingly short supply.

Yet the amounts dissipated in fraud or overpayment are, in aggregate, small relative to the value added by Britain's corporations. The important issues of corporate governance lie deeper. What is the relationship between the structure of rules, laws, and conventional practices within which companies operate and their style of management and the decisions which they make? There are increasingly widespread claims that the incentives, pressures, and restraints on British managers lead to short-term decision-making, and to failures to invest in physical equipment, in people, and in the development of businesses, and that these factors are ultimately profoundly damaging to Britain's economic performance (Hutton 1995). The different environment within which German and Japanese companies operate may be an element in the economic success of those countries.

With the collapse of socialism and centralized planning, attention is focused on different styles of capitalism (Albert 1991; Blinder 1995; Hampden-Turner and Trompenaars 1994). Corporate governance both exemplifies and influences these styles. Privatization and the extension of contracting out blur the traditional demarcations between the public and private sectors. The nature and legitimacy of organizations which, whatever their legal structure, provide what everyone continues to think of as a public service—water, transport, health, education—need careful attention. It is principally with issues such as these that this chapter is concerned. Our conclusions do, however, have implications for the regulation of companies and for the setting of executive pay.

The nature of the corporation

The 1985 Companies Act introduced into British law a distinction between a limited company and a PLC. The distinction has little practical significance (a PLC must have a share capital of £50,000 and may, but need not, offer its shares to the public). Many people think, mistakenly, that the distinction between a PLC and other firms corresponds to that between quoted and unquoted companies.

The reason for the distinction is that it already existed in several other European countries. The French regime is perhaps the one to express the objective most clearly. Most large French companies have the status of *société anonyme*, and any with more than fifty shareholders must. The governance structure of a *société anonyme* is the subject of detailed statutory prescription. The artisan who trades under a corporate vehicle mainly in order to limit his personal exposure to the risks of his trade will normally operate through a SARL (*société à responsabilité limité*). A SARL is subject to minimal regulation, mostly concerned with registration. Germany maintains a similar distinction between the *Aktiengesellschaft* (AG) and the *Gesellschaft mit beschränkter Haftung* (GmbH). As in France, the structure and organization of the AG, and also of the large GmbH, is the subject of detailed statutory prescription.

British law, by contrast, makes no real distinction between ICI and BT on the one hand and the incorporated local plumber or garage on the other. Indeed, British statute law is virtually silent on how corporations are to be organized. Since the corporation is regarded as a creation of private contract, obligations on companies are mainly there to prevent abuse of the privilege of limited liability, and concern formal matters such as registration and audit. Corporate governance is a matter for the company itself to determine and to describe in its articles of association. The legal system therefore provides, and is intended to provide, no more than a mechanism for the negotiation and enforcement of these contracts. The American position is broadly similar.

These differences between Britain and other European countries are not matters of accident. Nor are they just questions of law, though they are partly a product of the difference between the private law tradition of England, based around the enforcement of contract, and the administrative law general in continental Europe, where behaviour is regulated by public codes. They reflect basic differences in the ways large corporations are perceived in the countries concerned. In continental Europe, and in Japan, the corporation is an institution with personality, character, and aspirations of its own. Its objectives encompass the interests of a wide range of stakeholder groups—investors, employees, suppliers, customers, and managers—but cannot be equated with any of them. The corporation is therefore naturally perceived as a social institution, with public responsibilities, and a proper public interest in defining the ways in which it is run and governed. In the Anglo-American environment, the corporation is a private rather than a public body, defined by a set of relationships between principal and agent. Shareholder-owners, too busy and too numerous to undertake the responsibility themselves, hire salaried executives to manage their affairs.

We argue that much of the concern with corporate governance—a concern which is largely Anglo-American—arises from the tension between the Anglo-American model and the practical reality of how large corporations operate everywhere. We believe it is quite clear that the organic model of corporate behaviour—which gives to the corporation life independent from its shareholders or stakeholders—describes the actual behaviour of large companies and their managers far better than does the principal–agent perspective, and that this is as true in Britain and the United States as it is in Japan.

Yet the near unanimous view of those who criticize the present structure of corporate governance is that reality should be made to conform to the model.[3] The principal–agent structure should be made more effective, through closer shareholder involvement and supervision. All experience suggests that this is not very likely to happen, and would not improve the functioning of corporations if it did. The alternative approach—of adapting the model to reality rather than reality to the model—deserves equal consideration. After all, no one disputes that the German and Japanese models produce many successful companies.

Companies in Britain and the United States

The term governance invites comparison with political structures. Most experience of governance systems is derived from comparative politics. There are obvious resemblances between the system of corporate governance we

[3] This is as true of those who are fundamentally critical of current arrangements (e.g. Hutton 1995) as of those who broadly support them (Cadbury Committee 1992); and is equally reflected in intermediate positions such as Charkham (1994) or Sykes (1994).

have and entrenched authoritarian political systems, such as those which prevailed in Eastern Europe before the fall of the Berlin Wall.

The governing élite is self-perpetuating, in the sense that it appoints its own members by reference to its own criteria. The process of succession is normally internal and orderly, but from time to time there are peaceful palace revolutions and occasionally externally induced *coups d'état*. The hostile bid for the corporation parallels the military take-over of a government. There is a nominal process of accountability through election of directors, but in practice it is defunct. There are no genuine alternative candidates and incumbents are re-elected with overwhelming majorities. The formal ritual of the corporation's annual general meeting parallels the meaningless elections which routinely returned Mr Brezhnev and Herr Honecker to power. The flow of information about the affairs of the organization is managed by incumbents and, except in times of acute crisis, is uniformly favourable and optimistic in tone.

Authoritarian political structures sometimes work well. They offer opportunities to make rapid change and to impose firm leadership which more accountable systems lack. In the hands of honest leaders of determination and vision, they give opportunities for stability and long-term planning which democratic regimes often find difficult to achieve. One might cite the practical governance of Lee Kwan Yew's Singapore, although it is difficult to think of many other examples.

There is an important reason why this authoritarianism is less disastrous for companies than it has generally proved in politics. Many firms operate in competitive markets. So deficiencies in performance are more evident in corporations than in political systems, and internal and external pressures for reform and improvement build up more rapidly. Competition ultimately works for governments as well, and it was, above all, the failure of Eastern European regimes in economic competition that brought about their downfall, although the process took many years. But not all firms operate in competitive markets, and for these, such as privatized utilities, governance issues are still more acute.

For all but the most remarkable of men and women, authoritarian structures are insidiously corrupting. Leaders hang on to power too long, and many prefer to undermine those who might seek to replace them than to develop potential successors. Cults of personality develop, and are supported by sycophantic lieutenants. These are often associated with inappropriate accretion of privileges, and excessive fascination with the trappings of office. Slogans replace analysis, rallies replace debate. There is an alternation between periods of too little change and phases of instability in which there is too much. These features are today as commonplace in business as they were in politics. Authoritarian governance structures have a deservedly bad reputation.

And there is another way in which Anglo-American corporate governance curiously mirrors the Eastern Europe of the past. Both structures claimed legitimacy by reference to what was, in reality, empty rhetoric. Socialist bureaucrats purported to exercise power on behalf of the workers. They argued that their devotion to the interests of the workers was such that it did not matter that the workers were not involved in the process of government in any observable way; indeed, that to so involve them would inhibit the capacity of their leaders to promote their interests. The managers of many large British and American companies similarly defend their positions by claiming to act in the interests of the shareholders. Yet, if shareholder intervention (much of which is in fact ill informed, frivolous, or motivated by factors other than the interests of the company) seriously interferes with managerial prerogatives, it frequently encounters fierce resistance.[4]

Who owns the company?

It is often said that a company is owned by its shareholders. It is, however, not very clear what people mean when they say this. When I tell you that I own my house, you will infer that I decide who may enter it or live in it, and who not; that I determine how it will be furnished and decorated; and that I have the right to dispose of all or part of it and keep the proceeds for my own benefit. When I buy a share in BT I enjoy none of these rights in relation to BT, except a limited version of the last. As the ostensible owner, I have no right to access or to use its premises or assets, far less the ability to exclude non-owners; I take no part in decisions about the nature or direction of its business; when the company makes acquisitions or disposes of parts of itself, it seldom consults me; nor does it seek from me a share of the cost, or distribute to me a fraction of the proceeds.

So when we say 'BT is owned by its shareholders', as distinct from 'the shareholders of BT own their shares in BT', we use the word 'ownership' in a sense very different from that in which we ordinarily use the word 'own'. The dictionary definition of ownership emphasizes physical possession, something which is altogether absent from the relationship between BT and its shareholders. The problem is that the concept of ownership, clear cut in its application to simple tangible objects like toothbrushes and teapots, becomes elusive in its application to more complex constructions. Although I can, by contract, give to others many of the rights associated with ownership of my house, it is the ultimate capacity to expel them and occupy it myself which seems to be essential to ownership. It is a right which has no analogue in the case of an intangible asset, or a collection of assets.

This issue of the nature of ownership rights is given careful analysis by Grossman and Hart (1986). Their proposed definition is that the owner of an

---

[4] The hostility of General Motors' management in the 1980s to expressions of view by Ross Perot and the California Public Employees Retirement Scheme, the company's largely shareholders, illustrates the phenomenon very clearly. Note equally, however, that shareholder activism is mostly concerned with political rather than corporate issues.

asset is the person who enjoys those rights over it that have not been given to others by explicit contract. Some such rights will be those which were not provided for because contracts can never be exhaustive. When I hire a Hertz car, I acquire many of the rights normally associated with ownership, such as the right to determine where it is driven, but since Hertz retains all rights other than those explicitly conferred by the contract, no one doubts that Hertz continues to own it. Other rights are governed by implicit contract, and the issue here is who is arbiter of the implied terms.

One problem with this definition is that if it is applied to a firm, it is not the shareholders who appear to be the owners; it is the board of directors. And there is a common sense appeal to this. If we asked a visitor from another planet to guess who were the owners of a firm by observing behaviour rather than by reading textbooks in law or economics, there can be little doubt that he would point to the company's senior managers. The definition points directly to the paradox in Berle and Means's (1933) famous observation of the separation of ownership and control. If ownership does not imply control, what is meant by ownership?

Yet if the statement 'A company is owned by its shareholders' makes little sense, we should also be reluctant to say that 'A company is owned by its managers.' Perhaps a large corporation is not owned by anybody at all, at least in the normal sense of ownership—the one we use when we say, 'I own my house,' or 'I own my toothbrush.'

But does this matter? There are many things that function tolerably well yet do not appear to be owned by anybody, such as Oxford University or the River Thames. It is important that there should be statements of the various rights, obligations, and expectations which those who have interests in Oxford University and the River Thames enjoy. It is necessary that there should be mechanisms for resolving disputes over possibly conflicting claims. But so long as that is so, the fact that none of these rights or obligations amounts to ownership poses no particular problem. Indeed, the absence of any rights against these institutions sufficiently strong to constitute ownership may be important in enabling their usefulness to be enhanced and maintained. But many of the checks and balances that enable Oxford University, for example, to function reasonably satisfactorily do not apply to companies.

Certainly, no particular legal problem arises if the corporation is not owned by any particular group. As a legal matter, an English company does not appear to be owned by its shareholders, despite frequent statements to the contrary by corporate managers—a striking illustration of the substitution of rhetorical for real accountability. 'The company is at law a different person altogether from its subscribers.'[5] 'Shareholders are not, in the eye of the law, part owners of the undertaking. The undertaking is something different from the totality of the shareholdings.'[6]

[5] Lord Macnaghten in *Salomon* v. *Salomon & Co.* (1897, AC 22 HL).
[6] Evershed LJ in *Short* v. *Treasury Commissioners* (1948, AC 534 HL).

Many people find the suggestion that assets need not be owned by anyone a troubling one. We have been encouraged to believe that property ownership is the institution on which markets and capitalist organization are based: yet the claim is refuted by the observation that the most important of modern economic institutions cannot easily be described in those terms. Ownership is not necessarily important, and arguments about who 'owns' the company are irrelevant semantics when the essential facts about how corporations are run are not in dispute. In Charles Handy's phrase 'the myth of property gets in the way'.[7]

If a company is not 'owned' by its shareholders, and the shareholders are simply one of a number of stakeholder groups, all of whom enjoy claims against it, then there is no particular reason to think that the interests of shareholders do or should enjoy priority over the interests of these other stakeholders. From a legal perspective, even the rule that shareholders have exclusive claim to the residual assets in the event of liquidation (established in 1962) was reversed by the 1985 Companies Act, which entrenches the interests of employees and imposes on directors an explicit duty to strike a balance between their interests and those of other members.

The widespread perception that the purpose of British corporations is to maximize shareholder value is the product of a particular economic theory of the modern corporation rather than the structure of British company law. Although the description of the corporation as a nexus of contracts is an illuminating analogy, it is not a historical account of how such organizations came into being. It occupies the same status in relation to business life as Hobbes's Social Contract enjoys in political theory.

In the last decade, British and American companies have devoted far more attention to shareholder interests. This is not the result of changes in the law, or of more careful study of the fiduciary duties of directors of public companies, or of developments in economic theory. It has arisen from the threat of hostile take-over.

The alternative model

The divorce of ownership and control, the source of so much tension in Anglo-American corporate governance, is less marked, or at least different in form, in other jurisdictions. Of the 200 largest German companies, over 90 per cent have a shareholder (most commonly a bank or another company) with at least 25 per cent of the equity (Franks and Mayer 1990). Even in Britain (or the USA), concentration of ownership in large companies is not altogether absent (Nyman and Silberston 1978), but it is true that, by and large, shareholder control of corporations is now largely a myth in the Anglo-American world. It

---

[7] Handy, cited in Wheeler (1994). See also Royal Society of Arts (1995).

is tempting to conclude, on the other hand, that shareholder control of corporations is still a reality in Germany. That is a misleading oversimplification.

There is an extended German literature on the role of the corporation in society which is not easy reading for anyone brought up in an Anglo-American tradition. In sharp contrast to the shareholder agency model, this tradition originated a century ago with Gierke's concept of the 'Verbands-persönlichkeit', the corporate personality. For Gierke, as for some other German writers of his day, there was a mystical collectivism about this—the corporation sought to achieve a 'physio-spiritual unity'. While for obvious reasons this thinking is now unfashionable, that perspective continues to underpin the German view of the corporation. 'The social substratum to be personified is not simply a (static) social structure. Instead, it is an internal dynamics system, with selections of its own, and with a capacity for self-organization and self-reproduction' (Teubner 1988).

The role of concentrated shareholding in German companies needs to be seen in this light. Many of these shareholdings are controlled or influenced by banks or other major companies, and they certainly do not imply that large-scale German enterprises are closer to the model of owner-manager than British or American corporations. Rather these shareholdings are themselves evidence of the German conception of the company as a social institution; a community in itself and an organization in turn embedded in a community. This perception is reinforced by other widely noted institutions of the German market economy, such as the supervisory board, co-determination, and the co-operative relationships of the *Mittelstand* (the constellations of small enterprises which are such an important element in the success of German manufacturing business). It would be wrong to think that by reproducing these institutions we could automatically reproduce their effects. The institutions are the product of a different view of the corporation and its role in society.

The concept of the large company as social organization, rather than the product of private contract, emerges equally clearly in Japan. Japan does not have the difference in formal legal structure between major firms and owner-managed concerns which characterizes much of Europe, but the demarcation in operational structure and economic function between large and small companies in Japan is a factor noted by many commentators. The notion that the Japanese company is described by an agency relationship between shareholders and managers would be incomprehensible to most Japanese businessmen. 'We shall eliminate any untoward profit-seeking, shall constantly emphasise activities of real substance, and shall not seek expansion of size for the sake of size,' was the prospectus on which Sony began operations. It is difficult to imagine an Anglo-American company proffering a similar statement of intention. In Japan, 'Corporate growth is appreciated and sought after primarily for its contribution to utilising the enriching human resources and in creating promotion opportunities . . . workers identify their interests with those of the company which, as a consequence, is regarded as a sort of community' (Odagiri 1991: 106).

In other European countries, the same distinction between private and public company emerges in similar if not identical form. In France, many large corporations are part of a social and economic structure in which the boundaries between state and corporate bureaucracy are barely discernible to the non-Frenchman. Indeed, these formal boundaries have frequently shifted over the last fifteen years of nationalization and de-nationalization, with small effects on the operations concerned. In Italy, as in Spain or Greece, the large company is often not only a social institution but a political one. But most of what we have said about Anglo-American companies would apply equally to corporations in Australia, Canada, New Zealand, or, indeed, South Africa. While there are elements of caricature in the sharp distinction we have drawn between the corporate governance systems of the English-speaking world and those of the rest of the world, the differences are wide-ranging.

The trusteeship model of corporate governance

Thus there is an alternative to the shareholder agency model of the corporation. It recognizes the existence of corporate personality, and its economic and commercial importance. It accepts that the large public corporation is a social institution, not the creation of private contract. But if senior management are not the agents of the shareholders, what are they?

There is a well-established structure in English law to govern the behaviour of individuals or groups who control and manage assets they do not beneficially own; it is the concept of trusteeship.[8] Grossman and Hart have described the central role of what they call the owner as being the determination of the residual terms of incomplete contracts. What they define is exactly the historic function of the trustee. The settlor of property, unable to anticipate all the contingencies which might arise after his death, would appoint an honest man to determine what should be done in these circumstances. The concept is generalized to cover the governance of other institutions, such as Oxford University or the National Gallery.[9]

The notion that boards of directors are the trustees of the tangible and intangible assets of the corporation, rather than the agents of the shareholders, is one which the executives of most German and Japanese companies, and of many British firms, would immediately recognize. The duty of the trustee is to preserve and enhance the value of the assets under his control, and to balance fairly the various claims to the returns which these assets generate. The trusteeship model therefore differs from the agency model in two fundamental ways.

The responsibility of the trustees is to sustain the corporation's assets. This differs from the value of the corporation's shares. The difference comes not

[8] Goyder (1987) explains this concept and describes some legal history.
[9] The River Thames too had its conservators, whose functions have since been absorbed into the newly created regulatory agencies.

only because the stock market may value these assets incorrectly. It also arises because the assets of the corporation, for these purposes, include the skills of its employees, the expectations of customers and suppliers, and the company's reputation in the community. The objectives of managers as trustees therefore relate to the broader purposes of the corporation, and not simply to the financial interests of shareholders. Some British companies have seen it as entirely appropriate, in pursuit of shareholder value, to dispose completely of an existing collection of businesses and buy a new one. This course would seem inconceivable to a Japanese manager. A new vice-chancellor of Oxford University, or trustee of the National Gallery, who suggested that the University should become an international language school or that the Trafalgar Square site would make an excellent shop and restaurant complex, would be seen as having fundamentally misunderstood the nature of his responsibilities.

The concept of corporate personality acknowledges, as the principal-agent model cannot, the path-dependent nature of the behaviour of companies. Businesses are defined by a nexus of long-established trust relationships; the principal–agent model sees only a group of people who find it expedient every morning to renew their contracts with each other. Many of the ludicrous business books on the management of change see the Markovian nature of business evolution as a problem; yet for most successful companies, their history is a principal asset rather than a liability.

Thus the trusteeship model demands, as the agency model does not, the evolutionary development of the corporation around its core skills and activities because it is these skills and activities, rather than a set of financial claims, which are the essence of the company. This does not preclude diversification or divestment, but it restricts operations to areas that relate in an obvious way to the firm's distinctive capabilities. Deal-making, even if profitable, becomes again a function of financial markets rather than corporate management. Chandler (1990), in contrast to our views, places emphasis on the virtues of diversification. But we suspect that diversification is often sought by managers of companies in order to insure (however misguidedly) against risks to themselves rather than to insure against risks to shareholders.

The second fundamental difference between the agency model and the trusteeship model is that while the agency model expects the manager to attach priority to the current shareholder interest, the trustee has to balance the conflicting interests of current stakeholders and additionally to weigh the interests of present and future stakeholders. Thus future customers and employees, and the future interests of current suppliers, also come into account. These two distinct differences have the joint effect of materially shifting the balance of considerations in management towards long-term development of the capabilities of the business.

We believe that many non-executive directors already see their role in these terms. The trusteeship role is a more natural and appealing one than the position—which the agency model points towards—of shareholder spy in the boardroom, a function which would not be easy to perform and which most non-executive directors do not in fact perform, or aim to perform (Davis and Kay 1990).

Performance in the Anglo-American environment

The choice between structures of corporate governance ultimately depends not on legal theory but on economic performance. In this section, we consider the relationship between corporate governance and behaviour in two areas: strategies for the development of the business.

It is widely argued that the difference between Anglo-American and German-Japanese capital markets makes it more difficult for companies in the former to undertake long-term investments. Much of this argument is superficial or wrong. Fund managers may be monitored on their quarterly or annual performance; but that does not imply that companies will therefore operate on a quarterly or an annual basis. Indeed, that is to misunderstand the fundamental role of a stock market, which is to enable the time horizons of investors to be divorced from the time horizons of the firms in which they invest.

Perhaps more importantly, there are many examples of companies which have found it easy to access the British capital market for long-term investment. Pharmaceutical research and development often involves a ten-year time scale, but the industry is an unequivocal British success story, and funds have been readily available for both established quoted companies and start-up investments. The discovery of North Sea oil led to the development, in Britain, of project financing techniques which were widely imitated elsewhere.

What makes these industries different is that they have consistently delivered good returns to investors. If British capital markets denied funds to its car industry and were reluctant to support new civil aviation projects, it was mostly for good reason. Many myths about short termism have been effectively debunked by Marsh (1990). There are certainly grounds for criticizing the relationship between finance and industry in the UK. But the problem is less that the services of the capital market are insufficiently available to UK companies; rather it is that they are available too readily. If the Anglo-American company does not have a corporate personality, it is instead essentially a creation of the capital market.

The intellectual underpinning of this model is provided by the market for corporate control. Corporate governance is a market process rather than a political one; alternative teams of managers bid for the right to deploy corporate assets. Provided there is sufficient competition in the market for corporate control, transaction costs are low and assets will be delivered to the highest value users.

Problems arise because transaction costs are not low, and there are large asymmetries of information between insiders—incumbent corporate managers—and outsiders. Indeed, if these things were not true, it is not easy to see why firms would exist at all. To buy a company involves paying not only substantial fees to advisers, but a considerable control premium over the underlying value of the company.

Incumbent management will, or should, know more about the value of a company than outsiders. There are two relevant groups of outsiders: the company's existing stockholders, and prospective bidders. The problem for management is how, in the face of this information gap, they can make credible signals about the company's prospects to shareholders. There is substantial evidence that the market is not as irrational as many managers would argue, because most information feeds rapidly into prices,[10] but there is no escaping the fundamental disparity of information. Insider trading rules, designed to protect small investors by ensuring equality of information, have actually had the effect of reducing its amount.

Bidders face the problem of a 'winner's curse'; it is companies which overestimate the value of the assets they hope to acquire, not firms which underestimate them, which are likely to enter the auction. And there are many managers who have a natural inclination to overestimate the value which they will add to the operation of other companies. If transaction costs were low, then the correction of such mistakes would be rapid and inexpensive; but they are not.

So the costs of the market for corporate control, and the problems created by imperfect information, interact. Some bids function as the theory describes—replacing under-performing management by abler teams—and companies such as Hanson and BTR have built successful businesses by operating in this way. But others are the result of managerial self-aggrandizement, or temporary market under- or over-valuations, and in other cases the costs of dislodging incumbents prove to be too great. Taken as a whole, the evidence that this process adds any substantial value is slight.

That is important because in the Anglo-American environment, in contrast to that of Japan or Germany, merger and acquisition activity is central to business activity. Indeed, conversation with senior executives, or a perusal of the financial press, would suggest that corporate strategy consists of little else. The senior executive appears as a meta fund manager, juggling a portfolio of businesses as an investor juggles a portfolio of shares.[11] These preoccupations persist despite analysis which suggests that the contribution of corporate ownership to performance is almost negligible, and that competitive advantages are to be found in operating businesses, rather than in buying and selling them (Rumelt 1991; Campbell and Goold 1991).

---

[10] See Marsh (1994) for a survey.
[11] See Wright (1992) for a striking description.

Criteria for a model of corporate governance

It is often too easy to conclude that the grass is greener on the other side of the Channel, or the world, and the German-Japanese model is by no means free of weaknesses. 'Making bosses accountable to many stakeholders might make them accountable to none, as there would be no clear yardstick for judging their performance' (Bishop 1994). This problem is familiar from Britain's experience with nationalized industries, where the multiplicity of goals led to confusion between the concerns of government and those of the industry. It also enabled managers to conceal their lack of success in achieving any of these goals; or simply allowed them to pursue objectives such as expansion or technical excellence with little concern to balance these things against efficiency or value.

We see similar problems in private corporations operating under the stakeholder model. Philips is a good example of a company whose technical excellence was not matched by manufacturing efficiency or marketing effectiveness. What critics of the Anglo-American system commend as the ability to take a long-term view can easily become an opportunity to disregard external comment or criticism, however well founded. There are instances of similar under-performance in German companies, and the French PDG is often more autocractic than a British or American CEO. The sharpness and clarity of the objective of shareholder value maximization, and the greater prospects of monitoring performance against it, are reasons why that model is increasingly popular even outside its Anglo-American base. Part of the problem is that if there is atrophy in the Anglo-American system—a formal structure which has become empty—there can also be atrophy in the alternative. The German supervisory board may often be no more than an agreeable lunch club. The close relationships between the senior management of many large French companies and the agencies of the French government have sometimes been a source of strength, but it is not a structure which encourages self-criticism.

Any governance structure—political or corporate, democratic or authoritarian, American or Japanese—has a natural tendency to embrace those who share the basic values of those who currently operate it, and to reject those who do not. Moreover, such behaviour is easy to defend; is it not better to confine involvement to those who understand the business?

Yet there is something in these arguments. A board of directors clearly works better if it is cohesive, and can avoid reiterated argument about fundamental values on every specific proposal before it. Building societies have sometimes been arrogant and patronizing in their reaction to attempts to nominate directors by groups of members—in contrast to the normal building society and PLC practice of nomination by the existing directors. But it is difficult to believe that their operations would have been improved by the election to their boards of people who were often no more than vocal cranks. Attempts to bring reality into line with an impractical ideal of member democracy are not truly constructive directions of reform. Other experiments in the appointment of directors specifically charged to represent particular interests—whether shareholder spies in the boardroom or formal representatives of employees—have rarely proved a success. If unwelcome or unqualified members are appointed to a board, the likely practical consequence is that substantive decision-making will take place elsewhere.

Thus we can identify the delicate balancing of criteria which has to be achieved in a new model of corporate governance. It should give recognition and content to the trusteeship model which acknowledges corporate personality. It should allow managers to pursue multiple objectives, yet hold them responsible for their performance. It should encourage cohesion within an executive team, but be sufficiently open to outside influence to discourage introversion and ensure that success is rewarded and failure penalized. That basic objective of 'managerial freedom with accountability' is well set out in the Cadbury Report (1992).

It is important to recognize that the quest for perfection in systems of corporate governance is a hopeless one. We have emphasized the comparison between political systems and corporate governance. It has been wisely, and memorably, said that democracy is the worst form of government ever invented, except for every other form of government invented.

The future of corporate governance

The widely accepted consensus among those who have written about corporate governance in the last decade[12] is that the key requirement is to give content to the existing structure of notional accountability to shareholders. We are sceptical about this prescription. We doubt whether shareholders have either incentive or capacity to provide such monitoring. We doubt whether shareholder priority is an appropriate rule for the large corporation in any event. And we are not persuaded that the main lines of the proposed remedy—an enhanced role for non-executive directors, more extensive involvement of shareholders in major decisions, and the provision of fuller information about corporate affairs—represents a suitable monitoring mechanism. It is precisely the form of relationship which government, as controlling shareholder, traditionally enjoyed with nationalized industries, and its effect was to undermine management responsibility for corporate performance without providing stimulus to the effectiveness of corporations.

Moreover, there are dangers in an attempt to breathe artificial life into a model of accountability that has little practical reality. In the stultified authoritarian regimes of Eastern Europe, the rhetoric of popular democracy was used to provide spurious legitimacy for self-interested behaviour. The creation of supposedly independent remuneration committees by large

---

[12] See, for example, Cadbury Committee (1992); Monks and Minnow (1991); Bishop (1994); Charkham (1994).

companies in Britain and the United States has had precisely the same effect. The independence is generally a sham, and the institution has proved to be a mechanism not for restraining excess but for justifying it.

We therefore propose a new Companies Act. That Act should have several key elements.

- It would establish a distinction between the PLC—the social institution with corporate personality—and the owner-managed limited company. The principal criterion would be that any firm above a certain size or with a diffuse shareholding structure would be required to register as PLC; a similar obligation might apply to companies in a particular area of activity (schools, water supply) or to very large private firms even if they had few shareholders (Barings, Littlewoods).[13] The statutory duties of the directors of a PLC would be—as in fact they largely are now—to promote the business of the company and to balance the claims of investors, customers, suppliers, and employees.
- The Act should prescribe a governance framework for a PLC. A PLC should be required to have a board, with an independent chairman and a number (at least three) of independent directors. The definition of independence is primarily a financial one—an individual is independent if neither he nor his employer has received, or expects to receive, 'substantial'[14] remuneration from the company on whose board he sits (in salary or dividends).
- The Act should define the role and functions of the CEO (who should not also be the chairman), and possibly a small number of other senior officers of a PLC, and impose stringent requirements on the process by which they are selected. The independent directors would take the lead in this process, but they would be required to appoint a selection committee with other independent members drawn from other businesses and professional advisers (i.e. not just the independent directors themselves), and would be obliged to consult employees, investors, and suppliers and any relevant regulatory agencies. They would be expected to commission a report on the company's strategy and performance.
- The appointment of a CEO by this process should be for a fixed term of four years;[15] salary and any bonuses should be determined at the beginning of that period; the contract should expire after that period (it might, in exceptional circumstances, be determined) with a fixed and modest termination payment if it is not renewed; and, in any event, only one renewal of the contract of any individual should be permitted.[16]

[13] This creates an issue, or problem, of transition. Broadly, we envisage that a company must convert to PLC once it achieves a certain size or, more usually, its ownership becomes dispersed. This is a Rubicon: once the bridge is crossed, there is no going back.

[14] Judged by generous contemporary standards.

[15] For a similar proposal , although framed in the shareholder priority framework, see Lipton and Rosenblum (1991).

[16] Few corporate strategies cannot be expected to produce some result within four years. Experience with political systems suggests that a seven-year term is too long (France) and a

- The power of nomination of directors—executive or independent— should rest with the independent directors, but they should be obliged to consult stakeholders before appointing new independent directors. We do not, it will be noted, propose a supervisory board on German lines, since supervision on a month-by-month basis is inconsistent with the objective of freedom with accountability.

Our scheme as a whole has one dominant objective. That is to give executive management the greatest possible freedom to develop the business over a period of years in whatever way they think fit, while holding them rigorously responsible to all the parties involved in the business for their performance in the long run.

Under these measures hostile take-over becomes virtually impossible in practice, since ownership of a majority of shares confers no right to appoint executive management. However, the four-yearly review provides a fixed and clear opportunity for those with alternative proposals for the management and direction of a company to put these forward, and such proposals could (but need not) be coupled with an offer to the firm's shareholders.

A key consequence is a fundamental change in the relationship between chief executive and company. Provided the review is real, the creation of responsibility to a constituency should have the same effect on the style and behaviour of the chief executives of large corporations as the introduction of free elections has on the style and behaviour of politicians. As for politicians, the best may not need such a review; but most do. The one-renewal rule is modelled on the one instituted for presidents of the United States. Like Lady Thatcher, Lord King and Lord Weinstock would have left office with reputations immeasurably higher if they had been confined to an eight-year term; the number of CEOs for whom more than eight years is too long outnumbers considerably the number for whom it is too short.

A further advantage of such a limitation of term would be that it would establish a pool of able and experienced candidates for the role of company chairman. There may be corporations that would fail to benefit from the services of such a person, but not many. The political analogy is instructive here too: the political leaders who thought it necessary to combine the roles of prime minister and head of state were Hitler and Idi Amin, not Winston Churchill or Ludwig Erhard.

All this is not very different from what many well-managed companies currently do—or what others would like to do. It would, nevertheless, have a profound effect on corporate behaviour. And it would also have a profound effect on our recommendations for the newly marketized economies of Eastern Europe.

three-year term too short (Australia, New Zealand). There is a widespread consensus on four to five years.

14

The Customer Corporation

The stakeholding view of the nature and purposes of corporations applies most forcefully to monopoly public utilities. This chapter analyses some of the problems of utility regulation and proposes a stakeholding alternative.

The regulation of privatized utilities in Britain is widely criticised today.[1] The criticism comes from many quarters. Customers resent their money being handed out in excessive salaries and dividends. Academics are now widely critical of the (RPI-x) formula which was once a proud British innovation. A curious alliance of politicians and senior industry executives is concerned to suggest that the regulatory process is insufficiently accountable.

Much of this criticism of regulators is misconceived. On balance, regulators have done a better job than could reasonably have been expected. The problems of utility regulation are mostly not the fault of the regulators. They arise directly from the failure to address a range of fundamental structural issues about the management of utilities at the time of privatization. If people are trying to push water up hill, the correct response is not to berate them for incompetence, or to look for ingenious devices to help; it is to point the finger at those who gave them the job to do in the first place. We should address our criticisms to the politicians who devised the framework rather than at the regulators who struggle to operate within it.

The deficiencies of that framework are of three main kinds, and they have been cumulative in their effect. All have a common fundamental cause, which is that the principal concern in all privatizations (with the partial exception of electricity and buses) was to achieve a successful flotation. That was largely perceived as an end in itself. To the extent that the architects of the programme thought beyond that, it was simply assumed that the change in ownership would bring about the desired results.

The first weakness is that the terms on which utilities were privatized were much too favourable to firms and their shareholders, and gave insufficient

---

[1] The Institute of Economic Affairs lecture delivered at the RSA in London on 31 Oct. 1995.

attention to the interests of customers. The second is that no explicit mechanism was put in place for securing a substantial share of the expected efficiency gains for customers. Even if—as can be argued—such a mechanism was implicit, the absence of a clear relationship was bound to leave customers dissatisfied. The third, and deepest, of the problems is that the privatized utilities lack what political theorists term legitimacy—a popularly acceptable basis for the power they exercise. Much concern has recently been expressed over the accountability of the regulators. But popular opinion is not concerned with the accountability of the regulators. It is concerned with the accountability of the companies themselves, and it is right. It is this absence of legitimacy which explains why privatization remains unpopular with the public even as it has started to deliver benefits to them, in the form of lower prices. It is also why attempts to extend privatization further, in post and railways, in health and education, have ground to a halt.

This chapter develops these propositions and argues that attempts to add bells and whistles, or more accurately balls and chains, to the current regulatory system are certain to fail. They will increase rather than reduce dissatisfaction with the current structure. The right answer is a partial retreat from privatization. It is an acceptance that the governance structure of the PLC is not suitable for the governance of monopoly utilities even if it is appropriate for firms which operate in competitive markets (it is not clear it is appropriate for them either, but that is a matter for another day).

The basic reform proposal developed here is a very simple one, though far-reaching. At present, the conventional view is that the primary duty of corporate boards is to the shareholders of the company, and their obligations to customers arise incidentally to the fulfilment of that obligation.[2] In a competitive market, the interests of shareholders can only be achieved by meeting the expectations of customers. But this is not true for a firm which does not face a competitive market, such as a monopoly utility. For such a company, the legal position should be the other way around. The purpose of a privatized utility should be to serve its customers, and its obligations to shareholders exist only to the extent necessary to ensure that the company can meet that primary purpose. This change would have implications for the appointment and conduct of boards, for the financing of companies, and for the role of the regulator.

From my knowledge of the managers of privatized utilities, I believe that this change would reflect the ways in which the vast majority wish to behave and the ways in which they, in the main, do behave. To remove the tension between their aspirations and the expectations of the capital market would be to the long-run benefit of everyone. Some utility executives will see this as a major erosion of the management freedom which privatization has given to

[2] The legal duties of directors of privatized utility companies are to some degree imposed by the Companies Act, derive to a larger extent from common law doctrine on the responsibilities of directors, and are also defined by industry-specific statutes. This structure is opaque and potentially contradictory.

them. The intention, and the effect, would be precisely the reverse. The only hope of maintaining that freedom, and the efficiency gains which have been derived from it, is to find a structure which legitimizes it more effectively. Decisions as to what level of renewal investment is necessary, which new activities will benefit customers, how improvements in service quality should be balanced against price increases, are all best taken not by politicians, or regulators, or referenda among customers, but by utility managers themselves. What we need is a framework that both encourages and allows them to make these decisions in an environment which focuses unambiguously on the interests of customers. The alternative, which is already in progress, will be a continued erosion of management autonomy through expansion of the scale and scope of regulation and from increasing direct political intervention.

The achievements of privatization

Before turning to the supposed failures of regulation, it is well to begin with the successes of privatization.

There have been substantial improvements in efficiency in all those firms which were publicly owned when the privatization experiment began in the early 1980s. Most of this improvement, possibly all of it, has come from reductions in manning levels. The most remarkable achievements have been from those formerly state-owned firms operating in a competitive environment: steel, airways, the two electricity generating companies. Telecom and gas were slower to slim their work-force, but have begun to do so as competition has become more effective. The pace of change has been less marked in water and electricity distribution, and in these industries there are probably large improvements yet to come.

In broad terms, these changes have been achieved without loss of output or service levels. To a much greater extent than had been realized, nationalized industries had become employers of large amounts of unnecessary unskilled labour. The CEGB, widely regarded as one of the most efficient of nationalized industries, can now be seen to have been grossly over-manned. Other countries have had similar experiences in the restructuring of their public sectors. It is, however, important to recognize that competition, rather than ownership as such, seems to have been the key element. Not only have changes happened more quickly in competitive environments than in others, but substantial productivity gains have also been made in the same period in other industries, such as the Post Office, which remained in state ownership.

These efficiency gains have revealed clearly the negative effects of traditional 'accountability' which takes the form of detailed supervision of management actions and of firms' investment plans and operating activities. Such accountability had, in practice, undermined the responsibility of the managers of the businesses concerned for the consequences of their actions without effectively transferring it to the supervisory civil servants or politicians.

The recent fracas over prison management is an unambiguous reminder of the weaknesses of this structure as a means of organizing industrial activities or, for that matter, anything else. Greater freedom to manage has everywhere led to improvements in morale and performance.

Almost all utilities have become more customer focused, in terms of attention to service quality and relationships with customers. British Telecom's redesignation of 'subscribers' as 'customers' is in a sense only symbolic, but represents a real change; customers may now have a choice, and even those utilities which remain monopolies are more inclined to treat customers as if they did have a choice. The influence of employees on British nationalized industries was substantial, but implicit rather than explicit, and hence essentially negative. It operated to prevent change in the structure of organizations, in working practices, and in the range and nature of services provided. There was also an excessive emphasis on technical issues relative to those of marketing and finance, reflecting political love of the grandiose and the wide influence of equipment suppliers. Electricity generation illustrates the nature of change here. The CEGB focused on large, state-of-the-art generating sets, few of which were ever built to time or budget. Since privatization, all new capacity (apart from Sizewell B, an overhang from the old days) has taken the form of small, combined-cycle gas turbines, which can be built rapidly on well-established principles.

Privatization has given utilities more investment freedom. The results of this have been more mixed. Most have taken the opportunity to diversify, either internationally, or outside the core business. Since utilities see limited prospects for growth within the core business, internal and external pressures to do this have been substantial. Very few of these diversifications have been in any way successful. Companies have also been able to invest far more in their core businesses, and this has been particularly true in telecoms and in water. Arguably, a systematic bias towards under-investment has been replaced by a systematic bias towards over-investment. And the problem of monitoring investment, and securing effective discipline without depriving consumers of necessary capital expenditure, has been changed in form but not in substance. In water, in particular, the appraisal of investment programmes by the regulator, at once detailed and arbitrary, comes more and more to resemble the methods of Treasury scrutiny and control which were applied in public ownership. No better answers have been found in gas and electricity.

There is a substantial positive balance to be recorded. It is possible that many of the gains which have occurred in the last decade could have been made without privatization. It is, however, a matter of historical record that they were not made without privatization, and that they have now been realized. It is also possible that the effect of reducing manpower levels, which is by far the most important consequence of the programme, has been to replace disguised unemployment by actual unemployment. Nevertheless, there is no going back, nor should there be.

The problem of legitimacy

Privatization is, and has remained, an unpopular policy. A recent opinion poll showed that the proportion of the electorate which disapproved of water privatization had risen from 71 per cent at flotation to 75 per cent now. In its early stages, the main popular attraction of privatization was the quick and generally substantial gains which small investors made on the shares and there were few, if any, customer benefits. In electricity and water, the process of preparing the industry for privatization led to higher prices than would otherwise have been imposed.

With longer experience of privatization, the combination of efficiency gains by the industries and a tighter regulatory regime has led to significant price reductions. Increases in the x factors in telecoms and gas produced lower consumer prices in nominal terms in the second five-year phase of price regulation. Competition in electricity generation led rapidly to falling prices, and substantial reductions in distribution charges are now in progress. Although water costs will continue to increase in real terms in the second five-year period the rise will be much less than in the first quinquennium.

Although these things might have been expected to win more support for the framework of privatization and regulation, criticism has grown rather than diminished. Coincident developments have not helped. The share options which were awarded at flotation have produced unacceptably large gains for senior executives of privatized utilities. Although the salaries of these executives are not high by the—admittedly generous—standards of private industry generally, many people still remember that the same jobs were done only a short time ago, often by the same people, for relatively modest remuneration.

The fundamental problem which privatized utilities face is that which political scientists recognize as the issue of legitimacy: 'What gives them the right to do that?' Legitimacy can stem from many sources: traditional authority, direct election, proper and accepted delegation from those whose authority is itself legitimate. Unsatisfactory though the performance of nationalized industries was in many respects, their legitimacy was not in doubt. But this is not true of their successors. Legitimacy is rarely a problem for institutions which are seen to be doing a good job. But, as Fukuyama (1992: 18) puts it, 'Legitimate regimes have a fund of goodwill that excuses them from short-term mistakes, even serious ones.' The weakness of privatized industries is that they enjoy no such goodwill.

The drought of summer 1995 illustrated precisely that. No reasonable person could blame either privatization or the managers of water companies for the absence of rain. Yet the result of water shortages was to unleash a further wave of hostility against the privatized industry. That hostility was not confined to newspapers, or politicians, but widely felt and expressed. In earlier droughts, such as that of 1976, there was a general perception of common cause between water suppliers and their customers. Under the current structure, that perception no longer exists although the actual behaviour of the suppliers is virtually unchanged.

An instructive demonstration of these issues of legitimacy was provided at the recent annual general meeting of British Gas. An ill-timed announcement of a substantial pay rise for the company's chief executive provoked controversy. The AGM provoked a barrage of hostile criticism of the company and its management. In the end, the chairman used institutional proxies, overwhelmingly supportive of the management, to defeat all critical resolutions by large majorities.

In a real sense, the institution of the AGM—a meeting of the company's shareholders—was being abused. The representatives of the shareholders included, for example, Ken Livingstone, a left-wing Labour MP purportedly representing an American institutional shareholder. Livingstone was not, in fact, there to express concern for the interests of shareholders, and nor were most of those present at the AGM. He was there to make a political speech on what he considered a matter of public interest.

But it is difficult to argue that Livingstone's interest was not a proper one. It is not a good answer to the criticism levied at the company, and at its relative treatment of its own managers, employees, and customers, to say that these things are a private matter between the company and its shareholders. They are not. It is a better answer to say that the regulator is the vehicle through which the public interest in these questions is expressed. But the regulator, correctly, argued that few of the matters in dispute lay within her jurisdiction.

And the vote which vindicated British Gas management turns out, under scrutiny, to be an unsatisfactory affair. The billions of votes which supported the board were in fact cast by a small group—well under 100—of city investment managers, who had been assiduously cultivated by the British Gas chairman in the weeks preceding the AGM. These individuals were not themselves beneficial owners of claims against British Gas, and in so far as they had proper authority to act on behalf of those who were, it is not at all clear that such authority extended to matters such as these. It is very likely that the views of the beneficial owners, pensioners and holders of life policies, were closer to those which were expressed at the meeting than to the votes that were cast on their behalf. But even if it were practical to canvass the opinions of those who directly or indirectly owned the shares, no one can seriously believe that seeking these opinions would be a good way to run the company. The whole procedure might be from *Alice in Wonderland*: nothing is what it seems, no one is what they say they are.

In the early years of privatization, it could be argued that the unpopularity of privatized industries was a transitional issue, and that once the structure was properly understood it would be more widely accepted. The moral of the British Gas fiasco is that it is wrong to think that the problem is one of education and explanation. On the contrary, the more closely the structure is studied, the less defensible it becomes.

Profit sharing

If the considerable efficiency advantages which utility privatization has brought about are to be maintained, the link between firm performance and customer benefit must be clearly established. At present, the utility retains all benefits up to the time of the next periodic review, at which time an indeterminate fraction of efficiency gains is passed on to customers. It is essential that the lag be shortened and the connection made explicit.

The most obvious method of achieving this is a mechanism for sharing profits between shareholders and customers. The attraction of a system of profit sharing is that it represents a relatively modest reform which appears to answer some of the central criticisms of the current regime.

On closer examination, however, the scope of the reform is wider than it appears at first sight, and its effectiveness in defusing customer criticism of the current arrangements more doubtful. The measures adopted by several water companies, and the industry-wide agreement on a programme of leakage control, are examples of voluntary profit-sharing arrangements, and both represent constructive responses to recent customer criticism. But the limitations of voluntary arrangements are obvious. Unless very modest in scale— and the profit-sharing proposals put forward so far have been very modest in scale—they create tensions between companies which choose to behave in this way and those which do not, and they put the managers of companies faced with hostile take-overs in an untenable position. Unless very limited in amount, profit sharing is only possible within the framework of broadly agreed industry parameters.

That leads directly to the need to design a profit-sharing formula. There are two main alternatives. One is sharing relative to the starting level. The other is sharing of profits in excess of the amount projected in the regulator's determination of price caps. Such a formula will also need to prescribe the proportions in which profits are to be shared, and also to define whether its operation is symmetric: do customers face increased charges if profits fall or are below the anticipated level? It is probably not realistic to believe that the mechanism could, in practice, operate symmetrically. But the effect of asymmetric operation is to worsen significantly the risk profile of returns faced by the company, and hence to raise its cost of capital and the overall cost of the company's activities.

The simplest method of profit sharing is to propose that a fraction of all profits in excess of today's level be allocated, not to dividends, but to lower customer charges. The great advantage of such a scheme is its simplicity. One consequence is an effective 'tax' on investment by the regulated company. The source of the difficulty is that reported profit is both a return on capital employed and a return to the effectiveness with which the firm operates. This was the paradox evident in the Monopolies and Mergers Commission report on *South West Water*, where the obligation on the company to reinvest heavily in infrastructure improvements necessarily led, under the mechanism for price-setting, not only to steady and substantial increases in charges but also to steady and substantial rises in profits. It would be possible—indeed necessary—to allow for this in the determination of price caps. There is a substantial element of illusion in this—the obligation on the firm to share profits is compensated for by an offsetting adjustment in the level of profits allowed. But the illusion may nevertheless be helpful.

A more logically coherent approach involves sharing of profits in excess of (or conceivably below) the levels provided for in price-setting. This approach would demand that the regulator be more explicit about the basis of his or her calculations than has generally been the case in past reviews, where elements of judgement have conditioned the final determination. Some would see this as an advantage. I believe it would be the opposite. Under the present regime, the regulator is able to make qualitative judgements about the efficiency levels achieved by companies and about the extent to which companies are taking advantage of the information asymmetry. The loss of the opportunity to do so would aggravate gaming behaviour between regulator and regulatee. It would also probably increase the incidence of MMC appeal and legal challenge.

Any profit-sharing proposal demands definition of the base of profits. The base should be the profits of the regulated activity. Until now, this has not been entirely clear, and a number of regulatory reviews have taken into account the overall profitability of the enterprise, and not just its profits from regulated functions. The effect of this, however, is to impose an ill-defined tax on the firm's non-core functions. Not only is this undesirable, but the converse implication—that regulated customers should share the losses from unsuccessful diversification—is unacceptable. The game has been further changed, fundamentally, by the acquisition of regulated utilities by conglomerates with a wide spread of operations. There has to be a watertight boundary between Hanson's tobacco business and the activities of Eastern Electricity and this must carry over into distinctions between Eastern's first-tier supply business and its other operations. Any extension of profit sharing therefore requires ring-fencing arrangements between regulated and non-regulated activities, of a kind which currently exist in water but more loosely, if at all, in other industries. Such ring-fencing inevitably involves regulatory scrutiny of all transactions which cross the ring-fence. These include, in particular, financing transactions and it will become necessary to review, and possible to prescribe, the financial structure of the regulated business with the overall PLC. Further measures of these kinds are probably now inevitable, whether or not explicit profit sharing is introduced, and would best be undertaken on a common basis across regulated industries.

The most substantial group of issues to be tackled in implementing profit sharing is that concerned with the measurement of profits. These problems concern both the base level (however defined) and the figures actually reported. The question is whether current accounting practice and standards are sufficiently robust to allow the difference between base profits and actual profits to bear the importance which it would come to enjoy under an explicit rule-based profit-sharing scheme.

This apparently rather technical question is in fact fundamental. Under almost any profit-sharing formula, the impact of changes even in the timing of reported profitability is likely to have a significant impact on the division of gains between customers and shareholders. Issues such as the treatment of redundancy costs, pension holidays, and expenditure of a quasi-capital nature, such as computer system enhancement, have already been the subject of extended discussion in regulatory reviews. These questions, which are at present no more than relevant background, would instead become central to the functioning of the regulatory mechanism. Worse, firms and their accountants would have every incentive to proliferate issues of this kind. It is difficult to see how a conscientious regulator could, in the final analysis, avoid employing his own auditors; not only for the historic accounts but also for the preparation of projections for the setting of price caps.

The attractions of a general profit-sharing mechanism diminish on closer examination. Such a scheme is likely to aggravate the problem of gaming between regulator and regulatee, and to lead to a significant increase in the instrusiveness of regulation. It is also likely to provide friction and disputes which may take us further from, rather than closer to, the fundamental objective of strengthening customer support for, and involvement in, the present system.

The basic problem is familiar from general experience of non-market-based control formulae, such as the Common Agricultural Policy, British local government finance, or more widely in East European central planning. A common, and natural, response to criticisms of the simple formula, and the distortions of behaviour created by it, is to modify the formula to meet these specific concerns. Unfortunately, the modifications simply generate new concerns, and increase incentives to sophisticated management of the formula, relative to simple management of the business. The results are ones which continue to fail to meet the underlying objectives while, at the same time, involving ever more frequent intrusion in day-to-day behaviour. This was the history of British nationalization.

The issue is therefore whether the basic objectives—of preserving and enhancing management autonomy while clarifying and increasing commitment to customers—can be achieved by a different path of reform.

The customer corporation

An alternative mechanism of profit sharing is one which creates a link between dividends paid to shareholders and charges to customers. The merit of this proposal is that it creates an automatic alignment of the interests of customers, investors, and the regulator. The adversarial system described above, in which the regulator's concern for customers is pitched against the company's concern for shareholders, neither generates the quality of information needed for regulation nor provides adequate incentives to efficiency or protection to customers.

But a share whose dividend entitlement depends on charges to customers, rather than on the earnings of the company, is fundamentally different in character from a conventional equity. At this point, the economic question of the shape of the regulatory formula and the political issue of the legitimacy of privatized corporations come directly together.

The conventional view is that a company exists to maximize profits for its shareholders. Of course, a company which considered exclusively the interests of its shareholders would not survive for long. For a firm which operates in a competitive market, the only way in which it can serve the interests of its shareholders is by identifying and meeting the interests of its customers.

But a monopoly utility is different. A firm with a legal or practical monopoly of electricity distribution can do well for its shareholders whether it satisfies its customers or not, and that is why the profits earned by utilities are inevitably a matter of controversy. I therefore suggest that the ordering be reversed. The customer corporation is one whose primary objective is to produce services of the quality demanded by its customers at the lowest possible prices. But since it will operate in a competitive capital market, it will be obliged to consider the interests of investors in doing so.

It is important to understand that putting customers first is the natural instinct of the vast majority of managers of privatized utilities. Few of them leap out of bed looking forward to the prospect of another day enhancing shareholder value; but the motivation to do a good job for customers is generally extremely strong. Many such managers will volunteer that the opportunity to give priority to customer interests, with greater freedom from union influence and political restriction, has been the principal benefit of privatization.

It is an extraordinary feature of current arrangements that, far from encouraging this emphasis on the consumer, the structure invites managers of utilities to fight against it. It encourages, even requires, that they pursue shareholder value, with the regulator as customer advocate, in the essentially adversarial relationship between companies and regulator described above. It presupposes a priority of shareholder interests which would not necessarily be defended even by the shareholders of these companies themselves. If we truly believed that a water company put the interests of its shareholders ahead of its customers, we would prefer not to have to drink their water.

The companies often do not behave as the model would have them behave, but why do we encourage this futile tension in the first place? The customer corporation leaves managers free to do what they mostly want to do and what we want them to do. It removes an apparent divergence of interest between companies and the public which is quite unnecessary and which has created much of the discontent with the performance of privatization and regulation.

In advocating customer corporations, I emphatically do not propose either that management should be elected by customers or that customers should 'own' the business. It is essential that these firms are run by teams with common interests, values, and identity. Although Yorkshire Water's response was heavy-handed and inept, the election to the board of Diana Scott (the vocal chair of the company's Customer Service Committee who subsequently sought election to the board) would not have served the best long-term interests of that company's customers. If the board of a company is not united in purpose and objective, it rarely functions effectively, and the practical consequence is that substantive decisions are made outside it.

The customer interest is likely to be better served by professional managers committed to that interest, and accountable for it, than by representatives of consumers (who are, in the main, rendered unrepresentative by their very willingness to undertake the task). We should learn from the competitive failure of the co-operative movement. Much of the problem was that customers were not, in fact, interested in exercising control, which reverted to employees and politicians. The present method of board selection and election of public companies generally is considerably less than ideal, but it functions tolerably well in practice, and there is no urgent need to change it. The board of a customer corporation should, however, be encouraged to be widely representative of the community in which it operates. (Its non-executive directors should not be exclusively businessmen, or exclusively members of any political party, or exclusively anything for that matter.) Such a requirement should be part of the customer corporation statute.

The following activities are some of those which would be appropriate for customer corporations:

- water and sewerage services;
- electricity distribution in England and Wales;
- the National Grid;
- electricity distribution and transmission in Scotland and Northern Ireland;
- British Gas Transco;
- airport non-trading functions;
- Railtrack;
- the Post Office;
- BT Network Services;
- the BBC.

There is no reason why a customer corporation could not be 'owned' by a PLC, in the specific sense that all voting securities of the customer corporation would be owned by the PLC. And given the current starting point we visualize that most customer corporations would, in fact, be owned by a PLC. Thus, Eastern Electricity Customer Corporation might be wholly 'owned' by Hanson PLC or by Eastern Group PLC. 'Ownership' would, however, only relate to the securities of the customer corporation concerned. The PLC would not 'own' the assets or revenue streams of the customer corporation and would not be able to use these assets or revenue streams as security for its own borrowings, although it would, of course, be able to use its shares in the customer corporation and its dividends from them for these purposes. The customer corporation would not be permitted to undertake any activities other than those prescribed in its licence, although a PLC which owned it would enjoy the normal freedoms. This would imply ring-fencing the monopoly utility activities of the customer corporation, and any transactions between the customer corporation and its PLC parent would be the subject of specific regulatory approval. Arrangements of this kind already exist in the water industry, but would need to be introduced into other utilities.

The financial structure of a customer corporation

I expect to be told that no one would invest in a customer corporation, and certainly at first sight it would seem that a move to order interests of customers ahead of shareholders would make it more difficult to raise money from shareholders. This view is superficial. Customer corporations would certainly attract investment, and because of their low-risk character it is likely that they would do so more cheaply than do privatized utilities under the current system of regulation.

The recent regulatory reviews have put the cost of capital to the regulated water and electricity industries at around 6 per cent to 7 per cent in real terms. The activities concerned are inherently of very low risk—the monopoly supply of electricity and water under a regime which requires the regulator to secure a reasonable rate of return on the assets involved. This return is above what might be expected for such a low-risk activity, since the government's risk-free debt offers a rate of return around 3 per cent to 4 per cent in real terms. The difference is accounted for by the greater insecurity of investment in utility PLCs.

Uncertainty about the earnings streams of activities such as water and electricity distribution arises from two main sources. One is the possibility of divergence between the regulator's efficiency target and the actual outcome. The other is uncertainty about the evolution of the regulatory regime itself. If these sources of uncertainty were removed or reduced—as would be true for a customer corporation—than the cost of capital would be reduced correspondingly.

What does this mean in practice for the capital structure of a customer corporation? A customer corporation could be expected to carry considerably more debt in its balance sheet than do the existing utility PLCs. Indeed, this is already true of the utility PLCs themselves and restructuring to increase gearing is in progress. The debt of these companies might be provided by the parent PLC (subject to the regulatory oversight described above) or raised directly by the customer corporation.

The equity of customer corporations might take two forms: indexed preferred stock, and ordinary shares. Indexed preferred stock (IPS) would carry a dividend coupon linked to the RPI, but the dividend could be passed in circumstances which would lead the company into loss. It would, in any event, have priority over the payment of any ordinary dividend and the holders would acquire voting rights over the company if dividends were not paid on the due date.

The existing security most similar to the indexed preferred stock of a customer corporation is the permanent interest-bearing shares (PIBS) which are used as subordinated capital by building societies. PIBS offer fixed rather than indexed dividends, and there is no reason why customer corporations could not issue PIBS, but the indexed revenue stream implied by the current regulatory control makes IPS particularly appropriate. PIBS command a premium of 1 per cent to 2 per cent over equivalent government stock. The security offered by the IPS of a customer corporation would generally be substantially greater than that attached to PIBS, and it seems realistic to believe that IPS could be issued on yields of between 5 per cent and 6 per cent. Anglian Water's indexed loan stock, with greater security, currently yields 4.55 per cent.

That leaves the ordinary securities of the customer corporation. As described above, these might be directly held by individuals and institutions, or wholly owned by a PLC whose shares were in turn owned by individuals and institutions. In either case, the ordinary shareholders would enjoy the usual voting rights attached to such shares and would be entitled to a stream of dividends. There are at least three possible ways in which such dividends might be determined.

One possibility is that the ordinary shares might themselves have indexed dividends. In this case they would be further subordinated to IPS. The attraction of this is that it is simple and minimizes the need for regulatory oversight. The weakness is that ordinary shareholders have little incentive to take an interest in the company's efficiency. Their concern need not extend beyond ensuring that the company is not in danger of being unable to meet the dividend payments on its equity.

An alternative is that the directors of the customer corporation might set dividends by reference to what they consider reasonable, in all the circumstances and in the light of their statutory duties. If this sounds, and is, vague, it is nevertheless exactly the mechanism by which the dividend policies of PLCs are determined today. As the dividend policies of the PLC are, in a loose sense, subject to shareholder supervision and, in a formal sense, subject to shareholder approval, so it would seem appropriate for the dividend policies of the customer corporation to be the subject of regulatory oversight. The interests of customers would be protected by the statutory obligations of the company and the ultimate ability of the regulator or of the customers themselves to seek legal enforcement of them. The interests of shareholders would be protected by the company's need to secure continued access to the capital markets.

Would shareholders be willing to hold securities whose rights are thus ill defined? The evidence of other markets suggests that so long as conventions and competition secure adequate returns, there is little practical problem. In practice, a broad framework for dividend policy could be agreed; for example, real dividend growth might normally be in line with output volume, subject to variation upward or downward for exceptional performance, with that performance judged in relation to customer price and service quality.

Another version would make that relationship explicit. For example, changes in dividend levels might be linked to changes in customer charges, so that dividends would rise when charges fell, and vice versa. Differences between companies in the proposed charge increases and reductions would be translated into differences in the operating value of equity. It would be necessary to prescribe a formula for measuring charges, and to define how it would be adjusted for variations in service quality. The weakness of this system is that the reliance on a formula reintroduces, although in a much attenuated form, some of the gaming between regulator and company which I have criticized above. It is, however, best in allowing companies which believe they can do better for customers to bid for control of the customer corporation, but automatically restricts the class of potential bidders to those who believe they can achieve this (and allows them to profit from the acquisition only to the extent they do).

There are advantages and disadvantages to each of these mechanisms, and no doubt other mechanisms, and other advantages and disadvantages, would emerge over time. Once the general principle is accepted, there is no reason why each company should not find its own distinctive solution.

Regulating the customer corporation

The essence of these proposals is that many of the duties of the regulator are taken over by the board of the customer corporation itself. The intention is to replace a regime based on a battle between managers representing shareholders and a regulator representing customers with one in which a customer-oriented management makes the trade-offs for itself. Ideally, this might remove the need for regulation altogether. That would be to go too far. But there are overwhelming advantages from a shift from a relationship between regulator and regulatee which is fundamentally adversarial by one in which both parties are pursuing broadly similar objectives. The result would be a much more light-handed system of regulation than we currently have.

One of the regulator's principal duties would be to assemble and publish information on the comparative performance of firms. There is no good reason why any information about the activities or performance of a customer corporation should be commercially confidential, so that publication would be a key element in promoting performance. In effect, the regulator's job would be to point the finger at firms with poor relative performance—a more informal, but probably more effective, mechanism of comparative competition.

A key function for the regulator would be to police the ring-fence between the customer corporation and the owners of its securities. The objective would be that such transactions would be subject to the same rigorous evaluation that is applied to transactions involving trustees. The regulator would also provide, as to a degree is the case today, an important buffer between political influence and operational management of utilities; not eliminating that influence, but preventing it constraining day-to-day management.

Conclusions

On balance, the credit ledger of privatization far exceeds the debits. The task for the next decade is to find a structure which preserves these gains while meeting the criticisms which are fairly levelled at the existing arrangements.

I have argued that the key to this is to move to a structure which entrenches clear priority for consumer interests in monopoly utilities while maintaining and in general enhancing the freedom of operational management which has been the most valuable product of the last decade of privatization and regulation. The customer corporation is a vehicle for achieving that.

It recognizes fully the consumer interest, while minimizing the need for politicians and regulator to second guess what are best taken as managerial decisions. It is less novel than it sounds. It is, in reality, a modernization of the statutory water company framework, which was by no means unsuccessful in Britain for over a century; the companies were, on average, more efficient than their public sector counterparts but suffered none of the problems of legitimacy which have dogged their privatized successors. There are other historical and institutional parallels. Indeed, one of the attractions of the customer corporation framework is its relevance to schools, hospitals, and other state activities for which full privatization is inconceivable but a dilution of unproductive structures of political and bureaucratic control essential.

15

......

Inclusive Economies

The final chapter in this section extends the logic of the earlier chapters a stage further. If private ownership is not characteristic of the most important of modern economic institutions—the large corporation—then is private ownership truly central to capitalism? In this chapter, I question the conventional linkage between liberal individualism and market economics.

The triumph of the New Right

In an extraordinary reversal of a hundred earlier years of history, the last two decades have seen the revival of faith in market forces.[1] Deregulation and privatization have become a universal agenda: the need to contract the economic role of government is almost a cliché: the centrally planned economies of Eastern Europe collapsed under the weight of their own incompetence.

This victory of systems has been paralleled in the battle of ideas. The intellectual apologists for markets—no longer apologetic—are mostly American, although the doctrines they preach are partly attributed to the Austrian Hayek and, implausibly, to Adam Smith, the eighteenth-century Scot who founded modern economics. They include political philosophers such as Robert Nozick and Ayn Rand: aggressive free-market economists such as Gary Becker and George Stigler, both based at the University of Chicago: and another school of economists, led by James Buchanan of the University of Virginia, who have developed a sceptical view of government and government action labelled the theory of public choice.

These doctrines were popularized in Britain by the Institute of Economic Affairs. They found a ready hearing in the 1980s under radical right-wing governments in both Britain and the United States. Ignoring considerable differences of expression and emphasis, I will label this collection of individualist

[1] *Prospect* (May 1996).

philosophers, neo-classical economists, and conservative politicians 'The New Right'. Their missionaries range widely through the former Communist countries and the less developed world.

The premisses of the New Right are austere. The most important of social institutions is private property. Self-interest is the central human emotion, insecurity the engine of progress. Government is inherently coercive and corrupt. Fairness and justice mean respect for other people's property. Trust is established by good attorneys and watertight contracts. If there is a role for nobler sentiments, like altruism, goodness, sincerity, and confidence, it is in our family lives, not in commerce: the social responsibility of business is to maximize its profits.

Perhaps this harsh view of human nature is no more than a realistic one. There is ample unhappy experience to justify the New Right position. The dictators of Eastern Europe who seized economic power on behalf of the people mostly used it to maintain their own power and privileges. African politicians who took control of their economies frequently stole what they controlled. As we look at the many ecological disasters in the former Soviet Union, we understand that the environment is best protected when somebody owns it.

The New Right position is, however, self-reinforcing. People who are told there is no need to apologize for selfish behaviour tend to behave selfishly. Perhaps Ivan Boesky went too far in proclaiming that greed was good—or so the courts though when they sent him to prison—but he captured the spirit of an age. Senior executives justify their large salaries and generous stock options by reference to fairness and market forces: which mean no more than that everyone else is doing it. Thirty years ago, such behaviour was constrained by unwritten codes of behaviour, and corporate managers were no more expected to use their positions to help themselves to the money which passed through their hands than were judges or policemen. Thirty years ago, high levels of unemployment, or homeless people sleeping in the streets, were assumed to be politically unacceptable. Today these things are not only politically acceptable but politically accepted.

Even if these New Right doctrines are persuasive, they remain unattractive to most intelligent and sensitive people. Perhaps economic efficiency, market forces, selfishness, insecurity, and progress go hand in hand. Perhaps uncertainty, homelessness, and growing inequality are the price we have to pay for high and rising output. We have to accept that the best way to protect our savings and get our cars and pot noodles is to satisfy the demands of greedy executives and financiers. We may wish it were otherwise; but experience has shown that appeals to nobler feelings are not enough to fill the shelves of the supermarket or load the video recorder. We must just be thankful that there is more to life than economics.

But these claims of the New Right are false. The association of market economics and philosophical individualism which is at the heart of the New Right argument is unnecessary. Libertarian philosophy needs to be defended in its own terms, and does not acquire legitimacy from the success of capitalism. It is possible to believe that competitive markets are an effective and efficient system of organization and yet to reject the value system of the New Right, which applauds selfishness and glorifies private property.

The social context of markets

Markets are essentially social institutions and operate within a social context. Yet we operate with models of markets which appear to deny that: even though by this denial we are quite unable to explain facts about the world of obvious and central significance. Switzerland and Japan, respectively the richest and the fastest growing of major economies, are not by any stretch of the imagination individualistic societies. Indeed, among the world's most successful economies, individualism seems to be the exception rather than the rule.

And there is the awkward fact that the most important of modern economic institutions is the large corporation. We go through contortions to avoid confronting this. Economists describe companies by a principal agent–model, in which shareholders, too numerous and too busy to manage the company themselves, hire salaried managers to mind the store. Business journalists treat huge large firms as extensions of the personalities of individuals: General Electric *is* Jack Welch, Microsoft *is* Bill Gates. Neither of these descriptions bears the faintest resemblance to the reality of corporate bureaucracies. Our schema has no room for the irrefutable fact that large companies are social institutions with character and personality of their own, and that it is on the nature of that character and personality that their performance depends.

The individualistic context is not the only social context within which markets can function and it is not at all apparent that it is one in which markets function well. Individualism, as an economic system, centres around the establishment and exercise of private property rights. The costs of this form of organization are high. Since the definition of property rights is of overriding importance, much time and effort is devoted to it. This means litigation, with the direct costs it imposes, and the indirect costs of attempting to write agreements that will protect against litigation. If rich individuals dispute property rights in the courts, poor people dispute them in the street. So individualism is associated with high levels of criminal behaviour, and this too has indirect costs as those who have property defend themselves against those who have not. Since trading in property rights is encouraged, individualistic societies have over-extended financial services sectors in which considerable talent is devoted to activities of no real value.

And individualistic societies do not, in the main, manage well activities which either need to be undertaken collectively or which usually are undertaken collectively. Commodities like environmental services and education are inefficiently provided and inadequately supplied. Politics degenerates into a clash between conflicting economic interest groups. And individualistic societies are less successful in those commercial activities in which success depends on trust and co-operation between individuals and firms.

The individualistic model of markets implies too much litigation, high levels of crime, too much expenditure on financial services, an ineffectual and inadequate public sector, a political system structured around the representation of economic interest groups, and an absence of trust in commercial relationships. It is not an accident that this is a list of the principal social and economic problems confronting the United States.

It is also a list of areas in which non-individualistic market economies, like Japan, Norway, Singapore, or Switzerland, perform markedly better. All have low crime rates. The absence of lawyers in the conduct of Japanese business is as marked as their obtrusive presence in America. Singapore and Switzerland have important financial services sectors, to be sure, but mainly because foreigners find their institutions more reliable than those of their home country. Public education operates to high standards, the streets are clean, and, save in parts of Japan, the atmosphere unpolluted. And trust and co-operation in business yield hard-nosed commercial advantages. Above all, Japan, Norway, Singapore, and Switzerland are rich.

There are two important qualifications to what can easily sound like an anti-American tirade. Once is that there are advantages as well as disadvantages to an individualistic model of capitalism. The US economy has its own extraordinary strengths. Its record of both technical and organizational innovation is far ahead of any other country, and that capacity for innovation is closely associated with its individualistic culture. American business is wonderfully open to new ideas and there is little social or behavioural resistance to change. Individuals and organizations are free to experiment, and there is no disgrace and little penalty in failure.

The second is that although the USA is certainly the most individualistic of successful economies, it is still not very individualistic. Trust, co-operation, mutual respect, and collective action are all important to US commerce. The most individualist of modern economies is probably Nigeria, and it does not work. The key point is that the United States is at one end of the spectrum of effective market economies. The mistake is to univeralize a stylized version of the US economic system into a general model of how markets do and should operate everywhere.

The inclusive economy

We need a label to attach to non-individualistic market economies like those of Japan, Norway, Singapore, and Switzerland. There are several around—social markets, stakeholding or communitarian societies, Rhenan or alpine economies. These have different nuances, different emphases. I shall describe them as *inclusive economies*.

This term captures best the essential differences between the New Right philosophy and its alternatives. The New Right stresses autonomy—the right of the individual to pursue freely his or her own interests and objectives. The alternative is to emphasize inclusion—the right, and also the requirement, to be part of a community. The injustice that most concerns the New Right is coercion—a term which is used to cover taxation and economic regulation as well as more direct restrictions on personal freedom. But another injustice is that of exclusion—the inability of some to participate in an economy and a society which they would dearly like to join. In practice, autonomy is often a synonym for poverty.

In inclusive economies, there is no incompatibility between the functioning of markets and the existence of shared values, collective activity and institutions, and broadly accepted concepts of fairness. The commercial behaviour of individuals and firms is judged by reference to outcomes, not just by legitimacy of process. The exercise of property and other economic rights is not absolute, but conditioned by prevailing social values. It is not just that there is no incompatibility between markets and fairness, shared values and collective activities. These things are of central importance in making markets work.

That makes it sound as though inclusive economies rely heavily on appeals to our better nature. They do not. We have learnt, through hard experience, that altruism as a basis for business behaviour does not work. Inclusive economies impose sanctions on those who engage in inappropriate or unacceptable behaviour. These sanctions are social and commercial, not legal. They are not coercive, in the sense in which libertarians understand coercion. No one puts you in prison if you fail to observe the conventions of Swiss or Japanese business behaviour. You simply are not very successful. The coercion is more subtle, but entirely real. Some people find it oppressive.

But inclusion encourages the developmental of trust, and confidence. Inclusive societies foster co-operative behaviour, which stimulates the acquisition of skills, the exchange of information, and flexibility in response within firms and between firms and their suppliers. Above all, inclusive societies provide security. They offer social security, in the narrow sense of the phrase. More importantly, they offer the security that comes from the stability of business relationships—in employment, as customer or supplier, in finance. It is in this rather indirect, but profound, sense that inclusive economies encourage long-term behaviour and individualistic societies do not.

The result is not just that inclusive economies are kinder and gentler and altogether nicer places to live—although mostly they are. Trust, confidence, co-operation, and security have tangible commercial benefits. These features of inclusive economies are the source of their international competitive advantage. They are the basis of high levels of product quality based on a combination of assembly line discipline and exceptional component reliability. They enable firms to undertake just-in-time inventory management. They enable information to be shared in trust-dependent areas of financial services. They allow fast and co-operative reactions to changing fashions or changing markets. It is the resulting close relationships along the chain of production which have enabled firms to shorten model cycles. These factors are the source of Japanese hegemony in automobiles and audio equipment and Swiss leadership in production engineering.

The costs of individualism

But security has direct as well as instrumental value. This is the most important political issue of the moment. In objective respects, the performance of the British economy today is remarkable—low inflation, falling unemployment, stable growth. The widely noted absence of a 'feel-good factor' is a description of the sharply increased economic insecurity faced by individuals in Britain today: mainly the result of waves of 'down-sizing' and restructuring by corporations and public agencies, partly the product of fluctuations in asset prices, especially in the housing market.

The conventional view is that such insecurity is an inevitable product of technological change and international competition. And indeed it is true, particularly in the public sector and privatized industries, that many job losses have been the result of the elimination of long-term over-manning. But the widely expressed view that large companies 'cannot afford' to provide job security any more fails to stand up to scrutiny. The period since the early 1980s has seen a steady increase in stock prices, dividends, and in the share of profits in national income. It is not that companies cannot afford to provide job security. It is that in the face of changes in social attitudes, and pressures from the capital market, they have increasingly chosen not to.

At the same time, the social legitimization of individualistic behaviour has meant that the returns earned by successful organizations are concentrated on fewer people. 'Lean and mean' is the slogan. Its specific implication is that when companies create wealth, they are increasingly encouraged to distribute it to those who deem themselves to be responsible for that success. So the spread of rewards is widened: and in the economy as a whole we see well-paid people working harder than they wish and others, not necessarily less able, unable to find jobs at the going wage or salary.

The effect of these changes has been to widen pre-tax and benefit income differentials and to transfer much of the cost of structural change in the economy from the shareholders of corporations to individuals. Much of that cost then falls, via the benefit system, to the state. Housing benefit, unemployment, and social security expenditure directly or indirectly attributable to job losses have been the most significant elements of growth in public spending in the last decade. The rise in public expenditure is a direct and immediate consequence of the costs of individualism.

This seems paradoxical. The reason we find it so is that our thinking has been conditioned by a debate in which it is assumed that economic power can be exercised only by individuals or by the state. These are the terms of a traditional right–left, capitalist–socialist, liberalist–planner dichotomy. Both sides of the political spectrum have traditionally accepted this characterization, disagreeing only on where the lines should be drawn: socialists finding the concentration of economic power in the hands of individuals offensive, the New Right believing that its exercise by the state is coercive.

Yet once we understand that most economic activity is conducted through intermediate institutions which are controlled neither by government nor individuals, and that social values are a more important constraint on commercial behaviour than rules and regulations, this polarization becomes inappropriate and the terms of the argument sterile. When we attack the social role of intermediate institutions in the name of individualism, as we have done, we may find that we increase rather than reduce the economic role of the state.

This is true of state regulation as of public expenditure. Are Switzerland and Japan more or less regulated economies than the United States? The answer to that question is not straightforward. Neither country has anything which resembles the rule book of the Securities and Exchange Commission. Both would find quite ludicrous the hundreds of pages of codes and protocols which have been produced as the basis for the deregulation (*sic*) of the American telecommunications industry. Yet this absence of formal regulation is accompanied by, and made possible by, extensive self-regulation—regulation by values rather than by rules.

For this reason, there may be, and frequently is, less state regulation of economic activity in inclusive societies than in individualistic ones. The British financial services sector is an obvious example of the substitution of an elaborate system of formal regulation for an older tradition of self-regulation based on tacit rules and shared values. It is by virtue of such substitutions that the present government has established more new agencies of economic regulation than any before it.

Thus, the pursuit of individualism, far from rolling back the frontiers of the state, may create a need for greater state expenditure and more extensive government regulation. In both Britain and the United States today, the right observes with anger and bewilderment that the role of government and its share of national income are no less than they were when the Thatcher and Reagan experiments began. They are angry because they do not realize what they have done. It does not follow that a greater emphasis on the rights of individuals diminishes the functions of government, and what has in fact happened is the opposite.

Governance in inclusive economies

The individualistic era in Britain, in particular, was a reaction to a period of corporatist excess: but the alternative to individualism need not be corporatism. There is a world of difference between a market in which economic behaviour is influenced by widely shared values, and a centralized economy which is directed by those who purport to determine what these values are. That is why even though corporatists may use the language of inclusion, their objectives are opposite. It is important that the values of an inclusive economy are emergent rather than directed.

If there are clear levers of economic power, ideologues and interest groups will devote resources to capturing them. Often they will succeed, and the market degenerates into the regulatory state of the New Right or the centrally planned economies of the old left.

All market economies are vulnerable to this. We need only look across the channel to Germany and France to see the negative influence of organized economic interest groups—the farming lobby, the managers of large public and private bureaucracies, the *cheminots* of SNCF—who advance their own aims using the rhetoric of social solidarity. But at least they use that rhetoric. In the individualistic United States there is no need even to pretend. Washington is the lobbying capital of the world, most of that lobbying is entirely shameless, and the success of a congressman is measured by how many goodies he brings home to his district—or simply by how much he can raise to finance his re-election.

The most effective of inclusive economies operate within a fuzzy governance structure. Switzerland and Japan achieve this same outcome, but in entirely different ways. The chaotic, multi-level Swiss democracy precludes the exercise of much economic power by any single authority. In Japan, most centralizing institutions lost this authority as a result of the Second World War and Allied occupation, thus allowing the strongly consensual nature of Japanese society to flourish at the level of the corporation and its keiretsu. The lack of clarity about how these societies are run proves to be an economic virtue, not a vice, requiring adherence to a widely accepted set of social values while preventing any group from taking control of their nature or evolution.

What these examples emphasize is the strongly path-dependent nature of the evolution of market economies. The social contexts within which the successful market economies of the world operate are very varied—as between the United States and Japan, Norway and Korea, Singapore and Switzerland. The distinctive competitive success of each of these economies—the United States in international branding and technical innovation, the Japanese in reliable production line manufacturing, the Swiss in financial services and sophisticated engineering—are each associated with the specific context with which their markets operate. That variety is to the substantial economic advantage of the world as a whole.

Even if it were possible to identify one of these models as the most effective, the dependence of each model on its own history and culture means that the attempt to transplant it to other environments would be self-defeating. We see these problems of transplantation in the uneasy process of economic reform in Eastern Europe.

The road to reform

The objective is not simply to be more like Singapore, or more like Switzerland, or more like Japan. Rather we should observe that there are many different social environments within which market economies operate and that aggressive individualism is not the only one, nor the best. While there are strong elements of individualism in British society, these are also very different strands of thought: a long recognition that property confers obligations as well as rights, a substantial tradition of public duty and public service, and an approach to political and economic crisis more often characterized by solidarity than recrimination. A free-market economy does not require us to disparage these things, still less to discard them.

Governments cannot legislate for the social context of markets. But political debate can influence attitudes, and if the terms of that debate have contributed to the rise of selfish individualism in the last two decades the same mechanisms can be used in the opposite direction. One might begin, therefore, by asserting that unashamed self-interest is a vice, not a virtue, that the usefulness of an activity is not necessarily measured by its profitability: that what someone earns is not an indicator of the value of their talents, still less of their moral stature: and that no widely accepted body of economic doctrine (the works of Adam Smith included) has ever asserted otherwise.

Profit is central to a market economy, but not its object. If we admire Bill Gates as the most successful businessman of the 1980s, it is because he changed the world, not because he made several billion pounds: just as we admire the Olympic athlete for the achievement that won the gold medal, not for her possession of it. Only if we dispose of the notion that the functioning of markets depends on base and contemptible aspects of human behaviour will we create a market economy that commands wide and continuing support.

If changing attitudes and expectations is long and difficult, there is much that government can do to promote the growth and legitimize the status of intermediate institutions—organizations which are not controlled by single individuals or small groups, but which are not directed by government.

Such intermediate institutions are of many kinds. Perhaps the most important are local governments and public companies. Then there are autonomous bodies engaged in welfare provision, like occupational pension schemes. Others are involved in the delivery of goods and services: housing associations, passenger transport executives, universities, training and enterprise councils. The fissuring of the traditional state has added to the number of such intermediate institutions, privatized utilities, NHS trusts and opted-out schools, public sector management functions spun off as 'next steps' agencies.

We have done this without much systematic thought to the governance structures or the financial organization of the new vehicles which have emerged. Nor, for that matter, do we have a coherent view of the governance of the old. Our approach to them is schizophrenic. We are not sure what local government is for: we try to pretend that public companies are private companies, even to the extent of using the two terms synonymously: we disparage other intermediate institutions as quangos. We applaud their lack of autonomy and complain about their lack of accountability, often failing to recognize that these may be opposite sides of the same coin.

What is needed is to define a clear but limited range of organizational forms. The central current problem is that we have only one robust organizational form other than direct state ownership and control, which is the PLC. That has led to its adoption in contexts where the objective of greater autonomy from central government is desirable, but the PLC form itself inappropriate, such as water supply businesses or Railtrack. It has created constitutional paralysis in activities for which the public at large finds private ownership unacceptable, such as the Post Office and the BBC.

Even historically successful commercial organizations which are not PLCs are finding themselves forced into that mould by the absence of adequate legal support for any other—as with mutual building societies and insurance companies, Lloyd's of London, and accountancy partnerships. These structural issues are not very difficult to solve when we recognize that intermediate institutions are not anomalous, but central to modern economies. What we need is to develop a variety of structures which give them autonomy but achieve accountability and legitimacy.

The most effective means of accountability is the measurement of managerial or organizational performance relative to others engaged in similar activities. And the legitimacy of organizations which are manifestly delivering the goods and services which their customers want is rarely questioned. That is why competitive markets are often, though not always, sufficient answers to issues of accountability and legitimacy. The less it is possible, or desirable, for institutions to operate in competitive markets, the more extensive the need for accountability and legitimacy to be handled in other ways.

The policy agenda

The problems of individualistic societies help us to identify issues for inclusive economies. Richard Freeman's article in February's *Prospect* described a US prison population proportionately five times higher than that of the UK, itself close to the top of the league for developed countries. That is a forceful reminder that it is the inclusion of potentially disaffected communities, not the vigorous enforcement of the right to private property, which is the only long-term solution to crime.

And then there is the litigation disease which, having swept the United States, threatens us too. Commercial behaviour is often best governed by people's need to go on doing business with each other, not by the terms of a formal contract. That is what facilitates speedy response and the sharing of information in inclusive economies. You do not have a right to do something merely because it is not against the law, and those liberal individualists who think that invite, and are getting, an extensive and intrusive legal system. The language of rights—perhaps because it has become the only political language available—has begun to be misused by the political left as well as the New Right. We are in danger of forgetting that if there is a problem of sexual harassment or of how we treat the disabled it is about values and behaviour, not about procedure, process, and entitlement to compensation.

The emphasis on trading in individualistic economies imposes a variety of costs. The problem is that we need to have markets in stocks, bonds, foreign currencies, even derivatives: but what we need is only a small fraction of the volume of trading in them which takes place. In inclusive societies, the main restraint on the growth of these activities is simply that they do not command very much respect. In individualistic societies this sanction has declined, and we are even encouraged to believe that what is profitable is demonstrated to be valuable by that fact alone. But it is quite difficult to justify market economies as a means of creating wealth when the largest rewards so obviously go to those who trade in existing assets.

This fever has spread back to the industrial and commercial companies, whose senior executives are increasingly obsessed with deal-making. Their constant concern is merging and de-merging, buying and selling bits of their corporate portfolios: the preoccupation of German or Japanese managers is with the development of their operating businesses, and they expect that to be the principal source of their companies' growth. We need to put sand in the wheels of these mechanisms—not to bring them to a halt, because there is no example of a successful modern economy without efficient financial institutions, but to slow the pace at which they revolve.

The privatization of public utilities has produced substantial improvements in the efficiency of the firms concerned, by giving managers commercial freedom in the day-to-day management of the business. Yet their continuing unpopularity is evidence of a governance structure that lacks legitimacy. The attempt to establish a 'regulatory contract', under which firms maximize profit subject to an external constraint, is an unavoidable source of dissatisfaction, since under it companies succeed when they earn more profit than the regulator allowed. The right answer is to move away from the PLC framework, and to retain the advantages of managerial autonomy and commercial discipline in a framework focused on customers rather than the capital market. Here, as so often, we suffer from confusion between the establishment of market discipline and the institution of private ownership. London's sewers are no more private property than its streets—but we ought to pay for both of them.

And we should recognize the central role which intermediate institutions can play in the provision of social security. The only major success of UK welfare policy over the past thirty years has been the occupational pension system, which has delivered for a minority, but what is becoming a substantial minority, effective security in old age. The system survived a vigorous attack from the New Right, who tried to return its assets to the control of individuals, rarely to their advantage. We need to learn the lessons from that: we need a public–private partnership to develop similar benefits for those who do not spend long periods with a particular employer, and we should recognize that by far the most efficient provider of unemployment insurance is employers themselves.

I have chosen this small number, but wide range, of examples—crime, litigation, financial services, public utilities, social welfare—to demonstrate that there are many issues on which it is possible to take principled, market-oriented positions which differ radically from the New Right agenda. The merits of market organization are clear. The price mechanism has been shown to be superior to central planning and direction in managing the information and control systems needed for the functioning of a complex modern economy. Competition is a powerful stimulus to efficiency, innovation, and customer service. We can believe these things, and should, without feeling obliged to accept the political agenda of libertarian individualists. The language of inclusion provides the basis for doing so.

USING ECONOMICS

This section is concerned to illustrate the range of ways in which economic analysis can be applied to business problems. I have chosen a selection to cover a wide range.

- Chapter 16 uses economics to answer a variety of market problems and paradoxes.
  - Why does Nigel Mansell earn more than fifty times as much as the Prime Minister?
  - What do a solicitor at Linklaters and Paines and a packet of Persil have in common?
  - Why is an American hotel room cheaper than one in Tokyo but more expensive than one in India?
  - Why do some prices rise faster than others?
  - Why was it right for Marks & Spencer to sell financial services but wrong for BT to buy an equipment manufacturer?
- Chapter 17 uses the resource-based theory of strategy to analyse the market positions of a number of firms.
- Chapter 18 analyses one of the most remarkable product introductions of the decade—the opening of the Channel Tunnel—and asks how the tunnel should set its prices.
- Chapter 19 looks to the uncertain and disputed future of the media industries, and uses the framework developed in Part II to point out some directions—and destroy some conventional wisdoms.
- Chapter 20 uses economics to explore the nature of competitive advantage in a number of industries—the Lloyd's insurance market, insolvency, retain financial services, and international advertising—and asks what does, and does not, lead to changes in levels of industrial concentration.

16

Applying Economics

Economics is about the real world, or it is nothing at all. From time to time, I used a Daily Telegraph *column to explore the economics of an everyday issue—like the cab fare to Heathrow (Chapter 4). This chapter contains several other articles in the same vein. I have also included an essay from the* Spectator, *on one of the strongest examples of what David Henderson has called DIY economics—the fallacies which people who have not studied economics know to be self-evident truths. The fallacy here is the primacy of manufacturing over other forms of economic activity*

JUST REWARDS

Potential applicants for the post of the government's Chief Economic Adviser—on £76,000 per year—might be wondering, as they prepare their curriculum vitae and contact their two referees, how it compares with other top salaries.[1] Table 16.1 gives them some help.

The facts there are difficult to interpret. Probably most people would agree that all are jobs which should be paid more than national average earnings of £13,700 per year. But how much more? If the Prime Minister is paid six times as much as the man in the street, the chairman of British Telecom is paid seven times as much as the Prime Minister. The pattern of top earnings shown lacks any apparent rhyme or reason. The one clear common feature is that top people who work for the state are paid considerably less than top people who work in the private sector.

Is it just market forces at work? Not entirely. It is a safe bet that there would be well-qualified applicants for every one of these jobs at salaries considerably below the current level (except perhaps for the chairmanship of British Rail). And it is also a safe bet that the present incumbents would all be willing

---

[1] *Daily Telegraph* (17 June 1991).

Table 16.1. Top earnings (£)

Person	Job	Pay
Nigel Mansell	Racing driver	5,364,864
Sir Ian McLaurin	Chief executive, Tesco	1,480,000
Gary Lineker	Professional footballer	644,000
Iain Vallance	Chief executive, BT	536,303
Sir Jeremy Morse	Chairman, Lloyds Bank	212,712
Robin Leigh-Pemberton	Governor, Bank of England	155,019
Sir Terence Burns	Permanent Secretary, Treasury	96,210
Sir Peter de la Billiere KCB, CBE, DSO, MC	General, army	95,750
John Major	Prime Minister	72,533
George Carey	Archbishop of Canterbury	37,800
Professor Aaron Klug	Biochemist, Cambridge University	34,296

to do these jobs for less than they are currently paid. In contrast to the man in the street, most well-paid people enjoy their jobs.

So what does fix top salaries? Some top earners possess truly unique talents. This is most obviously true of Mansell and Lineker, and to a lesser degree of the kinds of ability that make a top barrister or a Nobel Laureate. These are people who can, clearly and indisputably, achieve things that are beyond the capacities of anyone else. But such individuals are rare. John Major is not prime minister because he is the Gazza of Parliament Square or the Gielgud of the front benches. That might have been true of Lloyd George or Churchill, or even of Margaret Thatcher. But few prime ministers are Churchills, few generals are Napoleons, and few chief executives are Rockefellers, or even Hansons. Most are very competent at their job, but there are many others who could do the job comparably well. They hold their posts, as John Major does, because they happened to be the best and most suitable candidates for a particular position in a particular organization on a particular day.

Yet even for those who possess it, unique talent is not enough to guarantee high earnings. For the owner to derive full benefit, there must be many—preferably rich—potential buyers rather than a single one. That is why top barristers are paid much more than top surgeons. It is also why even outstanding prime ministers are not paid well. You generally have the option of being prime minister of only one country. And it also has to be possible to exclude those who do not pay for your talent from enjoying the benefits of it, which is why Gascoigne and Madonna do so much better than Mozart or Isaac Newton. Football grounds and pop concert venues can be surrounded by stewards and barbed wire. But you can enjoy Mozart's music even if Mozart is not there; and Isaac Newton's ideas are available to anyone who takes the trouble to read them.

Who fixes your pay is also important. We might think that those who determine their own salary would be paid more than those who have it determined for them. But mostly this is a factor which keeps pay down rather than keeps it up. The three worst-paid figures in the table—John Major, Archbishop Carey, and Professor Aaron Klug, Nobel prize winning biochemist at Cambridge—all influence their own remuneration. There is never an opportune moment to increase the prime minister's pay, the Church cannot be seen to pay even its archbishops well, and Cambridge, in a mood of misguided egalitarianism, is unwilling to admit that any of its professors could be any better than any other.

Better than fixing your own pay is to have it determined by your friends and business associates, and this is the key to the process of enrichment in the boardroom. Like the practice of the chairman of the selectors retiring while his son's claims to inclusion are considered, the delegation to remuneration committees normally achieves satisfactory results while sparing the beneficiary any embarrassment.

Remuneration committees, naturally and properly, look to comparable businesses, reproducing precisely the process which, applied across the economy as a whole, brought Britain to its knees in the early 1970s. There is a slight danger that it might help do so again—the view that if the company can afford to give the boss 30 per cent it can afford to give me 10 per cent—and a much greater danger to the public esteem which British businessmen began to regain in the 1980s.

Why does a process which is so obviously personally and corporately damaging continue? The answer probably lies more in egotism than in greed. The fact that unique talent may lead to high earnings does not mean that high earnings demonstrate unique talent. But this confusion, which was particularly prevalent in financial markets in the heady days of 1987, seems now to have extended to senior executives. The revival of an enterprise economy means that many people will make a lot of money, and there is nothing wrong with that. It does not follow, however, that those who do make a lot of money are performing the most valuable services to society. The Eurobond trader whose income is many times that of the Prime Minister is the lucky beneficiary of a market anomaly, not the just recipient of her deserts. Big Bang and events around it have disoriented our sense of just differentials, and we need to get these back under control.

And what, you may ask, of professors at the London Business School? The answer is £39,000 per year. But do not shed any tears. The Chief Economic Adviser is definitely not allowed to supplement his income by writing for the *Daily Telegraph*.

WHAT'S IN A NAME?

A rose by any other name would smell as sweet, thought Shakespeare.[2] Today's wordsmiths know better. Wolff Olins, it is reported, charged £500,000 for naming Eurotunnel's cross-channel service Le Shuttle. And for encouraging British Telecom to cast off its dowdy and parochial image and call itself BT, they earned more from a single acronym than Shakespeare from all his plays. Such is the power of market forces.

The brand imperative is a reiterated theme of modern business. The shelves of off-licences are crowded with designer lagers. Liquid detergent, variously labelled as six brands of washing-up liquid, ten of body gel, and twenty types of shampoo, seems to fill half the supermarket. Nestlé paid twice what anyone had previously thought Rowntree was worth to get hold of names like Kit Kat and Polo, and told the Monopolies and Mergers Commission that their own Nescafé trademark was worth at least £250 million in the UK alone.

So what's in a name? Shakespeare, as usual, got to the heart of the matter. It is necessary to distinguish between a brand and the name of a product, and if Eurotunnel had understood that better they might have been able to save the £½ million for the benefit of their hard-pressed shareholders. A rose by any other name would truly smell as sweet. While we think now that if a rose had been called a pong we would be less likely to give our loved one six pongs when we are inexplicably late home, the reality is that if language had evolved that way we would now associate the name pong with romance, elegance, and the fragrance of an English country garden in midsummer. We buy a refrigerator for the things it does, not for its (unappealing) name, and if we use Eurotunnel's product we will use it because it takes us from Folkestone to Sangatte in 35 minutes, not because it is called Le Shuttle.

Some brands are little more than labels. When you buy a can of soup you want to know that the soup is the same as the soup you liked last week, and that is what the label that says Heinz Cream of Tomato tells you. Few people would buy an unlabelled can from a shelf headed 'soup'. But unless the taste of that soup is irreproducible by other firms, such a brand will not sell for a much higher price than other soups. Nor does it.

A brand is established when an object sells for more than the price of a functionally equivalent product, and it is then, and only then, that a company has an asset, or has established a market position which it is worth spending money to create. But what are the reasons for paying more for something when an identical object will do the same job?

One reason—and the commonest reason—is the quality certification function of the brand. For most goods we buy, we find out most of what we need to know about the characteristics of the product before we buy it (a lettuce) or immediately after we consume it (the designer lager). But some are long-term experience goods, whose quality emerges only slowly. Only time will tell

<hr>

[2] *Daily Telegraph* (13 July 1992).

whether your accountant or lawyer is any good. You rarely find out quickly whether your bank is solvent, your life insurance was a good investment, your underarm deodorant is really working, your dog or cat food gives vitality to your pet, or your baldness cure is really promoting the regrowth of your hair. It is for these types of commodities that brands are most necessary, if consumers are to have the confidence to buy, where they are the most difficult to establish, and where, once established, they command the highest price premium and achieve the greatest profitability.

Hence some of the most powerful of brands—Price Waterhouse, Barclays, Prudential, Persil, and Winalot. At most airports, you will find local firms offering the same cars on the same contracts as Hertz and Avis at lower prices. Probably, they are offering the same service. But you know that Hertz and Avis have high maintenance standards and that their cars are not reconditioned insurance write-offs. So you buy the Hertz brand for the same reason as you buy a Linklaters lawyer or a packet of Persil—the name is an assurance of quality when that quality is not easy to assess for yourself. And notice how advertising plays on that uncertainty—you may not be able to tell Persil-washed clothes from others but your mother-in-law can.

Now not all brands are about quality certification. There are some goods we use to signal information about ourselves to people we have only just met—like clothes, cars, drinks, and cigarettes. Bank managers wear suits because it is conventional that bank managers wear suits, not because the functions of a bank manager could not be performed perfectly adequately by a man in jeans. But a bank manager who wore jeans would immediately be telling us that he or she was an unconventional kind of bank manager. So we tell others things about ourselves by the clothes we wear, the cars we climb out of, the drinks we consume, and where the signal is associated with a proprietary product (an Armani suit rather than just a suit) then the owner of that product has a valuable asset.

For the signal to work, there has to be a cost to giving a misleading signal. The advertisements seek to associate Levi jeans with handsome men, but this is not a very enduring signal, because anyone can buy a pair of Levi jeans for £25 whether they are handsome or not. In fact, the most sustained of signals are those of affluence—Dom Perignon champagne, diamonds, Rolls Royce cars—where the exclusive nature of the signal is preserved by its price.

And then there are some brands that are truly irreproducible recipes. No one, it seems, has quite reproduced the flavour of Coke, the taste of Kit Kat, or the precise texture of Pedigree Chum. No one can legally reproduce the product that is Zantac. Eurotunnel is offering a unique product, and in many respects an exciting one—the first tangible, physical connection between Britain and the rest of Europe. It is on the attractiveness of that, not on the costly services of their marketing men, that the fortunes of Eurotunnel will depend.

REFLECTIONS FROM THE SEASIDE

Not many people think about economics when they lie on the beach. But economics is never far away, and with the holiday snaps go the inevitable stories about what things cost.[3] Wine was cheap. Taxis were expensive. Leather goods were wonderful value. But you should have seen what they charged for marmalade. If you go to the United States today, everything seems a bargain; but if you visit Japan, even goods made in Japan seem to cost a fortune. Why do prices vary so much across countries? And why, despite all the talk of a single market, a borderless Europe, and a common currency, do they continue to vary so much?

As Oscar Wilde said, economists know the price of everything and the value of nothing. They make a distinction between tradable and non-tradable goods. Tradable items can be made anywhere and used anywhere, but non-tradable goods have to be consumed where they are produced. So bottles of wine, leather goods, and Sony Walkmen are tradeable; and taxis, ready-mix concrete, telephone calls, and a glass of wine in a bar are all non-tradable. As a general but by no means invariable rule, manufactures are tradable but services are not.

If a good is non-tradable, its price is likely to be different everywhere it is produced and sold. A hotel room in Bourton-on-the-Water will be priced very differently from a hotel room in Frankfurt, since neither suppliers nor customers can readily substitute one for the other. Since non-tradable goods are often labour-intensive services, they tend to cost more in high-income countries than in low-income ones. So Scandinavia has some of the most expensive taxis and laundries in the world, and India has some of the cheapest.

The distinction between tradable and non-tradable goods has another important effect. In a country—Japan—which is particularly good at producing tradable goods, the price of tradable items like cars and electronics tends to be low relative to the price of non-tradables like restaurants and rail tickets. Because the exchange rate is determined by what happens in the tradable goods market, Japanese restaurants and rail tickets seem extraordinarily expensive. In Japan, everything seems dear and services particularly dear; in the United States and Australia, with large balance of payments difficulties, everything seems cheap and services, although not at bargain basement prices, are much cheaper than you would expect to find in these rich countries.

For tradable goods, however, you would expect international competition to equalize prices everywhere. And indeed for some commodities—mostly industrial products like crude oil or steel—this is true. But there are more exceptions to this rule than there are goods which follow it.

One major group of exceptions is for commodities where free trade is not allowed. Agricultural products are at the top of this list. The absence of free

[3] *Daily Telegraph* (24 Aug. 1992).

trade allows food to remain much more costly in Europe than in North America or the Antipodes where governments offer much less protection to their local farmers. In Norway, Switzerland, or Japan, where uneconomic agriculture is even more heavily supported, food is more costly still.

And then governments distort the market further by imposing taxes. That is why petrol, although a homogeneous commodity, is expensive in Italy and cheap in Luxembourg and why every alcoholic drink in Sweden is priced like liquid gold. A good rule of thumb is that countries are inclined to impose lower taxes on things they make than on things they do not, which is why Gauloises are cheap in France, wine costs very little in Italy, and ouzo is a snip in Greece.

You might think that if government did not distort the market, prices of tradables would be similar everywhere. But for branded goods, this is far from being the case. Your Sony Walkman, or your computer, will be a great deal cheaper in the United States than it is here. It is cheaper to purchase your washing machine in Britain than in France (or even in Italy, where it was probably made); but buy your car in Belgium, your pharmaceuticals in France, your life insurance in England, and your compact discs in Germany.

What is happening here is that manufacturers are taking advantage of differences between markets to practise price discrimination. Sometimes there are differences in competitive conditions, so that importers have been ready to follow the relatively high level of UK car prices which have been set by relatively high-cost UK producers. But stay out of the hands of the cartelized insurance industries of continental Europe, and get your cover in London instead. Sometimes the differences are in the way products are positioned. Whisky is a mass market commodity in Scotland and a niche product elsewhere, and it is priced accordingly in these different environments. If you want to buy cornflakes or baked beans in Britain, you will find them in aggressively priced bins at the front of the store. If you want to buy them in other countries, you will probably have to visit a delicatessen and pay the same sort of prices that you would expect to pay here for escargots or gnocchi.

So will 1992, and the coming of the single market, change all this? Will there then be a single price for olive oil from Belfast to Brindisi and ouzo as cheap, or as expensive, in Thurso as in Thessalonika? For Alfred Marshall and the nineteenth-century economists, a single market was characterized by the law of one price. But the single market the European Commission has set out to create is not a single market in Marshall's sense; it is a legal, not a commercial, concept. The coming of 1992 will not affect the price of non-tradable goods; it will reduce only slightly differences in the levels of national taxes; and it will only marginally inhibit the ability of manufacturers to continue to segment the market as they choose. Until the European Commission can harmonize our productivity and our preferences, our incomes and our weather, we will still go on holiday in search of a bargain and come home horrified by how much familiar items appear to cost.

FALLING PRICES

Price competition continues to break out everywhere.[4] Sainsbury has committed itself to a new, more aggressive attitude to its retail competitors, while the makers of the branded goods it sells are getting together to resist copycat products that look similar, do the same job, and cost considerably less. The gas regulator promises us the opportunity to get competing quotes for our gas supplies within two years from now. And we see the results as overall price rises continue to be less than anyone is expecting.

There are several causes at work. What is happening in our supermarkets is mostly a simple reflection of supply and demand. Over the last few years, everyone has been building too many superstores, each chain believing that it could continue to grow faster than the market as a whole. By the start of this decade, there was more retail space under construction than already existed. If you expand supply so much faster than demand, prices inevitably come under pressure, and now they have.

There is another factor at work in the food-retailing business. And, like excess capacity, it affects many other industries as well. One of the fashionable management stories of the 1980s was 'quality is free'. Improving product quality was said to be a certain route to higher margins and higher returns. So chains like Asda and Gateway set off up-market in emulation of Tesco and Sainsbury. Lacking either the retailing skills or the reputation with customers that Tesco and Sainsbury enjoyed, their attempts were not a success. Left alone to satisfy the bottom end of the market, Kwik Save earned handsome returns.

But this could not last, and did not. The profits of Kwik Save attracted new entrants, like Aldi and Costco, while the erstwhile advocates of the quality is free philosophy were forced to recognize that quality was not free at all. In reality it cost more than many of their customers were willing or able to pay. The result has been a shift back down market, and a new emphasis on price competition right across the food market.

The same phenomenon is at work in the market for branded goods. If quality was one fad of the 1980s, brands were another, and closely related, one. The idea was that a few words from the Marlboro cowboy, a modest expenditure in fancy packaging and advertising, or a promise of a lifestyle to match Julia Roberts or Richard Gere would enable companies to extract a large price premium for even the most mundane of products. It worked for a bit, but not much and not for long. However glamorous your stars or your advertising copywriters, if your product does not offer value for money you will be faced with competition from products which do. And that is what the firms who stuffed their balance sheets with imaginary valuations of their brands have steadily discovered.

Price competition has also been the result of deregulation. When you could only buy your telephone or your electricity from one company, there was no

---

[4] *Daily Telegraph* (16 May 1994).

role for price competition, and the only question was how much the national-ized industry chose to raise its charges by every year. Now you can get com-peting offers, charges are governed by regulators who insist that customers get the benefit of efficiency improvements, and prices have come down as a result. Other markets illustrate a more subtle version of the same phenom-enon. For many years professionals, like lawyers and accountants, main-tained restrictions on advertising and marketing. They argued that to allow their members to tout for business would undermine their ethics and their standing and the confidence the public placed in their services. It was a seductive argument, but also a self-serving one. There is no point in being cheap if you are not allowed to tell your customers that you are cheap, so rules against advertising were an effective barrier to price competition.

Today, these rules have gone. Ernst and Young proffer their services on massive hoardings at Heathrow Airport, solicitors place small ads saying 'any house conveyed for £250', and opticians' windows are as full as Dixons' with posters urging you to buy now while stocks and special offers last. Price com-petition has entered areas where only a decade ago price competition was almost unthinkable. Did you ever think that there would be a loan sale at your credit card company, or a cash-back offer from your building society?

And all this has helped to undermine the conventional wisdom that prices always go up. Nowhere is this more true than in the property market. Bricks and mortar were the most secure of investments, and while house prices might sometimes rise faster, sometimes slower, they could only move in one direction. Tenants happily signed leases containing upward-only rent reviews thinking they were giving nothing away. Now, we have a generation of first-time buyers who caught a cold in the housing market by following the advice—so wise for their parents—that they should buy the largest house they could as soon as they could. And—less widely noticed—we have a generation of industrial and commercial companies which have liabilities, sometimes for decades ahead, to pay rents which are far in excess of the cost or the value of equivalent property today. They show rather less enthusiasm for putting these undoubted liabilities in their balance sheets than they applied to the rather more ephemeral values of their brands.

There is one simple principle underlying all this: the stronger the competi-tion, the stronger is the downward pressure on prices. Look over twenty years and ask what prices have gone up by less than inflation, and you will point to television sets, cars (when you adjust price for quality), and air fares—all of them the subject of international competition. Ask instead what has hap-pened to products subject to less effective, and mainly domestic, competi-tion—beer, building costs, and rail fares. By comparing these lists you find the answer to those who do not understand that international competitiveness is the product of international competition.

Yet there is one striking exception to the explosion of price competition. After several years in which rapidly rising fares have made the Channel cross-ing the most costly short sea journey in the world, the tunnel comes in with charges which top any of them. Wait until the tunnel actually has its full capacity to offer. You will see these fares come tumbling down.

BLESSED ARE THE METAL BASHERS

Manufacturing is back in fashion. John Major, we are told, 'believes passionately' in the need to expand our industrial base.[5] He was, he says, in a minority in the Thatcherite 1980s (not many people recall his expressing these minority views). But he is in a minority no longer. Under his predecessor, the director-general of the Confederation of British Industry was once a barely tolerated visitor to Downing Street; today, the CBI's leader, Howard Davies, has an open door to No. 10. A report in Saturday's *Daily Telegraph* quoted a Treasury mandarin as saying, 'He's almost a member of the Cabinet. Sometimes it seems like it.'

The cult of manufacturing is one of the strangest of economic phenomena. It is a funny thing for people to become passionate about. As with all religions, manufacturing worshippers have their creed, their rules, and their responses. 'It is time for the government to recognize the importance of manufacturing industry.' (The congregation, clad in grey suits, will nod and murmur assent.) 'You cannot build an economy on insurance and hairdressing. (The congregation will snort and throw its hands in the air.) The cult has infiltrated deeply into society. It has its Department of State, its select committees, its trade associations.

Not all manufactured objects are equally revered. Pharmaceuticals and computers will just about do, but not films or books. The manufacture that is prized above all others is steel. Eastern Europe, where the cult was particularly influential, has so much steel-making capacity that if operated efficiently it would destabilize the world market for decades to come. In its last year of existence, the former Soviet Union produced more steel than the United States (and perhaps a tenth of US output of other things). Goodness knows what they did with it all. Presumably it is still rusting away somewhere. It is all bad luck on people for whom making steel is an ordinary business activity; their commercial steel is squeezed out by the planners' steel. Few cults have as their prophets both Lenin and Andrew Carnegie.

Now Lenin and perhaps also Carnegie were influenced by the labour theory of value: output is measured by the amount of hard physical toil that goes into it. That is why steel is the cult's most important symbol. Think of a steelworks and immediately the mind is filled with images of flaming furnaces, muscled men stripped to the waist and covered in a mixture of sweat and grease, wrestling to bring nature under control. Actually a modern steel plant is not

---

[5] *Spectator* (4 Sept. 1993).

like that at all, but since few manufacturing worshippers have ever been to one it does not matter.

In common with many other religions, the cult of manufacturing is irredeemably masculine. It is male manual labour that counts. George Orwell's account of the life of a *plongeur* describes work as physically demanding as can be imagined. But no manufacturing worshipper would ever think that washing-up was real work (even though, properly costed and accounted for, it would be one of Britain's largest industries). Washing-up is a woman's job. It is no accident that the service industry which heads the list for derision is hairdressing, a profession entered only by men of questionable masculinity.

And that explains why some non-manufacturing activities are ranked on a par with steel-making: mining, for example. Recall the extraordinary reaction last autumn to the announcement of pit closures in 1992. The government's plaintive cries that the coal was not needed, that there was already more stockpiled coal than anyone could use, were universally dismissed as irrelevant or absurd. The economic value of coal is self-evident. To question it is to devalue the efforts of the men who seize it from the ground. Arthur Scargill's repeated references to 'the cheapest deep-mined coal in Europe' is characteristic of the debate. Only deep-mined coal really counts. The effete coal that can be shovelled from a hill by a man with a bulldozer is not real coal, even though it burns just as well and the electricity it produces is just the same.

The activities that manufacturing worshippers value have a clear group of common characteristics. They involve arduous and unpleasant labour and they are mainly produced by men. Ideally man is set against the elements. So steel-making and vehicle assembly are key manufacturing activities, and pharmaceuticals and publishing (profitable export industries though they may be) do not really count. The people who work for them probably wear suits, and are as likely to be women as men.

Mining and agriculture meet the criteria that define real work; insurance, tourism, and hairdressing do not. As a result, governments around the world protect and subsidize their car and steel industries, their farms, and their mines. The world has a surplus of car- and steel-making capacity, agricultural products, and coal. It is very difficult to make a profitable living in any of these businesses. Drugs and books, insurance and hair salons, which are not deemed to be equally important, can be left to the ordinary laws of supply and demand. They are businesses you can make money in.

In primitive societies men hunted for food, made simple implements, and gathered fuel. Women stayed behind to rear their (preferably male) children. Securing sufficient food and fuel took all the hours of the day. The families of men who were vigorous and proficient in these activities thrived, while those with idle or inept husbands did not. There was then a real sense in which agriculture, energy, and basic manufacturing were primary activities and others secondary. If the primary ones were insufficiently successful, the secondary ones could not take place at all.

But the world, believe it or not, has changed. In Britain in 1993 it is no longer necessary to hunt all day in order to find enough to eat. As a matter of fact, in order to be able to hunt at all you need to spend the rest of the year earning a great deal of money in a merchant bank, and most of the people who hunt have already eaten far too much. The value of economic activities no longer turns on what they contributed to the Stone Age man's needs for food and shelter. It is derived from what other people are willing to pay for them. That is why Bill Clinton's hair stylist earns more than a steel worker.

Yet the spread of economic ideas lags far behind. As Keynes observed, practical men who believe themselves exempt from any intellectual influence are usually the slaves of some defunct economist—about 10,000 years defunct in this case.

17

The Strategic Audit

This essay is drawn from the American version of Foundations of Corporate Success, *published there as* Why Firms Succeed. *It illustrates, through a number of corporate examples, some issues in the practical application of the resource-based theory of strategy.*

Assessing strategy

One measure of success within the corporation is to be invited to its strategy weekend.[1] The strategy weekend is a ritual observed by many companies in which senior management retreat to the country to contemplate the issues which face them, with a detachment which daily routines render impossible. There are as many routines for conducting these events as there are corporations which conduct them.

One company, like many, began its strategy weekend with a discussion of the corporate plan. Within minutes, there was a heated exchange across the table between the vice-president for strategic planning and the CEO of one of the principal operating businesses. The CEO picked up the firm's planning document. It was not an easy task. The book contained printouts of key financial variables for each division of the corporation over the next five years, and ran to several hundred pages.

'What is this for?' asked the CEO. 'Is it a forecast? If so, it's not a good one. Does it provide targets? Then why are there no penalties for failing to meet them? Four of my staff spent six months preparing data for this, and I haven't had occasion to refer to them once.' The planning vice-president, equally angry, snapped back at him, 'You don't really think you can go on running this business by the seat of your pants?' Yet, as they later acknowledged, both were right. The CEO had to acknowledge that something longer term was needed to guide day-to-day operating decisions; the planning VP that the corporate plan was not it. Like many other corporations, this firm had begun

---

[1] *Why Firms Succeed*, ch. 14, edited.

strategic planning in the 1960s; like many other corporations, this firm had discovered that these elaborate planning documents had little influence on the way it actually conducted its affairs.

Another weekend. This British company had flown in an American facilitator to manage its weekend. First, he posed for them what he saw as the key issue: 'Do we want to be Europe's leading firm in our industry, or not?' The assembled executives responded enthusiastically in the affirmative. But the plan to be Europe's leading firm quickly encountered a snag; the firm's weakness in Germany. The solution was clear—a German acquisition. Within half an hour, discussion had focused on plans for buying a German company. Plans which that company has subsequently, but unprofitably, implemented. As so many corporations did in the 1980s, that firm has discovered that establishing a mission, or creating a vision, is not at all the same as achieving its profitable implementation.

That emphasis on implementation, so characteristic of more recent strategy discussions, was reflected in another strategy weekend. A consulting group, specializing in the management of change, were introducing their work by means of a video: 'The Circle of Quality'. The circle of quality ran from higher quality to larger sales, through scale economies to lower costs which, combined with the additional revenues from greater output, would establish a virtuous circle of ever-increasing quality and ever-rising profits.

The firm in question was a water supply business. Improvements in the quality of output would lead to negligible impact on its sales. Increased sales imply higher costs, not lower, because water resources are scarce. Revenues would not rise as most customers paid the company a fixed sum for water regardless of what they consumed. Higher quality might be appropriate, but for that company would inevitably mean additional costs without additional revenues. The video was irrelevant to the point of absurdity for this particular business.

The first company's strategy had become immersed in the numerical detail of its strategic plan. The second was in the process of formulating a vision no different from the vision that was formulated by many other firms in its business, and no more capable of realization. The third had fallen victim to the practice of reciting fashionable slogans—'go global', 'improve quality', 'empower', 're-engineer'—without regard to the specifics of the business concerned. What should they have done instead?

Identifying distinctive capabilities

Meaningful strategy begins from the question, 'What are this firm's distinctive capabilities?' That provokes debate no less heated, but more structured and more conclusive, than 'What is our mission?', or 'What business are we in?'

When Finserco, a leading retail financial services company, set about analysing its distinctive capabilities, there was no shortage of suggestions.

The marketing group stressed the novelties in its product range, the human resources vice-president argued that its competitive advantage lay in its internal architecture, and the business services division emphasized its information technology. Yet the analysis and debate at Finserco's strategy weekend revealed that these capabilities, although real capabilities of the company, were not truly distinctive.

The firm had made many minor innovations in product design, but those that appealed to customers were usually quickly picked up by others in the industry, and several of Finserco's competitors were also pushing through these sorts of product changes; no one was really prepared to argue that Finserco had a reputation for innovation. Employee relations were good, it was true, despite some recent problems; but the same was true for all of Finserco's principal competitors. Finserco was in a service business, and the quality of its products relied on the processing of several hundred thousand transactions every day at very high levels of accuracy. In their business, you could not stay among the market leaders unless you had a well-trained, committed work-force, but that very fact meant it was no one's distinctive capability.

What Finserco's management eventually focused on in seeking the company's distinctive capabilities was two principal features of its business: its reputation and its branch network. Market research confirmed what everyone around Finserco instinctively knew: customers trusted Finserco. It was not just that they were sure the company would still be there when they wanted their money back. They believed in the quality of its service and its products and that the advice they got in its branches was honest and not the biased product of commission-hungry sales people. Most surveys put Finserco number one or two in its peer group—well ahead, the executive group noted, of firms which today were providing services not very different from Finserco's but which had not in the past maintained the same quality of customer relationship. And although there was concern about the cost of Finserco's retail branches, it was clear to all that these were a strategic asset. The amount which one overseas bank had been willing to pay to acquire a comparable chain was one good indicator of that; so was the expenditure which another had been ready to make in an unsuccessful attempt to build something similar on a greenfield basis.

Bankcorp, another financial services firm, came to very different conclusions about itself. Whatever the VP for marketing and communications might say, Bankcorp did not have a name in the market-place, outside its narrow regional origins, which rivalled that of Finserco. Bankcorp's rapid expansion had been based essentially on one single element in its market position: it had the lowest cost processing capability in the business. Some called this innovation—certainly no one had yet been able to match the quality of Bankcorp's technology. But the CEO, who had come up through the operations group, preferred to emphasize architecture. It was, he argued, the interaction between the systems people and the day-to-day users in the business (which, he argued, had been possible because Bankcorp was based outside the major financial centres and so had much lower turnover of head office staff) which no one else in the industry had been able to replicate effectively.

Discussion of Universal Airlines' distinctive capabilities began with a long discourse on the importance of the brand, replete with the latest in marketing jargon. The chief of operations, a former pilot, brought the discussion down to earth with the same definitive confidence he had shown when he had brought his passengers down to earth. 'You know very well', he said, 'that the only reason passengers prefer our flights to others at the same price and the same time is the frequent flyer points.' The executive group tossed around various possible distinctive capabilities, concluding that there were not many in the airline business. The financial director's laconic observation that perhaps that was why no one seemed to make any money was not regarded as helpful. The firm's main distinctive capability, the group concluded, was its hub—the large regional airport which was its historic base and from which over half the flights were designated under the Universal Airlines name.

The CEO of Sonico, who had recently been recruited from the finance group of a large multinational, was all the more uncertain what she had inherited as she saw the senior management group assembled for the first time. She compared the chaotic enthusiasm of the technologists with the arrogant indifference of the sales-force, and knew that neither would have been tolerated for long in her last company. But she knew that these two groups represented the distinctive capabilities of Sonico, which made specialist sound equipment for the popular music business. The creative technical team bubbled with ideas; for people with interests in this area, a job with Sonico offered all they wanted or needed. Occasionally, individuals or small groups would leave to do their own thing, but there was no team of remotely comparable size or quality. And the sales people's ability to relate these technical skills to the idiosyncratic and demanding requirements of users was the other element in Sonico's competitive advantage. The external architecture of its customer relationships complemented the internal architecture that produced its technology.

Popular Energy, like many utilities, was both excited and overwhelmed by the range of opportunities created by the new world of privatization and deregulation. In common with many firms in its position, it had suffered from early ill-considered diversification; now it was emphasizing its core business. But what was that core business? The management of Popular Energy began the search for a definition by identifying the firm's distinctive capabilities.

The company enjoyed the considerable strategic asset of a distribution monopoly within its local area. Beyond that, it was forced to conclude that its distinctive capabilities were limited. While it had relationships with its customers, they were not deep, and were capable of being reproduced by others. Its regional focus might be important; it was the second largest company with a head office in its area, it was well regarded in the community, and it had, in the broad sense of the word, good political connections. It was also a leader, not only nationally but internationally, in a specialist technology which had been needed to deal with a particular local problem.

Matching markets to distinctive capabilities

Identifying distinctive capabilities is the first stage of formulating strategy. Matching markets to these distinctive capabilities comes next. Are the markets in which the company operates all ones in which its distinctive capabilities add value? Are there others, which it is not yet in, where they might create competitive advantage?

Finserco had identified clearly that its distinctive capabilities were to be found in its reputation and its branches. Its strategic focus followed directly from that. Both Finserco's distinctive capabilities related mainly to its existing customer base, or at least to its existing geographic area. The principal choice it faced—should it sell a broader range of services to its existing customers, or seek by geographical expansion to sell its established product range to new customers?—was therefore easily resolved. It could add far more value by attaching its name and reputation to new services than it could by selling its old ones in markets where it enjoyed no competitive advantage.

Although most of the executive group was excited by the prospect of expanding Finserco's product range, there was a group which was disappointed at the brake that had been put on geographic expansion. After all, they argued, if their predecessors had taken the same view, Finserco would still be a company with one branch in a single small town. But a consensus was quickly reached. Everyone agreed to rule out the major overseas acquisition which some advisers had been urging on them. The Finserco name would simply add no value there. But a controlled process of organic expansion which gradually enlarged the area in which the Finserco name was known was to be part of its strategy. That process was, it was accepted, one that would take many years to come to fruition.

Bankcorp reached just the opposite conclusions. Its systems could be applied widely; what is needed was the local presence that would bring in the business. Extending its product range would stretch its capabilities, but adding greater volume to its current processing capabilities would increase its cost advantage still further. Bankcorp agreed to establish a dedicated acquisitions team to speed up the pace at which new firms in different geographical areas could be absorbed into its organization.

Could it be right that two firms in the same industry could reach such different conclusions about the appropriate directions of their strategy? It would have been much more worrying if they had reached identical conclusions, because that would have raised serious questions over the viability of both companies' plans. Strategy based on distinctive capabilities will, of necessity, take corporations in directions as distinctive as their capabilities.

Universal Airlines' analysis had emphasized the critical role of its hub. Its analysis of markets began from there. The markets for business travellers to and from that catchment area were its principal clientele. Universal also catered for leisure traffic originating in that catchment area, and had segmented the market effectively to offer attractive fares to these customers while preserving its premium business rates. The market for leisure traffic *to* the hub was met much less effectively, and a strategy for tackling that market was assigned as a priority for the marketing department.

The heated debate was over the CEO's plan to move into hotels. He emphasized the intensity of competition in the airline business, argued that greater stability of earnings was essential to the future of the corporation, and stressed the links between demand for air travel and demand for hotel services.' Three-quarters of our passengers check into a hotel,' he noted. 'We're missing a great selling opportunity—and one our competitors are taking.' But pressed to explain why Universal Airlines' distinctive capabilities were relevant to providing overnight hospitality, he finally conceded that his opponents had the better of the argument. 'Perhaps that's why airlines lose even more money per dollar in hotels than they do flying,' commented the finance director.

Sonico's CEO had come into the business with ambitious plans to use the company as a base for developing the sort of multinational conglomerate business with which she was familiar. Looking around her, she understood that this notion had been a mistake. Her people were currently doing precisely those things that they could do better than anyone else. The scope of the business exactly matched its distinctive capabilities. Her job was to preserve these distinctive capabilities, and that match.

And once Popular Energy had focused on its distinctive capabilities, its strategic directions were clear. It agreed to divest its assorted portfolio of world-wide energy ventures just as soon as it could obtain reasonable offers for them. Outside its central utility business, it would concentrate on specific niche opportunities. There was a chance to both rationalize and develop a forest products business in Popular Energy's home area. With its connections in the state capital, and the trust of the local people, Popular Energy could encounter little of the local opposition which had deterred others from going ahead. There was some opposition from a group which argued that Popular Energy had no skills in forest products. But it came to realize that skills and distinctive capabilities were not necessarily the same thing. Skills could be bought; there was no shortage of capable managers in the forest products sector. Distinctive capabilities were another matter. (Notice how Sonico answered the same question very differently. Sonico's skills were one of its distinctive capabilities, and could not be bought, or reproduced, by another company.) After a decade of searching, Popular Energy had finally come to terms with what it meant by its core business.

Sustaining and appropriating competitive advantage

Each company needed to consider how it was to sustain its distinctive capabilities, and how it would ensure that the resultant added value was appropriated for the benefit of its shareholders. Finserco was clear where its distinctive capabilities lay—in its name, and its reputation. There were threats to this. Other, non-financial, companies were using their reputation to get into financial services. But these were manageable problems, and there were strategies in place for managing them.

The most important element in sustaining Finserco's position was that every one of its employees who dealt with its customers should remember, every day, the origins of the company's added value—and their profits share. When Finserco's executives finished their discussion with an affirmation of their mission—how they communicated their distinctive capabilities and their strategy to their employees—that issue was at the centre of the thinking.

The appropriation issue was central to another of Finserco's discussions. In broadening its range of financial services products, Finserco would be moving aggressively into new business areas, such as insurance, whereas in the past it had been content to collect commissions as a relatively passive seller of other companies' products. How far should it take vertical integration? One school held that Finserco should acquire an established insurer; another, that it should buy in systems expertise initially as the basis for its own greenfield operations. 'What we need', it was argued, 'is to earn the manufacturer's profit as well as the distributor's margin.'

But when they approached the debate in terms of the analysis of added value, a different perspective emerged. There was no such thing as 'a manufacturer's profit'; there was already excess capacity in the insurance industry and a new entrant could not expect more than the cost of capital. Why then were the financial projections for Finserco's entry into insurance so attractive? They were attractive, not by virtue of any 'manufacturing profit', but because Finserco could add so much value in distribution. Now Finserco could add that value whether or not it was itself the manufacturer. The best option was to ensure that Finserco had full control over product design and development while shopping around for the cheapest provider of systems and underwriting. Given excess capacity among insurers, and the volume of output which Finserco could deliver, it could drive an exceptionally tough bargain. Against this strategy, the alternative of paying a bid premium for an insurance company looked very unattractive. Finserco had come to understand that so long as you control the point in the chain of production at which added value arises, you can leverage that to secure the added value from the whole chain without yourself needing to own all of it.

Bankcorp had many more concerns about the sustainability of its distinctive capability. Its systems were the best in the business, its technical team second to none. But retail financial services are not at the leading edge of information technology. There were other people in the industry just as good;

other teams with potentially comparable talents. Bankcorp was not at a technical frontier as Sonico was. Some of Bankcorp's executives projected the recent past into the indefinite future, and constructed visions of an ever-rosier future. The more realistic among them recognized that, sooner or later, some competitors would catch up. They might even leap ahead. However much they invested in technology, there was little they could do to stop that happening.

For the enthusiasts, this was defeatist talk. But the wise CEO reminded them that they were in the business of adding value, not winning medals for defying the odds. There were, he suggested, two main routes ahead. 'If your distinctive capability may fade, it is time to sell,' he said cynically. Specifically, a merger with a well-established player whose systems are not up to scratch could add value to both companies, and could almost certainly be done on terms which over-valued Bankcorp's possibly transitory capability relative to the more sustainable one. The market, not fully appreciating the nature of the different distinctive capabilities, was mistakenly projecting the recent experience of both companies into the indefinite future. Alternatively, the window of opportunity created by the firm's current technical superiority could be used to build a reputation-based distinctive capability that could persist even if the lead in systems had faded. That meant racing against time, and promoting the firm's name through an extensive advertising and sponsorship programme which current levels of profitability could easily accommodate. The firm's merger talks did not work out, and the second path is now its strategic priority.

The lesson that Finserco had debated earnestly—how integrated a producer do you need to be to maximize your added value—was one Sonico had resolved years before. In Sonico's early days of operations, it had operated almost entirely on bought-in components. There had been pressure to fabricate an increasing proportion in-house. A consultant's report had advised it that it should make for itself everything that was customized for Sonico's operations or whose quality was essential to the quality of the final product. That, the consultant argued, defined Sonico's 'core business'.

Sonico had rejected this proposal. It was not practical—it identified components for in-house manufacture which Sonico's technical people did not believe the company could make to the necessary standards without huge investment. Nor was it necessary; the quality and reliability achieved by some of Sonico's suppliers was enviable. Like Finserco, Sonico did not need to undertake the whole process to extract the added value from it.

The greatest danger to Sonico's position was that one of the giants of the electronics industries would invade its market. There were those who argued that Sonico's technical capabilities were so strong that no one could do this. But realism prevailed; if these firms spent enough money, they could. It would not be profitable for them to do that, another argument ran. But it did not matter—in the graphic phrase which had been quoted then, and was still remembered around the company, 'being in front of a steam-roller is uncomfortable even if the steam-roller shouldn't be there'.

What was vital to Sonico was to discourage such entry. That meant not being too greedy; remaining on good terms with the relevant technical divisions in the industry's giants; and ensuring that they knew enough about Sonico's business to meet its needs but not enough to make their own entry too easy. These principles had been laid down three or four years ago; and so far they had achieved Sonico's objectives.

Universal Airlines had emphasized the role of its hub as its principal distinctive capability. What threats were there to that? The prospect of another airline establishing a similar operation was remote. The greatest danger was probably that the market would move away from 'hub and spoke' operation, which had emerged as the principal means of airline operation since deregulation in the 1970s. The economics of smaller planes might become more favourable, or business travellers' preferences might move further towards point-to-point services. These were trends that needed to be watched, but problems did not seem imminent.

Universal had scheduling and code-sharing arrangements with a number of commuter airlines which brought passengers into its hub. There was a good deal of resentment at Universal at the profits which some of these companies had been making, especially while the airline business as a whole had been through such difficult times. Universal's operations director was, again, on top of the issue.

'Some commuter services', he argued, 'were provided by carpetbaggers with an aeroplane.' They would move elsewhere if the returns were better and, conversely, Universal could find equally good operators to replace them. Others were people with real routes, and connections, in their local community. 'Passengers are booking with them, not with us. Sometimes we add the value to the code share, sometimes the other fellow does.' Universal had to distinguish carefully between one and the other. 'We can deal toughly with the first sort of relationship; we need to treat the second with kid gloves.'

Adding value

The return on capital employed earned by my five companies varied considerably. Sonico's was the highest. The company added substantial value, and employed very little capital. Subject to some of the dangers which the analysis of its operations had identified, it might continue earning that rate of return for many years ahead; the company was one with a genuine distinctive capability. Sonico's shares had been a stunningly good investment for those who had held them for a decade or more (which included many of its senior management group). But today, these shares sold on a PE ratio well above the market average, and its market value was many times the book value of its assets. The good news about Sonico was fully in the price.

Bankcorp and Finserco also earned returns well in excess of any reasonable measure of the cost of capital in their businesses. Finserco's projections showed a steady decline in its ratio on assets as its diversification proceeded, and this worried some of its executives. But they were somewhat reassured when they focused on the fundamental objective of adding value. It is better to earn 20 per cent return on capital than to get 25 per cent on a business half the size, was how the argument was put to them. In Bankcorp, by contrast, the return they expected to earn on capital employed continued to hold up as they increased the geographical scope for their operations; they could, they believed, add as much value to their new businesses as they were doing on the old.

The four ways of looking at the capital employed in a business—current cost, historic cost, cash flow, and shareholder return—reduced effectively to two for Sonico, Finserco, and Bankcorp. The first three measures of current profitability and cash flow all gave very similar impressions of the business. The reason was that physical capital was not very important for any of these companies. But while the financial statements reflected the current position, the market was driven by expectations for the future. All three companies had out-performed the market over the last few years, as the stock market had come to appreciate the strength of their distinctive capabilities. Now, all enjoyed glamour ratings. Finserco had the lowest PE of the three, and its management suspected the market still underestimated the strength of its franchise when supplied to a wider range of products. Bankcorp—which had the most doubts of any of these firms about the sustainability of its distinctive capability—concluded its stock was probably fully valued.

But Universal Airlines and Popular Energy were both capital-hungry businesses. Their returns on capital were much lower, partly because their added value was spread over a much larger base, but more because it was doubtful if they added very much value. Popular Energy earned a respectable, but regulated, historic cost rate of return on its assets. As analysis made clear, its diversification programme had raised earnings per share; but these higher earnings had been obtained by using retained profits to generate returns which, although positive, were less than the cost of capital (which measured what the shareholders could have got by investing the money themselves). Popular Energy's refocusing of its business implied more shareholder value from higher dividends and slower growth; a return, in fact, to something closer to its traditional utility status. Not everyone in Popular Energy found the limitation of its horizons which an analysis of its distinctive capabilities produced easy to accept. After a decade in which costly strategic and financial advisers had told them that the world was at their feet, the narrower conception of the business seemed constraining. Yet the consequences of buying firms to which they had no real value to add were obvious—they had seen a declining return on capital, and a falling stock market rating. As their CEO summed it up, 'Running a utility well is one of the hardest management jobs, and now is the time we set about doing it.'

The financial appraisal of Universal Airlines was the most depressing of all. 'Over the last five years, we would have done better to sell our fleet and put the money in a bank, and our shareholders would have done better to sell their stock and put the money in a sock.' Yet Universal Airlines was a well-run business with some real distinctive capabilities. In the equation that says added value is the sum of competitive advantage and industry conditions, it was industry conditions that had let them down.

Would—could—too many planes go on chasing too few passengers indefinitely? Economic and commercial logic said no, but experience of the airline industry seemed to suggest otherwise. If, but only if, the business reaches an equilibrium in which the marginal firm is, just sufficiently profitable to stay in business, will Universal's competitive advantages enable it to add value.

Conclusions

I sat down with my notes to set out what these five companies—Finserco, Bankcorp, Sonico, Universal Airlines, and Popular Energy—had in common. But it is far more important to record what they did not have in common. Take every one of the slogans of the strategy business in the last two or three decades—'stick to the knitting', 'global', 'emphasize related diversification', 'focus on the core business', 'emphasize quality'—and you will find there were some of these companies for which each was appropriate and others for which it was not. The only extraordinary thing about that statement is that anyone could ever have thought otherwise.

But it is quite wrong to conclude that because there are no general solutions to management problems and no valid generic strategies, there are no general principles of good management. The fact that aspirin does not cure every disease does not mean that medicines are useless, and to respond to that discovery by looking for some other compound that will cure every disease is a foolish response. As the appropriate medicine is specific to the disease for which it is prescribed, the appropriate strategy is specific to the company which adopts it. It should not be a surprise that although Bankcorp and Finserco were in the same business the moves that were right for one were wrong for the other. Geographic diversification was right for Bankcorp and wrong for Finserco; extending the product line was right for Finserco but wrong for Bankcorp. Bankcorp was right to stress acquisition—and even to contemplate being acquired. Both would have been damaging to Finserco. The differences followed directly from the differences in their distinctive capabilities.

Not all firms have distinctive capabilities in all their markets. Indeed, some firms may not have distinctive capabilities at all. Most of us come to terms with the fact that we are not likely to win Olympic gold medals for anything. It is curious that we find this so much harder to accept of corporations. The hardest of business cases to handle in strategy classes are those of companies whose competitive advantages are inherently transitory—the result of an innovation which others will certainly follow, or a position that others will assuredly replicate. The extravagant claims made, if rarely realized, for strategic management, and the extraordinary powers attributed to charismatic CEOs, make us all reluctant to accept such obvious propositions as that IBM might have to settle for being a lesser corporation than it once was; there is nothing else that it can do.

So the firm's distinctive capabilities are those it has, not those it would like to have. All these companies found it difficult to keep these apart. 'If we are number one in processing, why shouldn't we be number one in customer service and number one in investment management?' asked a Bankcorp manager. It was as if the 100-metre gold medallist had said that since she was a gold medallist she could easily win the 1,500 metres in swimming and the long jump as well. Distinctive capabilities are rare; companies must identify and nurture them, but not exaggerate them.

18

Pricing the Tunnel

Eurotunnel crops up on many occasions in this book. There is a reason for this. It is an extremely simple company, with one production facility, a narrow and pre-defined product range, and even a limited lifespan. Yet at the same time, it displays a wide range of business issues and problems. This chapter, which was written with Alan Manning and Stefan Szymanski, is concerned with one specific, but critical, aspects of its operations—its pricing policy. It was written towards the end of 1989, when the tunnel was in its early stages of construction, and five years before it actually opened to traffic.

Eurotunnel's intentions on pricing are set out in its 1987 prospectus.[1] It will match the prices set by the ferries. It expects their level to be somewhat lower—perhaps 20 per cent lower—than at present. The ferries have declared an intention to base their response on low-cost competition on the short sea crossings. Neither of these strategies makes sense. The tunnel must price aggressively to secure volume, and by doing so it can secure profits considerably in excess of those shown in the prospectus, regardless of how the ferries respond. The ferries cannot compete effectively in direct opposition to the tunnel, and should concentrate their energies on other routes.

The competitive background

The tunnel will provide services in a well-established market for transport between the UK and continental Europe. The crossing can at present be made by air or by sea. The key markets, however, are those for accompanied vehicles—around 2.8 million cars per annum—and a similar number of lorries.

The market is more or less evenly divided between two principal operators, P. & O. and Sealink, with around 80–90 per cent of the market. The remainder

---

[1] *Business Strategy Review*, 1/1 (Spring 1990), edited.

is fought over by a competitive fringe (e.g. Sally Line, Brittany Ferries, Olau Line, etc.).

Although there is a high degree of concentration the existence of a competitive fringe ensures there is downward pressure on prices. Entry into the market is relatively cheap and failure need not be too costly (there is a well-developed second-hand market for ferries).

The Channel Tunnel will be a 31-mile twin-bore tunnel between Dover and Calais. It is scheduled to be opened in May 1993. The tunnel will offer two main services. Foot passengers and rail freight will be able to travel through the tunnel on scheduled services offered by BR and SNCF (the UK and French national rail companies). Through rail services will connect London to Paris, Brussels, and beyond. Eurotunnel will not charge travellers directly for this service and has negotiated a usage contract with BR and SNCF.

ET will also offer a shuttle service with specially designed trains carrying cars (with passengers), lorries, and coaches between Dover and Calais. The journey time through the tunnel is expected to be 35 minutes. The crossing time of the fastest ferry is around 70 minutes.

The capacity of the system will be very large. A rough calculation based on Eurotunnel figures suggest that maximum capacity in 1994 will be double to size of *total* 1994 cross-channel traffic demand (268 per cent of current demand). Even on Eurotunnel's own forecasts, the market size in 2010 will still be only 95 per cent of ET capacity. In principle at least, ET has the potential to satisfy the entire market for the foreseeable future. It also has first option on the construction of a further tunnel, which may, in the end, be an asset of considerable value.

The cost of constructing the tunnel was estimated at around £5 billion at the time of flotation in 1987. Since that time anticipated costs have risen substantially for reasons which are the subject of continuing, and unresolved, dispute between the company (ET PLC) and the contractors. At the time of writing total cost estimates have risen to between £7 billion and £8 billion, but since around £2 billion has already been spent, it is clear that suggestions of abandonment are far-fetched. Aside from the loss of face to all parties, it is apparent that if it was deemed profitable to construct a tunnel two years ago for £5 billion, then it is still worth spending £5 billion today to achieve the same result. This illustrates an important characteristic of ET's competitive position. The huge amount of capital which must be committed to its construction, once 'sunk', plays no further role in deciding how the tunnel should be operated, although of course it affects the financial position of ET PLC. The capital costs of the ferries are recoverable. Since they have a second-hand value, they can be sold up and used in some other activity if the Dover and Calais trip becomes unprofitable.

The costs which matter when deciding how to operate the tunnel and the ferries are marginal costs—which we discuss further below. According to our estimates, the tunnel has a marginal cost (the extra cost of carrying one more passenger, car, or lorry) around *one-tenth* of the ferries. This reflects the fact that the tunnel itself is a fixed hole in the ground with dedicated equipment and so the cost of running through another trainload of passengers or goods is very small. By contrast, running another ferry incurs substantial additional costs in the form of crew costs, fuel, port dues, and so on, and in the long run the full capital costs of operation must be remunerated or the ferries will be used elsewhere or not replaced.

In our analysis we have assumed that the tunnel is completed roughly on time and roughly within budget. This now seems increasingly unlikely. However, it does little to alter the nature of our results. Whilst higher construction costs or delayed opening will reduce the profits available for Eurotunnel's shareholders, this fact in itself should have no bearing on the way in which Eurotunnel attempts to generate the maximum level of profit possible, once it is opened.

Tactical competition

By tactical competition we mean price-setting behaviour which takes no account of the possible impact that current profitability may have on future profitability. Tactical competition means that day-to-day price-setting decisions are taken with a view to maximizing current profits. Thus it does not allow for price strategies designed to build market share at the expense of current income or to persuade competitors to leave the market or refrain from entering it. There are three factors which are central to the outcome of this tactical competition—relative product quality, substitutability, and relative costs.

1. Relative product quality

It is by no means clear whether a tunnel or a ferry crossing is a superior product. The tunnel will certainly be faster but a sea trip will often be more pleasant. For example, consumers will typically view the prospect of a sea crossing differently from a trip through a tunnel. Experience may change these perceptions but in the extreme, claustrophobes will never like travelling through a tunnel whilst agoraphobes will never happily choose to saunter on the open deck of a ferry. Product quality also depends on how well the product is adapted to its purposes. The tunnel will offer faster movement of freight between Dover and Calais but very little traffic originates at Dover or terminates at Calais. A crossing between Felixstowe and Zeebrugge is often a more appropriate routing.

We define an objective overall measure of service quality in each market segment by asking what relative prices would give each mode of operation an equal market share. If the tunnel would take 50 per cent of the market for accompanied cars at a price premium of 20 per cent, we judge that the tunnel's service is 20 per cent superior. If it needs to undercut ferry charges by 30 per cent to win 50 per cent of the market, then it is inferior by that amount.

Other things equal, the producer of a superior product can charge a higher price. But other things may not be equal. As we see below, it may b e that the tunnel should charge a lower price even if its product is superior. It is often better to take profits through volume than through price.

2. *Substitutability*

Tactical competition will also be influenced by the degree to which one product can be substituted for another. Substitutability and superiority/inferiority are quite distinct properties, although both are the characteristics of the underlying product. One good may be highly substitutable for another even though it is inferior—as with ordinary and long-life light bulbs, or alkaline and zinc-carbon batteries. And related products may be poor substitutes even if they are of equal quality in the sense defined above. Two washing powders may have similar-sized bands of loyal adherents, each of whom view their favourite product as clearly preferable. The powders are of equal quality but, in terms of customer perception, they are not easily substitutable.

Our measure of substitutability is the elasticity of substitution—the rate at which changes in relative prices bring about changes in market share. If the elasticity of substitution is high then, even if ferry and tunnel prices diverge by a small amount, a very large share of the market will go to the firm charging the lower price. If, on the other hand, the elasticity of substitution is low, then only very large differences in prices will cause customers to shift to the cheaper alternative. In the extreme, an infinite elasticity of substitution means that firms must charge identical prices if both are to stay in the market. A zero elasticity means that even if a competitor charged nothing, no customers would defect.

3. *Relative costs*

It is by no means clear whether a tunnel will increase or reduce the average cost of crossing the Channel. This depends not only on the size of final construction bills: it is also influenced by the ultimate level of demand for its services. This evaluation is relevant to an assessment of whether the tunnel should have been built, but not to tariff strategy now that the tunnel is certain to be built. But when setting prices it is marginal costs which are crucial, rather than fixed or average costs. Any price charged above marginal cost adds to profitability; but it never pays (in the short run at least) to charge below marginal cost. Of course, revenue over marginal cost is not pure profit; first it must cover fixed costs (such as the cost of construction of the ferries or the tunnel). However, the goal of the competitive firm must be to choose prices so as to maximize the surplus over marginal cost. If this surplus is insufficient to cover fixed costs then the firm faces bankruptcy, but this does not alter the argument since, by definition, any other price would actually reduce the surplus and therefore the likelihood of covering of fixed costs.

Relative marginal costs will therefore be crucial in determining profitability. As noted above, the marginal costs of the tunnel are much lower than those of the ferries. This is central to the competitive outcome.

The dynamics of market entry

Here we concentrate on the tunnel as entrant into the freight market. The prospectus envisages that the likely outcome of competition is that tariffs would fall by about 20 per cent. This implies that both tunnel and ferry would charge about £150 for an average truck.

We take this case as our starting point. The model used by the promoters suggests that the tunnel is an inferior product in the freight market, taking about 18 per cent of the overall market at equal prices. This reflects the unsuitability of the Dover–Calais route for most freight users. We need also to consider the extent of possible substitution. Our base assumption here is that this is relatively high. The freight market is decidedly a price-sensitive one. Note here again the importance of the distinction between substitutability and inferiority. Even if the tunnel is inferior for many users in this market, it is highly substitutable. They will always be ready to take advantage of it if the price is right.

On this basis, we show in Fig. 18.1 the net revenues the tunnel could anticipate from the freight market assuming that the ferry price is indeed £150. If

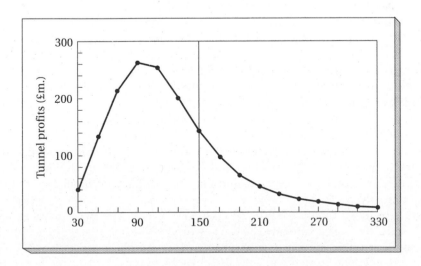

Fig. 18.1. Tunnel Profits for a Range of Tunnel Prices Given a Ferry Tariff of £150
Source: Business Strategy Review (OUP, Spring 1990)

the tunnel also charges £150, these net revenues are around £125 million per year. Fig. 18.1 also shows, however, the profits which the tunnel would make at alternative price levels.

As is general with such curves, the shape is an inverse v, rising to a maximum and then tailing off. Too low prices are insufficiently remunerative: too high prices damage volume. The position of the curve depends principally on the superiority or inferiority of the product. If the tunnel was a poorer substitute for the ferry (road access was worse than anticipated, for example), then the whole curve would shift to the right. The slope of the curve depends primarily on the substitutability of the product. If the two products are very good substitutes, then profits will be very sensitive to the price charged and the curve will slope steeply away from the maximum.

Figure 18.1 shows that if the ferries did indeed charge £150, it would pay the tunnel to undercut it substantially. The profit-maximizing price for the tunnel is about £87, little more than half the ferry level, and at this price it would take the lion's share of the traffic (around three-quarters of it). Profits would be approximately double the level implied in the prospectus projections. The additional volume is very attractive to the tunnel because its marginal costs of operation are so low. The tunnel could not expect, however, to price on this basis without some response from the ferries.

So in Fig. 18.2 we consider precisely the same question from the perspective of the ferries. We assume a single decision-maker for the ferries. (Agreement or merger between the two leading operators by 1993 is highly probable.[2]) What options are available to them if the tunnel price is £150 as in the prospectus scenario? The net revenue curve for the ferries has the same inverse v shape as that of the tunnel, but its position and slope are very different. This is because of the much higher variable cost base of the ferries. If the ferries match a tunnel price of £150 (as in the prospectus) they take most of the traffic and earn slightly more profits than the tunnel (around £150 million). Ferry revenues are much less sensitive to volumes than those of the tunnel, because of their higher costs. But for this reason it does not make sense for them to match the tunnel's price. It appears that if the tunnel did indeed charge £150, the best strategy for the ferries would be to concede volume to the tunnel and push their own price up to around £200. But, of course, this cannot be the final outcome.

We know that it is not attractive to the tunnel to charge £150: we suggested £87 was a better price. On the other hand, if the ferries did succeed in pushing up their prices to these levels it would make sense for the tunnel to follow, at least partially.

Thus we need to consider the pricing strategies of the two parties simultaneously. But we can already see the key qualitative features of the solution. Given the massive variable cost advantage of the tunnel, it must pursue a volume strategy. The best outcome for the ferries is to retreat into a niche market

[2] In 1993 the two operators in fact proposed such an agreement but were blocked by the Office of Fair Trading.

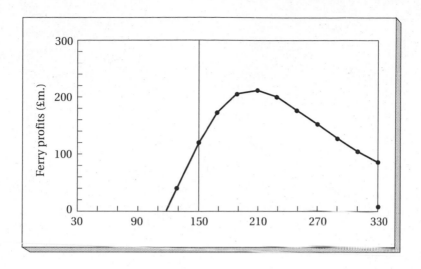

Fig. 18.2. Ferry Profits for a Range of Ferry Prices Given a Tunnel Tariff of £150
Source: *Business Strategy Review* (OUP, Spring 1990)

and take relatively high prices for those sectors of the market to which they can provide a premium product.

Figs. 18.3 and 18.4 summarize the strategies available to the two participants. Fig. 18.3 describes the 'reaction curve' of the tunnel—the most remu-

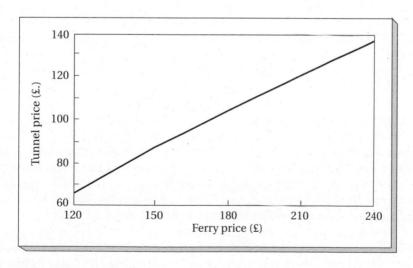

Fig. 18.3. Tunnel Reaction Curve
Source: *Business Strategy Review* (OUP Spring 1990)

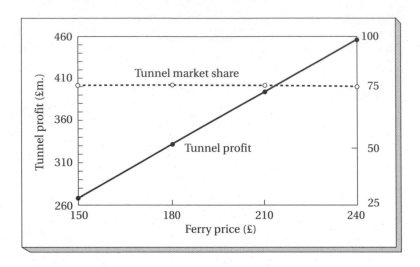

Fig. 18.4. Tunnel Profitability and Market Share on its Reaction Curve
Source: Business Strategy Review (OUP, Spring 1990)

nerative price for the tunnel—at each price which the ferries might set. Clearly, the higher the ferry price the higher the tunnel price should be. But whatever the ferry price is, it always pays the tunnel to undercut it. Since the tunnel is assumed to be both an inferior product and a lower-cost competitor this follows inescapably.

Fig. 18.4 shows the implications of this reaction curve for tunnel profits. The higher the price the ferries set, the higher is the level of tunnel profitability. Fig. 18.4 shows, however, that if the tunnel prices correctly its profits are very sensitive to the level of ferry pricing but its market share is not. Whatever the ferry tariff may be, the best strategy for the tunnel is to price aggressively to win volume.

In Fig. 18.5 and 18.6 we present the analogous options for the ferries. Fig. 18.5 shows the best price for the ferries to charge at different levels of tunnel tariff. The ferry prices rises with the tunnel price, but generally less rapidly. Fig. 18.6 shows how this determines the profit opportunities of the ferries. If the tunnel prices very aggressively—say at £75 or below—the competitive position of the ferries is hopeless. The ferries cannot match these prices: even at much higher prices, more in line with ferry costs, market share is very low. A viable market for the ferries remains only if the tunnel price is higher. As the tunnel price rises, the ferry price rises also, but not as rapidly, so the ferry benefits both from higher margins and from higher market share.

It always pays the tunnel to undercut—with its low marginal costs and inferior product; it always pays the ferries—with their much higher variable costs and variety of routes—to look for premium prices. Thus the two competitors' best strategies are potentially compatible. Fig. 18.7 shows this by bringing together the reaction curves of the two competitors.

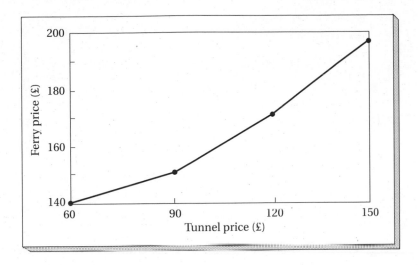

Fig. 18.5. Ferry Reaction Curve
Source: *Business Strategy Review* (OUP, Spring 1990)

There is a point at which the two reaction curves intersect. If the ferries set a price of £150, the best response for the tunnel is to charge £87. If the tunnel sets a price of £87, the best strategy for the ferries is to charge £150. It is easy to see from the diagram that this is the only pair of prices for which this

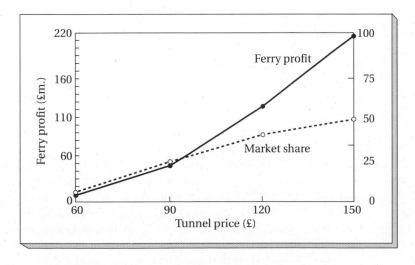

Fig. 18.6. Ferry Profitability and Market Share on its Reaction Curve
Source: *Business Strategy Review* (OUP, Spring 1990)

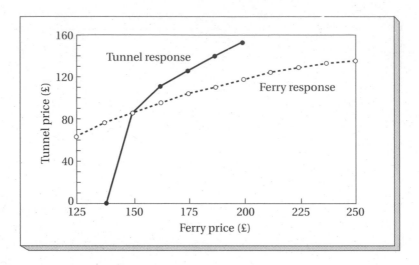

Fig. 18.7. Finding the Equilibrium Price Responses
Source: *Business Strategy Review* (OUP, Spring 1990)

property of mutual consistency of responses holds. If, for example, the tunnel charged £100, the ferries should charge £170: but if the ferries did charge £170, then the tunnel should set a tariff of £130. If the tunnel did charge £130, the ferries should alter their price, and so on. In technical terms, the tunnel price of £87 combined with a ferry price of £150 is a *Nash equilibrium* in strategies. It is the only Nash equilibrium for this particular competitive (non-co-operative) game.

Is such an outcome inevitable? Certainly it is profoundly unsatisfactory for the ferries. Their profits are less than half those they would earn in the prospectus scenario. Tunnel profits, by contrast, are twice as large. *But so long as the tunnel makes appropriate strategic responses, this is the best they can do.* If they were to try to cut prices further to meet the tunnel's competition, then the tunnel should reduce prices still further, and the ferries face the prospect of very low margins and low volumes. If the ferries raise prices, the tunnel will not follow them up fully, and the loss of ferry traffic will more than offset its higher profitability. The ferries earn more profits only if the tunnel makes a strategic mistake. The prospectus scenario (of equal tunnel and ferry prices) is an example of such a strategic mistake. In it, tunnel profits are much less than they should be, and the ferries benefit accordingly. But barring such an error by the tunnel there is no way in which the ferries can compete more effectively. Their only hope of making more profit is to co-operate with the tunnel, tacitly or explicitly.

We see no prospect of such an outcome in the freight market. Prices are set by individual negotiation between operators and large customers, and given the radically different cost structures of the two kinds of operator uncertainty about each other's actions would be an overwhelming obstacle to co-operative action. There are better prospects for keeping prices high in the consumer market, when fares are announced in public brochures, but here too the difference in costs makes concerted action difficult to achieve.

The ferries have very little to offer the tunnel through a collusive arrangement. Their prices are already high relative to the costs of the tunnel and higher ferry profits are only likely to increase the already excessive capacity in the market. Indeed, our analysis suggests that the future of the ferry companies is bleak. We consider some alternative ferry strategies further below.

Influencing market structure

Until now we have assumed that the goal of both parties is short-term profit maximization. We now consider price strategies which might sacrifice immediate profits for longer-term gains. We are concerned here with very short-term marketing activities. It might, for example, pay the tunnel to make introductory offers to gain publicity and familiarize potential customers with its product. Such product launches are common in many markets although probably unnecessary in this: few manufacturers can anticipate having their product introduction celebrated jointly by the Queen of England and the President of France.

Firms can derive long-term gains from short-term behaviour in two ways. They may force rivals to leave the market. Or they can establish a reputation which will deter potential competitors from entering the market or induce actual competitors to modify their behaviour. The strength of both these strategies depends on the extent of commitment to the market and the degree of irrevocability of decisions to enter or to leave the industry.

The construction of the tunnel is irreversible: never have costs been so literally sunk. Once completed, it is there to compete forever with alternative forms of transport, while a ferry can be used on many different routes. This is a source of financial weakness for the company but of competitive strength for the tunnel itself. In particular, it rules out the possibility of predatory action *against* the tunnel since such actions can never lead to the withdrawal of the tunnel (as distinct from Eurotunnel PLC) from the market. It is possible, and by no means improbable, that Eurotunnel PLC will face liquidation or financial reconstruction but the tunnel will continue to transport passengers.

This is an extreme example of a common phenomenon. Where the costs of market entry are large, incumbents must distinguish between the financial strength of the entrant and the competitive strength of the product. If entry occurs, a lower-cost product is unlikely to go away even if the company producing it fails to recover the costs of entry and loses money. The primary objective must be to deter entry, as indeed the ferries did for many years—a tunnel has been technically feasible for decades. But once entry has occurred (even if mistakenly) the nature of the market is forever changed.

Indeed Eurotunnel's financial weakness is in some respects a source of competitive strength. Because it has a huge burden of debt to carry it has to acquire a dominant market position or face acute refinancing problems. If the ferries themselves fear that ET may act as predator, they may rationally decide to quit the market rather than face future losses. Once ET achieves market dominance it will be able to deter potential competitors from entering the market, since it has already endured the substantial sunk costs of entry. A potential entrant, by contrast, will face at least some sunk costs in entering the market. When calculating the cost of competition, therefore, the entrant will always find it more expensive than ET and so long as ET does not set its prices too high this means that entry will never be profitable (even if ET is making substantial profits). This will be true for a ferry operation and also, at some distant date, for a prospective second tunnel.

It follows that the ferries have no long-term strategic threat which need disturb the tunnel but that the tunnel does against the ferries. The tunnel cannot force the ferries to quit the market altogether, but it can force the ferries off the short sea crossings from Britain to France and this is what it should seek to do.

Most 'strategic moves' involve costs as well as benefits if they cause the firm's profit levels to deviate from the short-run maximum. A reputation for being a 'tough character' or an aggressive competitor can act as a substitute for such strategic moves, but the problem with developing reputations is that they require the firm to take tough or aggressive actions, which in themselves may not be rational. Building a business on the basis of irrational decisions would seem to be a poor strategy. The only circumstance where strategic play can both be credible and make sense is where it involves sunk costs—irreversible investments which demonstrate the commitment of the firm to its market and deter competition from potential entrants. The cross-channel market is a striking example. The ferries have negligible sunk costs, and for all their aggressive talk their commitment to the market in the long term is by no means assured. ET, however, by sinking £7 billion into a hole in the ground which can only be recovered by charging tolls to cross the Channel have demonstrated their commitment to their market in dramatic form.

Conclusions

Our conclusions fall into two categories. There are those that arise from the techniques we have used for approaching this problem. There are also some general conclusions about likely strategy choices and outcomes in product launches.

The Channel Tunnel is unusually well documented in terms of the availability of public information, but the data available to us are probably no better than would normally be available to a firm introducing a new product. We have defined how the optimal reactions of competitors can be analysed, so that the response and counter-response which might otherwise take place in real time can be analysed and anticipated in advance. We have shown how the sensitivity of this solution to the key parameters—the perceived superiority/inferiority of the new product and the elasticity of substitution between it and its competitors—can be measured. We have stressed the key difference between superiority and substitutability.

This non-co-operative solution sets lower limits to profits and prices. We have considered the profitability of accommodations, and also the attractiveness of strategies designed to alter the structure of the market in the long term, by driving out the entrant or incumbent. We have also noted the possibility of market segmentation which, in this case, is more readily available to established firms than to the newcomer and may be an attractive response for them.

The naïve approach in what we describe as the prospectus scenario—price similar products similarly—is clearly inappropriate for a process innovator. A firm which owns a lower-cost technology must seek a dominant market share, and the superiority or inferiority of its product, and the degree of substitutability between it and established products, determines the level of prices at which it achieves this, but not the optimal outcome. Incumbents cannot compete effectively in the long run either by improving their product quality or by reducing their own variable costs (unless they reduce them to levels below those of the entrant, which is impossible in this case, and in most cases implausible). Their only viable strategy is product differentiation.

If accommodation is possible, it may be more profitable for all parties but, as we have seen, accommodation between competitors with very different cost structures is particularly difficult to achieve. And, paradoxically, firms with substantial sunk costs may be financially weak, but strong competitors none the less.

19

The Media Revolution

In this chapter, I use the framework of earlier sections, particularly Part II, to suggest how one of the most exciting and controversial of modern industries—audio-visual media—is likely to evolve.[1]

The widespread view that we live in a period of unprecedented technical and economic change is founded almost entirely on what has been happening in electronics and information technology. We can be certain that markets, and technology, will continue to change. The ultimate shape of that technology is something that cannot be known to anybody. Surprisingly, however, there are many who claim to know the ultimate shape of the industry. Indeed there is an emergent conventional wisdom. Let me sum it up.

Size, and global reach, are essential elements in success. Only international companies with large resources at their disposal will prosper. National fragmentation weakens international competitiveness. It is necessary for countries to enlarge the size of their domestic players through mergers and alliances in order to keep up in the new world.

These mergers and alliances must not just be horizontal, but also vertical. Firms must increase the scope of what they do. Unless they take control, by purchase or by alliance, of the new delivery mechanisms, they have little hope of surviving. Convergence of technologies means convergence of firms.

Free trade in audio-visual products inevitably means an increase in the dominance of the United States. (This view, interestingly, is held both by those who welcome it— the American companies involved—and by those in Europe who oppose it.) Finally, individuals and their talents and specialist skills are at risk in these new worlds and require greatly extended protection.

This morning, I wish to argue that all these propositions are certainly superficial and most of them are wrong.

At London Business School, where I teach, it is widely held that the pace of change in modern business is such that cases which are more than a few

[1] A lecture delivered to the European Business Information Conference in Milan on 27 Mar. 1996.

months old are already out of date. That is not a view to which I personally subscribe. I think there are a lot of enduring truths in management, many of which we do not yet know. While browsing through the London Business School archives recently I came across a particularly old case. Five hundred years old, in fact. Nevertheless it is written in what many of you will recognize as the authentic style of the Harvard Business School.

It was 1476, and Pius Third, Chief Executive Officer of the Roman Catholic Corporation, was pacing the floor of his elegant office in Rome, Italy. The Roman Catholic Corporation, with its principal competitor, Islamicorp, then dominated the world media market. The corporation was integrated through all stages of the industry, from production to dissemination, and enjoyed global reach.

Its factories, then known as monasteries, were located world-wide. Products were distributed through multi-media shows, called masses, which took place on synchronized dates right across the Roman Catholic Corporation's universe. Policy had recently favoured a dramatic increase in the size of its superstores. The new cathedrals, as they were known, had been rolled out across Europe and were attracting large audiences right across Roman Catholic Corporation's major markets.

But was what disturbing Pius was the news from England and Germany: the invention of printing. This revolutionary new technology threatened to change the whole market and industry within which Roman Catholic Corporation operated. Pius had commissioned a report on these developments, and it was that report, prepared by one of his aides, Signor Borgia, which threatened to shake even the sturdy foundations of RCC's Vatican City headquarters complex.

The lesson of the Borgia report was stark and clear. Borgia noted that the new technology implied massive economies of scale. In the old days, the only method of reproducing material was for monks to act as copyists. The set-up costs of the new printing technology were larger, but once incurred copy after copy could be run off at relatively low cost. From this, Borgia concluded that only a few large international players could survive, only those that had the volume to derive most benefit from scale economies. It was hardly likely, Borgia argued, that there would be further proliferation of new written media. The advantages of established literature were too great. There would be fewer books, and Roman Catholic Corporation and Islamicorp would tighten their dominance of the world market.

Next, Borgia noted that control of printing was the key to controlling the audio-visual market. The main threat to Roman Catholic Corporation came from this sector. Borgia painted a picture in which the Englishman, Caxton, would become Pope within a decade, unless Roman Catholic Corporation moved quickly, through acquisition and alliances, to get control of the printing presses.

Next, Borgia suggested that the boundaries which had traditionally existed between written and painted material, between literature and art, would soon vanish. The same technology would soon be able to reproduce both kinds of material. Convergent technology meant convergent firms and convergent content. Finally, he predicted that Latin would become a general world language within fifty years. The importance of scale economies and global reach meant that the dominant linguistic standard would sweep the world. How else could the inhabitants of a global village talk to each other?

Pius was shocked by Borgia's conclusions, but found them compelling. 'Smart man, Borgia', he thought. 'Must have him murdered before he gets too big for his Cardinal's hat.'

The Borgia report was, of course, wrong in almost all essentials. Appended to it in the London Business School files I found a later report from Johannes Keay, a poor British scholar who, one century later, had reviewed how printing had actually affected the world audio-visual market. Keay noted that, far from being more concentrated, the market had rapidly become more fragmented. Indeed some historians traced the long decline of the Roman Catholic Corporation, which had begun at around that time, directly to the invention of printing. Printing did not reinforce the dominance of Latin: printing destroyed it. There had been an explosion of material in vernacular languages. Art and literature, far from coming together, had in fact moved apart. Each had come to assume functions far beyond the religious and outside the control of the Church. And finally, printers had had very little influence on the way in which audio-visual markets had evolved.

Johannes Keay went on to explain why Borgia had got it so badly wrong. The most important point, he noted, was that the cheapness of the new technology was far more significant than the scale economies associated with it. The result of that cheapness was a proliferation of companies, activities, and products in the market-place. This proliferation led to all stages of production becoming highly competitive, and once such vigorous competition was universal there were no benefits from vertical integration. Printing and origination of both literary and artistic material had flourished outside the control of the traditional integrated suppliers.

You can go on from there to see the shape of the industry which did emerge from the printing revolution. It was organized on a tripartite structure, with the chain of production broken down into three main elements. First there is the talent which creates the original material. There is the delivery mechanism—in the case of books this includes both printing and bookselling—which provides the technical services needed for dissemination. And there is publishing, lying between the two. Publishers co-ordinate these functions, undertake product marketing, and bear the risks involved. Once, all these three stages of the audio-visual process had been controlled by the Roman Catholic Church: the emergence of competition broke up that structure.

Now it is not just books in which we observe that tripartite structure. In music too the three elements of the production chain—talent, publishing, delivery—are reflected in a division between artists, publishers, and those who disseminate material, either by pressing discs or by selling through retail outlets. In films also there is a tripartite structure. Originating talent lies among the artists—actors, writers, and directors. Delivery is undertaken by technicians, cinemas, and video duplicators. Studios—misnamed—in fact serve the same role in the film industry that publishers do for written media: they take on the functions of co-ordination, marketing, risk-taking. All the principal media industries are organized in this tripartite way.

Historically, however, electronic media have been organized differently. Since broadcasting began sixty years ago, integrated firms have controlled talent, publication, and delivery. The reason is straightforward. Terrestrial bandwidth, which has traditionally been the only way in which electronic signals could be delivered to customers, has been scarce and has been allocated by government. The people to whom it has been allocated have enjoyed market power which has enabled them to control the whole integrated production process. That scarcity is rapidly disappearing and will soon have vanished entirely. And that fact is the key to understanding why industry structure is changing, and how it will evolve.

I believe the likely outcome for electronic media will be, as it was with printing, the emergence of this tripartite structure. The services of origination, of publishing, and of delivery and dissemination, historically integrated, will start to come apart. In every industry—as was once true in this—the power in the value chain rests with those who control the point in it at which resources are scarce. This scarcity was, but is no longer, at the point of delivery. The winners in future markets will be those who have resources that will be scarce in the future. Let's look and see who they are.

At which stage of that tripartite structure are scarce resources truly to be found? The greatest scarcity is in originating talent. By that I do not mean that there is a shortage of material, but that there is scarcity of material of quality. Publishing, the second stage of the value chain, requires specialist skills. These specialist skills are also in limited supply. Control of the process does *not* lie with those who own the delivery mechanism, any more than print media are dominated by printers or by those who run bookshops. Those who believe that the future media giants will be Bell Atlantic or British Telecom have simply not understood either how traditional media markets work or how new ones will evolve.

This analysis gives us a broad indication of how media industries are likely to be structured in the future. Electronic publishing, like other forms of publishing, will find plenty of room for both large and small companies.There will be large companies with cross-media and international capabilities, and equally many smaller players whose strengths are based on understanding both the customers and the product in a particular niche. I do not believe that there is either reason or necessity for any publisher to be integrated into either talent or delivery, which require distinct skills—the creative talent of origination, or the engineering and organizational skills required to configure a telecommunications network. We will observe no more vertical integration here in the long run than we do in books or in music.

And what of US dominance? Perhaps the most remarkable thing about the invention of printing, as I have described, was the growth of material in both volume and variety. We can already see that the effect of electronic publishing is exactly the same. And we also know that when people can get local products at reasonable cost that is what, for much of the time, they prefer. The notion that electronic media are going to be controlled by a few standards and a few firms is wrong: we should be more concerned about the opposite. A better-founded fear is that there will be too much material around, and that we will be swamped and confronted by difficulties of selection. But that is why the future role of the publisher is so important. Brands, reputation, and quality certification, and the names, experience, and capabilities to deliver on these, are the real keys to future development.

In my introduction I said that there are many who look ahead at the future of electronic publishing and see a clear vision even if it is often a vision that they do not like. It is a world of big corporations, who talk with an American accent. The future lies with Microsoft, with Time Warner, with Bell Atlantic.

The mistake in all this, which is so characteristic generally of approaches to changes in business structure, is to project the immediate past into the indefinite future. We should remind ourselves that Microsoft did not exist twenty years ago. We should also ask ourselves how it is possible today to run a company that owns Time, Fortune, Warner studios, Warner music, and Little Brown publishers and loses money: the answer is that you are called Time Warner and you incurred massive debt to buy these excellent businesses for rather more than they are worth.

What I have tried to do today is to take a more detached view of history. One that emphasizes that the key to the future is cheap dissemination. One that believes that the result of this will actually be more pluralism, fragmentation, and above all variety of products and of firms. And it is a vision that emphasizes that the talents which will be truly scarce, and truly valuable, in that new world are the skills which are needed to guide others through that pluralism, fragmentation, and variety to what they really want and those things that have true and enduring value.

20

Firms and Industries

Most popular business literature describes success, but the study of failures is often more illuminating. This chapter begins with surveys of two industries—once hugely successful, recently in serious decline—the Lloyd's insurance market and the British horse-racing industry. The Saatchi story tells how a business which for a time epitomized 1980s Britain came to the edge of financial collapse. There is less doubt that the next market I consider—retail financial services—has a future, but plenty of room for doubt, and misunderstanding, about the nature of that future. And I conclude by examining two generic issues for all firms and all industry— what is the core business, and when do industries consolidate?

INSURANCE WITH COFFEE

When Edward Lloyd ran the coffee shop which was to become Lloyd's of London, he certainly did not envisage that his customers would end up suing each other.[1] But he did help to establish the peculiar character of an institution which was ultimately to behave in that way.

Lloyd's is, in essence, a network. A network is a somewhat unstructured group of business relationships in which information is exchanged and in which each trader draws, to some extent, on the collective skills of the totality. We find networks in areas as disparate as Silicon Valley, the knitwear firms of the Scottish borders, the metalworkers of the Brescia valley in northern Italy, or the groups of subcontractors which surround the leading Japanese automobile producers. The whole City of London is a financial services network.

As a means of doing business, networks have considerable advantages. They are flexible, and they can often combine the advantages of specialization and the massed resources of big organizations with the motivation and responsiveness of small firms. That is why many of these networks have been, and remain, successful.

[1] *Daily Telegraph* (9 Mar. 1992).

But networks also have problems and difficulties. They rely on the establishment of trust between the parties to the network, and on the similarity of their background. The rules of the game are generally informal, and implied. Networks operate, and have to operate, as clubs, with insiders and outsiders. This can work well. But these strengths of a network can also turn out to be weaknesses. Networks are good at making small changes, but bad at making big ones, which need a sense of central direction. The cohesion of the network, which is its value to insiders, can be a danger to outsiders. The same organizational structures which perform so well in sectors of Italian industry are the same ones which underpin the Mafia. The advantages of dealing through stable relationships with people one knows can degenerate into nepotism or old boy networks.

So the problem, and the challenge, for Lloyd's has been to find a mechanism for responding to major changes in the world insurance market, and to ensure that it can retain the advantages of a clublike organization without the incestuousness which can easily go with it. The current danger is that these long-term issues are overwhelmed by the urgency of Lloyd's immediate difficulties.

It is a fact that Lloyd's, like most of the world's general insurance industry, made huge losses in 1988 and bigger ones in 1989. It is a fact that Lloyd's, like most of the world's insurance industry, has to meet large and unpredictable bills for asbestosis and pollution claims from many years ago. There is no one, except the Names on the syndicates which incurred these losses, who is going to pick up the bill. No government will do it, other Names are not going to be willing to do it, and future members of Lloyd's will certainly not be willing to do it. The only hope of relief is to offset these past losses by profitable future trading. And the more people squabble about the past, the fainter the hope of achieving that is likely to be.

Because the fundamental problems of Lloyd's are not the ones posed by the 1988 losses. In the 1980s Lloyd's was largely successful in cleaning up its act, imposing a proper regulatory structure, expelling crooks, and eliminating baby syndicates. The problem was that a period in which too much had been taken out of the market in improper and illegal ways was followed by a period in which too much was taken out of the market in entirely proper and legal ways. The cost base of Lloyd's grew far faster than inflation, and faster than the market for Lloyd's products could stand. That cost escalation was in part the result of the churning that afflicts every financial market—the generation of transactions which increase costs but offers no substantive benefit to the final customer. In the life insurance market, churning is found when dubious salesmen propose the surrender of old policies and the taking out of new ones. In the stock market, brokers recommend endless and costly switching between securities. In the general insurance market, the same phenomenon was seen in the spiral of reinsurance and re-reinsurance. For Lloyd's that meant—and means—a cost structure which employed too many people, paid too much. It also means that risks had been allocated and reallocated so many different times that no one could know what the structure of the risks that had been taken on actually was.

Lloyd's will survive if, and only if, it can re-establish a profitable business. That is why, if the emphasis of the 1980s had to be on regulation, the emphasis of the 1990s has to be on management. The latest howls of outrage set the market back if they distract attention from that change of focus.

Networks are alternative forms of business organization to markets, or to hierarchies. If relationships cannot be built on trust, or confidence, the players must deal with each other on arm's length terms, or live in a world in which one party can tell the other what to do. There is no shortage of hierarchies in the world insurance market—that is how every major insurance company is organized, and Lloyd's particular distinctiveness is precisely that it is not organized like that. Perhaps Lloyd's must become an insurance market-place, with value for syndicate participation and corporate insurers as well as Names. But it must first try to make its existing structures work. The debate over Lloyd's is not just about the future of a London insurance market. It is over the capacity of flexible and innovative forms of business organization to survive in an increasingly pressured, regulated, and litigious world.

THE SPORT OF SHEIKHS

Horse-racing may be the sport of kings, or more recently sheikhs. But it is also a business.[2] Viewed as such, it is remarkably unprofitable. There are almost no other industries in which, over a long period of time, revenues have covered less than half of costs. There are also almost no other industries in which participation is such fun. The one fact explains the other.

Racing costs around £250 million a year to run. What racegoers contribute, and what sponsors pay in order to provide their name to races and their champagne to clients, amounts only to about £70 million. So racecourses (mostly) lose money; trainers (largely) lose money; and racehorse owners (almost invariably) lose money. Much the largest part of the difference between costs and revenues is made up by the losses of owners. Owning a racehorse will leave you no change from £200 per week. Most of that is the cost of training but you will have to add insurance, vet's fees, and the capital loss which almost all horses suffer over their racing career. Prize money in Britain covers only about one-quarter of these costs. That is why some of the biggest owners are looking increasingly at the larger prizes available in other countries.

Despite these losses, the number of horses in training increased steadily through the 1980s. If owning a horse (or part of a horse—only a minority of owners actually own a whole horse) has been a lousy investment, racehorse

---

[2] *Daily Telegraph* (3 Apr. 1992).

ownership is also a form of conspicuous consumption, and the 1980s were good years for conspicuous consumption. But the 1990s are not, and since 1989 the number of new horses being trained to race has been falling steadily.

And yet the strangest aspect of racing as a business is that it supports another, unconnected, but much larger business. The £250 million which racing costs to put on can be compared with the £4 billion which punters bet every year on the results. You do not have to ask permission, or pay, to bet on what someone else is doing. You can back one party or another to win the election, or bet on men arriving from outer space, without having to make any contribution to the costs of the election campaign or the necessary expenses of the men from outer space. So a £4 billion industry can use the product of a £250 million one and need pay nothing for the privilege.

It need pay nothing; but in reality off-course betting has paid an annual levy to racing since it was legalized in 1960. Since then the levy has grown, but government tax on betting has grown even faster. The levy has yielded between £30 million and £40 million to racing while betting tax now nets the government rather more than £300 million from racing.

But off-course betting is in long-term decline. Put your head around the door of a betting shop and you will see why. The problem is partly the result of regulation which prevents betting shops being made attractive lest they persuade anyone to go in. Control of betting in the UK is based on the principle of unstimulated demand and the environment of the shops is indeed one of unstimulated demand. The punters are typically those C2 social groups whose support, we are told, the Conservatives must retain if they are to do well. So gambling is very sensitive to the economic cycle. When times are good, people spend relatively more on gambling; when they are bad, gambling expenditure is one of the first things to be cut back.

The finances of the betting industry have been under pressure as well. Of the major chains, only Ladbrokes is in secure long-term ownership. Coral, another diversification error by Bass the brewer, is up for sale, and William Hill is part of the troubled Brent Walker empire. The other large force in bookmaking is the Tote, a bizarre organization run by Lord Wyatt, which enjoys a monopoly of pool betting on racing. For many years this monopoly has remained under-exploited. The Tote was the only legal means of off-course betting for decades but off-course betting did not thrive until Ladbrokes was allowed in on the act. More recently the Tote has used its modest profits to acquire for itself a chain of still more modestly profitable betting shops. The Tote's status is an arcane legal matter (akin to that of TSB before its flotation) and no one knows who owns it or its assets.

The declining fortunes of both racing and bookmaking came into direct collision when they tried to determine an appropriate levy for the next fiscal year. The bookmakers offered less, racing demanded more, and the government-appointed members of the Levy Board, which distributes the punters' largess, failed to persuade the two parties to split the difference. An unusual fairy godmother—the Treasury—came to the rescue with a 0.25 per cent reduction in betting duty which enabled both sides to get something out of the negotiations and allowed the Home Secretary to please everyone, something which home secretaries rarely find an opportunity to do.

But it is not wise to rely on fairy godmothers reappearing. Britain needs fewer, brighter racecourses with a range of facilities that will attract customers for 300 days a year, not ten. It needs prize money that is internationally competitive, and the people most likely to provide that prize money are bookmakers and their customers. The betting industry needs to shake off its dowdy appearance and attract customers who will still be customers in the twenty-first century. There is already a long list of great British industries—from shipbuilding to motor cycles—which have slid into terminal decline. Racing has a last chance to make sure it is not one of them (see Fig. 20.1).

Who pays for racing (£m.)

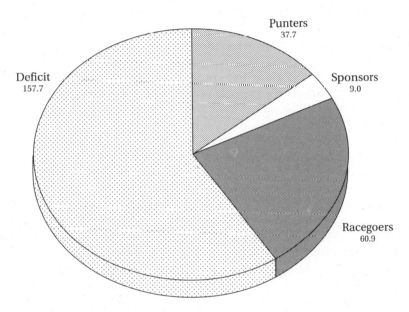

Fig. 20.1. Who Pays for Racing?

THE SAATCHI STORY

With the departure of Maurice Saatchi to establish his New Saatchi agency, one of the great episodes of hubris in British business history comes to an end.[3] Since one of the lessons is to think long and hard before listening to

---

[3] *Daily Telegraph* (17 Jan. 1995).

business school professors, it is worth taking a few moments to remember the story. Saatchi & Saatchi established itself in the 1970s as one of the most respected creative advertising agencies around. The agency became one of the best known in Britain, and played a major role in promoting Mrs Thatcher's election campaigns.

The guru who then came on the scene was Theodore Levitt, a Harvard Business School professor whose most famous work is called *The Marketing Imagination*. Levitt's key thesis has been that the thinking of businessmen is too often constrained by what they already do, and that they are too inclined to define their products in narrow, technical terms. From Levitt's perspective, the *Daily Telegraph* is not just a newspaper; it is a learning and entertainment experience. In future, customers will experience learning and entertainment in new ways, which is why the *DT* is now available on the Internet.

Levitt's early emphasis had been on seeing the product in the broadest possible context (see pp. 199–202 below). Don't think soap, think solutions to cleaning problems. But in the 1980s, together with many other American business people, Levitt discovered that there was a world outside the United States. It seems to have been the import of Japanese cars in large numbers, together with the resultant emergence of a large US trade deficit, which drew attention to this phenomenon. It is said that the newly appointed director of international operations of a major US corporation discovered only at the airport that you need a passport to travel outside the United States. That story tells it all; the old parochialism, the new *naïveté*.

A market has both a product and a geographic dimension. Levitt had begun by stressing the need to expand the product dimension. The need now, he argued, was to expand the geographic dimension. This wisdom was encapsulated in a 1983 article in the *Harvard Business Review*, and it was that article which fired Maurice Saatchi's imagination. Only those who visualized their market in global terms, Levitt claimed, could survive in the new business environment. Following this thesis, Saatchi determined to create the world's first truly global advertising business. Breaking the limits of the marketing imagination still further he aimed subsequently to establish the world's first multi-disciplinary consulting business. Levitt joined the Saatchi board. At the peak of the Saatchi myth, in 1987, Maurice made his famous pitch for Midland Bank. There could hardly be a less appropriate target for the global vision. Midland had been crippled by its disastrous foray into retail banking in the United States. In the end, Saatchi's experience was not to be so much better.

The realities of globalization are a bit more complicated, as is often the case with realities. There had been a massive internationalization of production of many kinds of manufactured goods. In the 1950s, the car industry was structured on essentially national lines. Most cars bought in Britain were made in Britain, and the equivalent was true in France, Germany, and the United States. All that has changed, and we now have a global car industry. It is slightly pedantic, but nevertheless important, to point out that this does not mean we have a global car market. The cars which are bought, the prices which are paid for them, and the ways in which they are sold still vary substantially between countries. Globalization is real, but it is important to understand what it means; and when you do understand what it means, you also understand that the day of the truly global advertising market is a long way off.

The basic Saatchi mistake was to misunderstand the nature of that company's competitive advantage. It rested on the company's creative team, the reputation that went with it, and the client relationships that went with it. Saatchi added nothing to most of the businesses it bought—which were mainly ones that already had these assets themselves. The final irony is that it remained to Maurice Saatchi himself to demonstrate that the truly valuable assets of an advertising agency—the team, the reputation, the relationships— do not belong to the company and its shareholders, but to those who work in it, and take them home with them every night. High public profile, and hyped slogans, are not a substitute for careful thinking about the specific nature of a business. If there is a role for business schools and their professors, that is where it is to be found.

BEST ADVICE

Amidst the flurries over the miss-selling of personal pensions and the formation of the Personal Investment Authority, there is one simple fact which it suits everyone to ignore.[4] Financial advice of high quality is simply too scarce and too expensive a commodity to be widely available.

It is easy to see why the regulatory objective is to ensure that everyone receives best advice. Everyone ought to be able to dine at the Ritz. And it is easy to see why the position of the regulators is that, give or take the occasional glitch which can be remedied by rapid retraining, everyone does receive best advice. Meals at the Ritz are what the industry provides.

But it is only necessary to consider what the average life insurance salesman earns to see that they are never going to produce advice of the highest quality. 'If you're so smart, why aren't you rich?' is not a silly question to address to people in the financial services business, and in fact people in the financial services business who are smart mostly are rich. True, there are also some life insurance salesmen who are rich, but that mostly reflects their sales abilities rather than their financial acumen. The disgraced—if insufficiently disgraced—Roger Levitt illustrates the problem. A salesman of genius, and a hopeless businessman.

To see the impossibility of the dream, look at other types of retailing. There was a time when you bought groceries or clothes from skilled, knowledgeable,

---

[4] *Daily Telegraph* (18 Apr. 1994).

tradespeople. Mostly, that time has gone. We pick our groceries or clothes from the shelves ourselves, and we take them as we find them. If the retailer is a good one, the shop assistants are polite, helpful, and friendly, but largely ignorant of what it is they are selling. Individual advice from knowledgeable tradesmen is available, in specialist food shops and boutiques, but only at the top end of the market with prices to match.

It is difficult to think of any commodities for which careful tailored advice is available to a mass market. If you go to a travel agent, you will quickly learn that people who can readily understand the intricacies of international air fares and timetables will not often be working as a clerk in a travel agency. They can hand you a package holiday brochure over the counter, and mostly do. And how much do you value the advice provided by a used car dealer or an estate agent? You can get personal assistance from your doctor (but the government pays for that) or from a lawyer (but only if the government pays for it, or if you are very rich). Mostly, we opt for self-service from Sainsbury or Marks & Spencer, and we wish they sold holidays, cars, and houses as well. Customized products simply cost too much for most people to want to buy.

So why does anyone think financial services are likely to be different, or ought to be different? Now the analogy is not exact. When you go to Marks & Spencer, you know you need a pair of socks and the question is simply which pair; when you buy financial services, you may not know whether you need a PEP or an endowment policy (if, indeed, you need either). And if you buy the wrong pair of socks, you find out pretty soon. If you buy the wrong pension, you may not find out until it is too late.

But the fundamental problem remains. Skilled financiers are paid even more than skilled grocers or skilled tailors, and their services are never going to be cheap. You cannot will the end of best advice without willing the means, who is going to provide it. And the notion that commission disclosure is an answer to this problem is a puzzling one. In a market where the central failure is that customers find it difficult to assimilate or understand the information they receive, why should we expect that giving them more information about the way the product is sold is going to help. Do we really think that printing 'We made fifty pence profit from selling these socks' on the label would help you find the right pair? Commission disclosure has little value unless you can judge the quality of the service, and the products, that go along with the commission. But if you could judge these things, the problem we are trying to solve would never have arisen in the first place.

So what is the answer? What has happened to socks does illustrate the way ahead. It is not feasible to provide a skilled clothing adviser for every customer, but it is possible to provide very highly skilled head office staff who buy clothes, or groceries, from the best value available on the market and ruthlessly pressure suppliers to make sure they provide just that. You do not get socks that are exquisitely matched to your skin tones and the size of your feet, but for most people the system is adequate. And in truth people probably differ less in their needs for financial services than they do in the clothes that suit them.

The future lies with banks and building societies developing their role as retailers. They will have to learn to exert the same tight central control over both their suppliers and their branches that supermarkets do (although the simplest of systems would stop you selling personal pensions to 56-year-old miners). And they will provide a product range that may not be ideal for everyone's needs but for most people will do well enough. And modern food and clothing retailers have found that paying staff by commission has simply ceased to be a sensible commercial practice. You give targets to managers, but not to sales assistants.

Our history is that we have pretended to a system which offered quality financial advice of a kind and level which could never conceivably have been delivered, and was too often in reality provided by commissioned salesmen who knew little more than their customers. Attempts to make the pretence a reality will fail. The future will see financial services sold in different ways.

THE CORE BUSINESS: DO PEACHES NEED CREAM?

Granada's bid for Forte is an audacious attempt to create Britain's largest leisure business—one that would stretch from Coronation Street to the Savoy Hotel, from Newport Pagnell service area to television rentals.[5]

But is there such a thing as a leisure business? Or is there just a range of different things that different people do with their spare time? In the last decade, many companies have posed the question 'what business are we in?'

The intellectual spur came from a series of articles by Ted Levitt (Levitt 1986), the American marketing guru behind Maurice Saatchi's aspirations to create a global business. Levitt blasted companies for what he described as 'marketing myopia'.

Railroads had gone into terminal decline, but only because they had limited their horizons to the tracks. After all, neither people nor goods had stopped moving. If only railroads had seen themselves as being in the transportation business—if they had been customer-oriented rather than product-oriented—they might still be prosperous today.

Levitt acknowledged that no amount of product improvement could have saved the buggy whip industry from Henry Ford's model T. But, he explained, if the buggy whip people had only appreciated that they too were in the transportation business, they might have survived as makers of fan belts.

Levitt's analysis of the petroleum industry was particularly forceful. Firms such as Exxon and Amoco, BP and Shell, had for too long laboured under the misapprehension that they were oil companies. Levitt told them they were in

[5] *Financial Times* (6 Oct. 1995; 1 Dec. 1995).

the energy business. If they continued to confine their attention to oil and gasoline, they risked going the way of the buggy whip manufacturers.

His advice was influential. Oil companies, fearful for the future of their markets after the 1974 oil shock, diversified into other energy markets. The results ranged from disappointing to the disastrous. Few of these activities survive.

The leading oil companies continue, as they always have, to make their considerable profits out of selling oil. And this should be no surprise. The Levitt thesis is fundamentally misconceived. The term 'business'—as in the question 'what business are we in'—conflates two distinct concepts: the market and the industry. The market is defined by consumer needs and markets reflect consumer demands. The industry is defined by related firm capabilities and industries are based on supply technologies.

Thus washing machines and laundries are in the same market, because both are means of cleaning clothes. Washing machines and refrigerators are products of the same industry, despite their wholly different purposes, because each is a white box with a motor and is sold through similar distribution channels.

Confusing the industry with the market is one of the most frequently repeated mistakes in corporate strategy. There was an energy market—coal and oil served similar purposes. But there was no energy industry—the skills needed to dig for coal were different from those needed to manage an integrated oil company, as firms who tried to do both discovered.

The buggy whip manufacturers might have made fan belts, but there is no reason to think that they would have been any good at these activities: no reason to think that they would have performed better than any other firm which saw airlines or automobile components as a new market opportunity. And the examples Levitt used to make his case in fact demonstrated his error. At the time he wrote, DuPont and Corning had continued to succeed in the nylon and glass businesses. But they had not done it by diversifying into substitutes like cotton or tinplate. What they had done was to find new uses for their core products and key skills. Levitt had simply confused the evolution of an industry with the evolution of a market.

So how should a firm define its core business? Is BT in the integrated provision of telecommunications products (as it once thought when it bought Mitel, a hardware supplier)? Or is it in the international provision of telecommunications services (as it next thought when it bought McCaw, an American cellular phone company)? Or is it in the business of global data transmission for multi-channels (the rationale of its current alliance with MCI)? Or is it just a phone company?

The way to resolve these questions is not necessarily inconclusive debate about whether buggy whips are instruments of correction or transportation accessories. Even if that question could be resolved, it would not tell their manufacturers whether to diversity into thumbscrews or motor cars. The right approach is to identify what are the distinctive skills and capabilities of the firm and ask what are the markets in which these yield competitive advantage.

Posing the question that way shows why it was right for Marks & Spencer to diversify into financial services (because that capitalized on their reputation with customers) but wrong for BT to own an equipment manufacturer.

And it also shows why there is no such thing as the leisure business. We have heard about the leisure business before—from Rank when it attempted to buy Watneys, from Bass when it mistakenly acquired Horizon Holidays. Package tours and an evening in the pub may represent alternative claims on consumer expenditure, but that does not mean that there is a leisure industry of which both are part.

AT&T is to be divided into three parts—equipment, global information systems, and telecommunications. The company's equipment manufacturing activities date back to the era when it enjoyed almost complete dominance of US telecommunications. AT&T's involvement in computers is more recent. The firm perceived (rightly) that the boundaries between data processing and data transmission were becoming blurred, and concluded (wrongly) that it should therefore blur them in managing its own business.

With the split up, AT&T has recognized two general lessons. Convergence of technology need not imply convergence of firms. And vertical integration which makes sense for a monopoly often loses its rationale when markets become competitive. These are lessons others would do well to learn.

Most of all, those behind the current wage of media mergers. They talk of nothing but integration and convergence. The merger of Disney and ABC/Capital Cities is hailed as the deal of the decade. Westinghouse has just bought CBS. And Time Warner has followed the pack with its acquisition of Ted Turner's media empire.

Michael Ovitz, heir apparent to the new Disney kingdom, boasts that attaching a studio to a network gives Disney distribution of its product. But will Disney, with a repertoire that its competitors would kill for, encounter any difficulty obtaining distribution of its product? Must Kellogg buy Sainsbury to get access to its shelves?

The fact that peaches and cream go well together is not a reason why dairy farmers should grow peaches. Nor does solicitors' need for pink tape mean that every law firm must acquire a ribbon manufacturer. It is hard to believe that industries could be restructured on the basis of arguments as superficial as these. Yet not only is that happening in the world's media business; its well-paid executives are hailed as business titans for perceiving these connections between products.

Now there can be good arguments for convergence and integration. Perhaps there are cost savings from combined production—feeding the cows with peaches might give you the joint product more cheaply than mixing them in the bowl. Perhaps the skills of the peach grower are readily applicable to dairy farming. And if the ability to make pink tape is a rare skill, then taking control of its producers may enable you to hold your legal rivals to ransom.

But absent these factors—significant cost savings from integrated manufacture, common distinctive capabilities, or the opportunity to lever market power from one market into another—integration and convergence give no advantage, and limit your ability to seek the most effective suppliers, distributors, and co-producers.

Firms should always ask whether a new activity extends the application of their distinctive capabilities. If it does not it is no more your business than it is anyone else's.

WHEN FIRMS CONSOLIDATE

The retail financial services scene is changing rapidly.[6] The last few months have seen the announcement of the merger between Lloyds and TSB, the acquisition of the Cheltenham and Gloucester and National and Provincial Building Societies, and the merger and planned conversion of the Halifax and Leeds. In the insurance sector, Norwich Union has proposed to demutualize to pursue acquisitions, while smaller companies, like Provident Mutual and London Life, have decided to throw in the towel. More of all these developments will follow.

Peter Birch, who runs Abbey National, has no doubt of the cause: 'Basic economics dictate that only companies which have a dominant market share will survive long term. Here I cite as example, Unilever and Procter & Gamble.' Mr Birch's example does not support his argument. The once dominant Unilever used to sell one packet of detergent in two in Britain. After years of decline, that figure had fallen last year to one in three, and following the Persil Power fiasco may now be as low as one in four. If there is any general lesson from basic economics, it is that dominant firms rarely maintain market share (Table 20.1).

Consolidation in financial services will happen, but not for Mr Birch's reasons. Competitive markets drive the weak into the cold, or into the arms of

Table 20.1. Market leadership, 1979–1986 (average of 54 industries)

	Share in 1979 (%)	Share in 1986 (%)	Change (%)
Leading firm	21.9	20.1	–2.1
Second firm	12.2	12.1	–0.1
Third–fifth firm	3.8	3.5	–0.3

Davies *et al.* (1991).

[6] *Financial Times* (20 Oct. 1995).

the strong. Where competition is weak, as for decades it was among banks and building societies and between life and general insurers, these tendencies are muted. Under-performing firms are protected by high prices and gentlemanly restraints on competition. That is why we have too many banks and building societies and too many insurers, many of them inadequately equipped to cope with a competitive world. In the 1980s, banks fought for market share, building societies stopped getting together to fix interest rates, and the tariff agreement and commissions agreement among insurance companies disappeared. The whole retail financial services sector became much more competitive, and what we are seeing is the working out of that process.

The relevant economic theory is that actions to increase competition usually have the apparently paradoxical effect of promoting consolidation. We saw this first after the 1956 Restrictive Practices Act abolished most cartels, and a wave of mergers followed. We saw it again when Edward Heath outlawed Resale Price Maintenance, and set the stage for the growth of Sainsbury and Tesco. That growth came about not because Sainsbury and Tesco were bigger than their rivals (the Co-op still dominated British food retailing at that time, and on the Birch theory would so so today). Sainsbury and Tesco grew not because they were big but because they were better, and a more competitive market allowed them to profit fully from their superior performance.

The end of the Net Book Agreement will lead to this consolidation in bookselling. Not necessarily to the same public benefit, since it is the wide range of bookshops, efficient and inefficient, which helps to sell books, and makes browsing a pleasure. But the rule that consolidation follows competition will apply here too, and the industry will focus around bigger claims.

Sometimes—where the cartel has been so strong that it has not only limited competition among established firms but has enabled them to keep new entrants out—fragmentation precedes consolidation. The US airline industry is a paradigm example. The initial response to deregulation was a frenzy of expansion and new entry. But the industry became even more concentrated than before. The difference was that the survivors were the efficient rather than the established. Delta, American, and United prospered; Eastern and Pan Am failed.

The same will happen in the European airline industry, as competition gathers pace. And in other European industries—like telecommunications and financial services—which, slowly wiping the sleep from their eyes, stumble into a more competitive era. There will ultimately be consolidation, but consolidation around the effective rather than the large. And—as in the US airline industry—some of the giants of the past who see even greater size and global alliances as the route to the future will not be there to see the future when it comes.

The British beer market is going through the same transformation. Increased competition following the Monopolies Commission report led to the seemingly contradictory forces of new entry and consolidation among the established players particularly in the retail sector. When all this has settled down, the industry though less vertically integrated will probably be more concentrated than before. But market share will be based on a company's effectiveness rather than historic position. That, not the durability of dominance, is the basic economics of industry structure.

REFERENCES

ABERNATHY, W. J., and HAYES, R. H. (1980), 'Managing our Way to Economic Decline', Harvard Business Review (July–Aug.), 67–77.

ALBERT, M. (1991), *Capitalisme contre capitalisme*, Paris: Seuil (*Capitalism against Capitalism* (1993), Whurr).

ALCHIAN, A., and DEMSETZ, H. (1972), 'Production, Information Costs and Economic Organization', *American Economic Review*, 62 (Dec.), 777–95.

ANSOFF, H. I. (1965), *Corporate Strategy*, New York: McGraw Hill.

BAIN, J. S. (1959), *Industrial Organization*, New York: Wiley.

BARSTOW, A. and HENSON, W. (trans.) (1991), *The BMW Story: A Company in its Time*, London: Sidgwick and Jackson.

BERLE, A. A., and MEANS, G. C. (1933), *The Modern Corporation and Private Property*, London: Harcourt Brace.

BISHOP, M. (1994), 'A Survey of Corporate Governance', *The Economist*, 29 January.

BLINDER, A. (1991), *Profit Maximisation and International Competition*, Amex Essay Prize Volume, Oxford: Oxford University Press.

—— (1995), 'Should the Formerly Socialist Economies Look East or West for a Model?', in J. P. Fitoussi (ed.), *Economics in a Changing World*, London: Macmillan.

Boston Consulting Group (1975), *Strategy Alternatives for the British Motorcycle Industry*, London: HMSO.

BURROUGH, B., and HELYAR, J. (1990), *Barbarians at the Gate*, New York: Harper & Row.

BUZZELL, R. D., and GALE, B. T. (1987), *The PIMS Principles*, New York: Free Press.

Cadbury Committee Report (1992), *Report of the Cadbury Committee on the Financial Aspects of Corporate Governance*, London: Gee.

CAMPBELL, A., and GOOLD, M. (1991), *Strategies and Styles*, Oxford: Oxford University Press.

CHAMBERLIN, E. H. (1993), *The Theory of Monopolistic Competition*, Cambridge, Mass.: Harvard University Press.

CHANDLER, A. (1990), *Scale and Scope*, Cambridge, Mass.: Harvard University Press.

CHARKHAM, J. (1994), *Keeping Good Company*, Oxford: Oxford University Press.

CONNER, K. (1991), 'A Historical Comparison of Resource-based Theory and Five Schools of Thought within Industrial Organization Economics: Do We have a New Theory of the Firm?', *Journal of Management*, 17: 121–54.

CORNSHAW, M., DAVIS, E., and KAY, J. (1994), 'On Being Stuck in the Middle', *British Journal of Management*, 5: 19–32.

CONYON, M., GREGG, P., and MACHIN, S. (1995), 'Taking care of business', *Economic Journal*, 105/430 (May), 704–14.

CRYSTAL, G. S. (1991), *In Search of Excess*, New York: Norton.

DAVID, P. A. (1986), 'Understanding the Economics of QWERTY: The Necessity of History', in W. N. Parker (ed.), *Economic History and the Modern Economist*, Oxford: Basil Blackwell.

DAVIES, S. *et al.* (1991), *The Dynamics of Market Leadership in UK Manufacturing Industry 1979–1986*, Centre for Business Strategy Report Series, London Business School.

DAVIS, E., and KAY, J. (1990), 'Corporate Governance, Takeovers and the Role of the Non-executive Director', *Business Strategy Review*, 1/3 (Autumn), 17–35.

DELL'OSSO, F. (1990), 'Defending a Dominant Position in a Technology Led Environment', *Business Strategy Review*, 1/2: 77–86.

—— and SZYMANSKI, S. (1991), 'Who are the Champions?', *Business Strategy Review*, 2/2: 113–80.

DIERICKX, I., and COOL, K. (1989), 'Asset Stock Accumulation and Sustainability of Competitive Advantage', *Management Science*, 35: 1504–11.

EDWARDS, J., KAY, J., and MAYER, C. (1987), *The Economic Analysis of Accounting Profitability*, Oxford: Clarendon Press.

FALLON, I. (1988), *The Brothers: The Rise and Rise of Saatchi & Saatchi*, London: Contemporary Books.

Financial Times (1989), 'Taking Groupe Bull by the Horns', 30 June, p. 29.

FRANKS, J., and MAYER, C. (1990), 'Capital Markets and Corporate Control: A Study of France, Germany and the UK', *Economic Policy* (Apr.), 191–231.

FUKUYAMA, F. (1992), *The End of History and the Last Man*, Harmondsworth: Penguin.

GOYDER, G. (1987), *The Just Enterprise*, London: Deutsch.

GROSSMAN, S., and HART, O. (1986), 'The Costs and Benefits of Ownership: A Theory of vertical and lateral integration', *Journal of Political Economy*, 94 (Aug.) 691–719.

HAMPDEN-TURNER, C., and TROMPENAARS, F. (1994), *The Seven Cultures of Capitalism*, London: Piatkus.

HART, O. (1988), 'Incomplete Contracts and the Theory of the Firm', *Journal of Law, Economics and Organization*, 4 (Spring), 119–40.

HBS (1978), *Notes on the Motorcycle Industry* (1974), Case 578–210.

—— (1985), *Komatsu Limited*, Case 9–385–277.

—— (1990), *Komatsu: Ryoichi Kawai's Leadership*, Case 9–390–037.

HUTTON, W. (1995), *The State We're In*, London: Jonathan Cape.

JOSKOW, P. (1975), 'Firm Decision Making Processes and Oligopoly Theory', *American Economic Review Papers and Proceedings*, 270–9.

KAY, J. A. (1976), 'Accountants, too, Could be Happy in a Golden Age', *Oxford Economic Papers*, 17: 66–80.

—— (1993), *Foundations of Corporate Success*, Oxford: Oxford University Press.

—— (1995), *Why Firms Succeed*, New York: Oxford University Press.

KOTLER, P. (1991), *Marketing Management*, Englewood Cliffs, NJ: Prentice Hall.

LEVITT, T. (1983), 'The Globalisation of Markets', *Harvard Business Review*, 1 (May–June), 92–101.

—— (1986), *The Marketing Imagination*, New York: Free Press.

LIPPMANN, S. A., and RUMELT, R. P. (1982), 'Uncertain Imitability: An Analysis of Interfirm Differences in Efficiency under Competition', *Bell Journal of Economics*, 23: 418–38.

LIPTON, M., and ROSENBLUM, S. A. (1991), 'A New System of Corporate Governance: The

Quinquennial Election of Directors', *University of Chicago Law Review*, 58/1 (Winter).

MacIntyre, A. (1981), *After Virtue*, London: Duckworth.

Macneil, I. R. (1980), *The New Social Contract: An Inquiry into Modern Contractual Relations*, New Haven: Yale University Press.

Marsh, P. (1990), *Short-termism on Trial*, International Fund Managers Association, London.

—— (1994), 'Market Assessment of Company Performance', in N. Dimsdale and M. Prevezer (eds.), *Capital Markets and Corporate Governance*, Oxford: Clarendon Press.

Marshall, A. (1890), *Principles of Economics*, London: Macmillan.

Monks, R. A. G., and Minnow, N. (1991), *Power and Accountability*, London: Harper Collins.

Mönnich, M. (1989), *BMW: Eine Deutsche Geschichte*, Vienna: Zsolnay.

Montgomery, C. A. (ed.) (1995), *Resource-based and Evolutionary Theories of the Firm*, Boston: Kluwer.

Moore, J. (1990), 'Property Rights and the Nature of the Firm', *Journal of Political Economy*, 98: 1119–58.

Moss Kanter, R. (1983), *The Change Masters*, London: Allen & Unwin.

—— (1989), *When Giants Learn to Dance*, New York: Simon and Schuster.

Nelson, R. R., and Winter, S. G. (1982), *An Evolutionary Theory of Economic Change*, Cambridge, Mass.: Harvard University Press.

Nyman, S., and Silberston, A. (1978), 'The Ownership and Control of Industry', *Oxford Economic Papers*, 3/1 (Mar.).

Odagiri, H. (1991), *Growth through Competition, Competition through Growth*, Oxford: Clarendon Press.

Ormerod, P. (1994), *The Death of Economics*, London: Faber & Faber.

Oster, S. (1990), *Modern Competitive Analysis*, New York: Oxford University Press.

Pascale, R. T. (1982), 'Perspectives on Strategy: The Real Story behind Honda's Success', *California Management Review*, 26/3: 47–72.

Penrose, E. T. (1959), *The Theory of the Growth of the Firm*, Oxford: Oxford University Press.

Peters, T. J., and Waterman, R. H. (1982), *In Search of Excellence*, New York: Harper and Row.

Porter, M. E. (1980), *Competitive Strategy*, New York: Free Press.

—— (1985), *Competitive Advantage*, New York: Free Press.

—— (1990), *The Competitive Advantage of Nations*, New York: Free Press.

Quinn, J. B., Mintzberg, and James, R. M. (1988), *The Strategy Process*, Englewood Cliffs, NJ: Prentice Hall.

Rasmussen, E. (1989), *Games and Information*, Oxford: Blackwell.

Ricardo, D. (1819), 'The Principles of Political Economy and Taxation', in P. Sraffa (ed.) (1961), Cambridge: Cambridge University Press.

Richardson, G. B. (1960), *Information and Investment*, Oxford: Oxford University Press.

—— (1972), 'The Organization of Industry', *Economic Journal*, 82: 883–96.

Royal Society of Arts (1995), *Tomorrow's Company*, London.

Rumelt, R. (1991), 'How Much does Industry Matter?', *Strategic Management Journal*, 12/3 (Mar.), 167–86.

Scherer, F. M. (1970), *Industrial Market Structure and Economic Performance*, Boston: Houghton-Mifflin.

Solomons, R. C. (1993), *Ethics and Excellence*, New York: Oxford University Press.

Sykes, A. (1994), 'Proposal for a Reformed System of Corporate Governance to Achieve Internationally Competitive Long-term Performance', in N. Dimsdale and M. Prevezer (eds.), *Capital Markets and Corporate Governance*, Oxford: Clarendon Press.

Teece, D. J., Rumelt, R. D., Posi, G. and Winter, S. G. (1994), 'Understanding Corporate Coherence: Theory and Evidence', *Journal of Economic Behaviour and Organisation*, 23: 1–30.

Teubner, G. (1988), 'Enterprise Corporation: New Industrial Policy and the Essence of the Legal Person', *American Journal of Company Law*, 36: 130–55.

Tirole, J. (1988), *The Theory of Industrial Organization*, Cambridge, Mass.: MIT Press.

Wernerfelt, B. (1984), 'A Resource Based View of the Firm', *Strategic Management Journal*, 5: 171–80.

—— (1989), 'From Critical Resources to Corporate Strategy', *Journal of General Management*, 14, 3: 4–12.

Wheeler, S. (ed.) (1994), *The Law of the Business Enterprise*, Oxford: Oxford University Press.

Wright, S. (1992), *Two Cheers for the Institutions*, London: Social Market Foundation.

INDEX